Rick Steves®

SNAPSHOT

Scottish Highlands

T0054190

CONTENTS

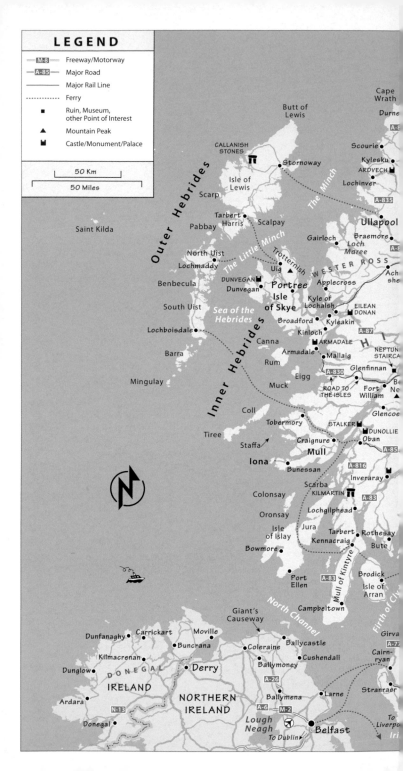

Inverness

Accommodations

1. Eildon Guesthouse
2. Dionard Guest Housese
3. Atholdene Guest House
4. Rossmount Guest House
5. The Ness Guest House
6. Ardconnel House & Crown Hotel Guest House
7. Heathmount Hotel
8. Glen Mhor Hotel
9. Castle View Guest House
10. Bazpackers Hostel & Inverness Student Hotel

Eateries & Other

11. Café 1
12. Number 27
13. La Tortilla
14. The Mustard Seed
15. Rose Street Foundry
16. Aspendos
17. Black Isle Brewery
18. MacGregor's Bar
19. Hootananny
20. Rocpool Restaurant
21. River House
22. The Kitchen Brasserie
23. The Gellions Pub
24. SoBar
25. Malt Room
26. Grocery
27. Leakey's Bookshop
28. Cabar Fèidh (Bagpipes)
29. Chisholms (Kilts)
30. Launderette (2)
31. Inverness Bike Tours

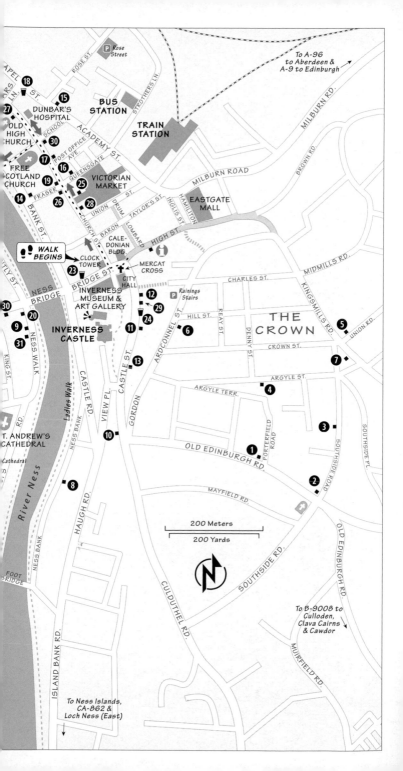

INTRODUCTION

This Snapshot guide, excerpted from my guidebook *Rick Steves Scotland,* introduces you to what many think of as traditional Scotland: the Highlands, with their weathered bluffs, countryside castles, whisky distilleries, deep lochs, heather-strewn moors, and lush green mountains called Munros. Here, during summer, towns host traditional Highland Games that deliver a full dose of Scottish culture. Once the home of rival clans, the region is now the domain of nature lovers, who revel in its sparsely populated countryside. And, along the west and north coasts, you'll discover some of Europe's most intriguing islands—mountainous, scenic, romantic, and indelibly Scottish. At these northern latitudes, mist drifts across craggy hillsides, and cold and drizzly weather isn't uncommon—even in midsummer.

In the Highlands you'll find Scottish culture distilled to its most potent brew. Whenever I want a taste of traditional Scotland, this is where I come.

To help you have the best trip possible, I've included the following topics in this book:

• **Planning Your Time,** with advice on how to make the most of your limited time

• **Orientation,** including tourist information (abbreviated as TI), tips on public transportation, local tour options, and helpful hints

• **Sights,** with ratings and strategies for meaningful and efficient visits

• **Sleeping and Eating,** with good-value recommendations in every price range

• **Connections,** with tips on trains, buses, ferries, and driving

Practicalities, near the end of this book, has information on money, staying connected, hotel reservations, transportation, and other helpful hints.

To travel smartly, read this little book in its entirety before you go. It's my hope that this guide will make your trip more meaningful and rewarding. Traveling like a temporary local, you'll get the absolute most out of every mile, minute, and dollar.

Happy travels!

Rick Steves

THE SCOTTISH HIGHLANDS

Filled with more natural and historical mystique than people, the Highlands are where Scottish dreams are set. Legends of Bonnie Prince Charlie linger around crumbling castles as tunes played by pipers in kilts swirl around tourists. Avid hikers—called "Munro baggers"—scale bald mountains, grizzled islanders man drizzly ferry crossings, and midges make life miserable (bring bug spray). The Highlands are the most mountainous, least inhabited, and—for many—most scenic and romantic part of Scotland.

The Highlands are covered with mountains, lochs, and glens, scarcely leaving a flat patch of land for building a big city. Geographically, the Highlands are defined by the Highland Boundary Fault, which slashes 130 miles diagonally through the middle of Scotland just north of the big cities of the more densely populated "Central Belt" (Glasgow and Edinburgh).

This geographic and cultural fault line is clearly visible on maps, and you can even see it in the actual landscape—especially around Loch Lomond and the Trossachs, where the transition from rolling Lowland hills to bald Highland mountains is almost too on-the-nose. Just beyond the fault, the Grampian Mountains (which include Cairngorms National Park) curve across the middle of Scotland; beyond that, the Caledonian Canal links the east and west coasts (slicing diagonally through the Great Glen, another geologic fault, from Oban to Inverness), with even more mountains to the north.

Though the Highlands' many "hills" are technically too short to be called "mountains," they do a convincing imitation. (Just don't say that to a Scot.) Scotland has 282 hills over 3,000 feet. A list of these was first compiled in 1891 by Sir Hugh Munro, and to this day the Scots call their high hills "Munros." (Hills from 2,500-3,000 feet are known as "Corbetts," and those from 2,000-2,500 are "Grahams.") Munro baggers love to tick these mini mountains off their list: According to the Munro Society, more than 5,000 intrepid hikers can brag that they've climbed all the Munros. (To get started, you'll find lots of good information at www.walkhighlands.co.uk/munros).

The Highlands occupy more than half of Scotland's area, but are populated by less than five percent of its people—a population density comparable to Russia's. Scotland's Hebrides Islands (among them Skye, Mull, Iona, and Staffa), while not, strictly speaking, in the Highlands, are often included simply because they share much of the same culture, clan history, and Celtic ties. (Orkney and Shetland, off the north coast of Scotland, are a world apart—they feel more Norwegian than Highlander.)

Inverness is the Highlands' de facto capital, and often claims to be the region's only city. (The east coast port city of Aberdeen—Scotland's third largest, and quadruple the size of Inverness—has its own Doric culture and dialect, and is usually considered its own animal.)

The Highlands are where you'll most likely see Gaelic—the old Celtic language that must legally accompany English on road signs. While few Highlanders actually speak Gaelic—and virtually no one speaks it as a first language—certain Gaelic words are used as a nod of respect to their heritage. *Fàilte* (welcome), *Slàinte mhath!* (cheers!—literally "good health"), and *tigh* (house—featured in many business names) are all common. If you're making friends in a Highland pub, ask your new mates to teach you some Gaelic words.

The Highlands are also the source of many Scottish superstitions, some of which persist in remote communities, where mischievous fairies and shape-shifting kelpies are still blamed for trouble. In the not-so-distant past, new parents feared that their newborn could be replaced by a devilish imposter called a changeling. Well into the 20th century, a midwife called a "howdie" would oversee key rituals: Before a birth, doors and windows would be unlocked and mirrors would be covered. And the day of the week a baby is born was charged with significance ("Monday's child is fair of face, Tuesday's child is full of grace...").

Many American superstitions and expressions originated in

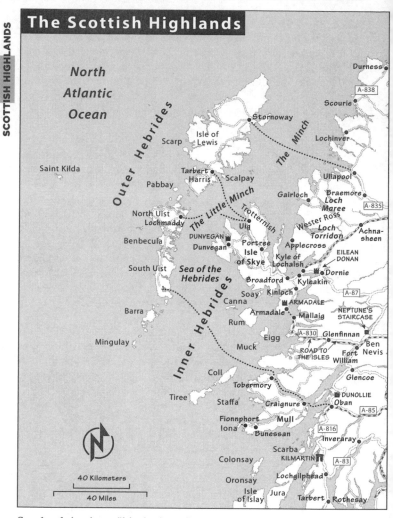

The Scottish Highlands

North Atlantic Ocean

Durness
A-838
Scourie
Lochinver
Stornoway
The Minch
Scarp
Isle of Lewis
Outer Hebrides
Ullapool
Saint Kilda
Braemore
Pabbay
Tarbert
Harris
Scalpay
Gairloch
Loch Maree
A-835
Wester Ross
The Little Minch
North Uist
Lochmaddy
Trotternish
Uig
Loch Torridon
Applecross
Achna-sheen
EILEAN DONAN
Benbecula
DUNVEGAN
Dunvegan
Portree
Isle of Skye
Kyle of Lochalsh
Dornie
South Uist
Sea of the Hebrides
Broadford
Kyleakin
A-87
Soay
Kinloch
Canna
Armadale
ARMADALE
Mallaig
NEPTUNE'S STAIRCASE
Barra
Rum
A-830 Glenfinnan
Ben Nevis
Mingulay
Eigg
ROAD TO THE ISLES
Fort William
Muck
Inner Hebrides
Glencoe
Coll
Tobermory
DUNOLLIE
Tiree
Staffa
Craignure
Oban
A-85
Fionnphort
Iona
Bunessan
Mull
A-816
Scarba
Inveraray
Colonsay
KILMARTIN
A-83
Oronsay
Lochgilphead
Isle of Islay
Jura
Tarbert
Rothesay

N

40 Kilometers

40 Miles

Scotland (such as "black sheep," based on the idea that a black sheep was terrible luck for the flock). Just as a baseball player might refuse to shave during a winning streak, many perfectly modern Highlanders carry a sprig of white heather for good luck at their wedding (and are careful not to cross two knives at the dinner table). And let's not even start with the Loch Ness monster...

In the summer, the Highlands swarm with tourists...and midges. These miniature mosquitoes—like "no-see-ums"—are bloodthirsty and determined. They can be an annoyance from late May through September, depending on the weather. Hot sun or a stiff breeze blows the tiny buggers away, but they thrive in damp, shady areas. Locals suggest blowing or brushing them off, rather

than swatting them—since killing them only seems to attract more (likely because of the smell of fresh blood). Scots say, "If you kill one midge, a million more will come to his funeral." Even if you don't usually travel with bug spray, consider bringing or buying some for a summer visit. Locals recommend Avon's Skin So Soft, which is effective against midges, but less potent than DEET-based bug repellants. The brand Smidge, while pricey, is also popular (sold at many outdoor shops).

Ticks are also numerous in the Highlands—and can carry Lyme disease and other ailments. When tramping through fields of brush or grass, experienced hikers tuck their pant legs into their socks to keep their skin covered. After a hike, inspect your clothes carefully and brush off any ticks that have hitched a ride. If you do get bitten by a tick, pull it out carefully (without squeezing, and trying to keep the head intact). If you notice a "bullseye" rash around the bite, seek medical attention without delay.

Keep an eye out for another, far more lovable Scottish animal: shaggy Highland cattle called "hairy coos." They're big and have impressive horns, but are best known for their adorable hair falling into their eyes (the hair protects them from Scotland's troublesome insects and unpredictable weather). Hairy coos graze on sparse vegetation that other animals ignore, and, with a heavy coat (rather than fat) to keep them insulated, they  produce a lean meat that resembles venison. Highland cattle meat is not commonly eaten, and the relatively few hairy coos you'll see are kept around mostly as a national symbol.

Seeing a herd of hairy coos at the side of the road is thrilling—they're often mobbed by shutterbug tourists. Most you see are females, with horns that curve distinctively upwards as they narrow. (If you get a close look, you can actually count the "rings" on a female's horns—one for each calf she's birthed.) Males' horns are directed straight ahead. Be respectful and keep your distance from these giant, usually docile animals; don't hop over a fence to approach them—they can become agitated, especially if you get too close to a mother and her calf. (To see some hairy coos up close in a safe setting, you can tour the Cladich Highland Cattle Farm near Loch Awe—see page 50.)

While the prickly, purple thistle is the official national flower, heather is the unofficial national shrub. This scrubby vegetation blankets much of the Highlands. It's usually a muddy reddish-brown color, but it bursts with purple flowers in late summer; the less common bell heather blooms in July. Heather is one of the few things that will grow in the inhospitable terrain of a moor, and it can be used to make dye, rope, thatch, and even beer (look for Fraoch Heather Ale).

Highlanders are an outdoorsy bunch. For a fun look at local athletics, check whether your trip coincides with one of the Highland Games that enliven Highland communities in summer (see the sidebar later in this chapter). And keep an eye out for the unique Highland sport of shinty: a brutal, fast-paced version of field hockey, played for keeps. Similar to Irish hurling, shinty is a full-contact sport that encourages tackling and fielding airborne balls, with players swinging their sticks (called camans) perilously through the air. The easiest place to see shinty is at Bught Park in Inverness (see page 121), but it's played across the Highlands.

PLANNING YOUR TIME

Here are three recommended Highland itineraries: two to three days, six days, and 10 or more days. These plans assume you're driving, but can be done (with some modifications) by bus. Think about how many castles you really need to see: One or two is enough for most people.

Two- to Three-Day Highland Highlights Blitz

This ridiculously fast-paced option squeezes the maximum Highland experience out of a few short days, and assumes you're starting from Glasgow or Edinburgh.

Day 1: In the morning, head up to the Highlands. (If coming from Edinburgh, consider a stop at Stirling Castle en route.) Drive along Loch Lomond and pause for lunch in Inveraray. Arrive in Oban in time for the day's last distillery tour (see page 22; book ahead). Have dinner and spend the night in Oban.

Day 2: Get an early start from Oban and make a beeline for Glencoe, where you can enjoy a quick, scenic drive up the valley and visit the folk museum. Then drive to Fort William and follow the Caledonian Canal to Inverness, stopping at Fort Augustus to see the locks (and have a late lunch). Zip along Loch Ness and overshoot Inverness on your way to the Culloden Battlefield (outside Inverness) in the late afternoon (carefully confirm the current closing time and plan around it). Finally, make good time south on the A-9 back to Edinburgh (3 hours, arriving late).

Day 3: To extend this plan, take your time getting to Inverness on Day 2 and spend the night there. Follow my self-guided Inverness Walk either that evening or the next morning. Leaving Inverness, tour Culloden Battlefield, visit Clava Cairns, then head south, stopping off at any place that appeals: The best options near the A-9 are Pitlochry and the Scottish Crannog Centre on Loch Tay, or take the more rugged eastern route to see the Speyside whisky area, Balmoral Castle and Ballater village, and Cairngorms mountain scenery. Or, if this is your best chance to see Stirling Castle or the Falkirk sights (Falkirk Wheel, Kelpies sculptures), fit them in on your way south.

Six-Day Highlands and Islands Loop

While you'll see the Highlands on the above itinerary, you'll whiz past the sights in a misty blur. This more reasonably paced plan is for those who want to slow down a bit.

Hiking the Highlands

Scotland is a hiker's paradise...as long as you bring rain gear. I've recommended a few hikes of varying degrees of difficulty throughout this book. Remember: Wear sturdy (ideally waterproof) shoes, and be prepared for any weather. For serious hikes, pick up good maps and get advice at local TIs or from a knowledgeable resident (such as your B&B host). Be sure to bring food, water, and bug spray to fend off midges. A good resource for hiking route tips is WalkHighlands.co.uk.

For a more in-depth experience, consider one of Scotland's famous multiday walks. These are the most popular:

West Highland Way: 95 miles, 5-10 days, Milngavie to Fort William by way of Loch Lomond, Glencoe, and Rannoch Moor

Great Glen Way: 79 miles, 5-6 days, Fort William to Inverness along the Caledonian Canal, Fort Augustus, and Loch Ness

John Muir Way: 134 miles, 9-10 days, coast to coast through the Central Belt of Scotland, from Helensburgh to Dunbar via Falkirk, the Firth of Forth, and Edinburgh

Day 1: Follow the plan for Day 1, above, sleeping in Oban (2 nights).

Day 2: Do an all-day island-hopping tour from Oban, with visits to Mull, Iona, and (if you choose) Staffa.

Day 3: From Oban, head up to Glencoe for its museum and valley views. Consider lingering for a (brief) hike. Then zip up to Fort William and take the "Road to the Isles" west (pausing in Glenfinnan to see its viaduct) to Mallaig. Take the ferry over the sea to Skye, then drive to Portree to sleep (2 nights).

Day 4: Spend today enjoying the Isle of Skye. In the morning, do the Trotternish Peninsula loop; in the afternoon, take your pick of options (Talisker Distillery, Dunvegan Castle, multiple hiking options).

Day 5: Leaving Portree, drive across the Skye Bridge for a photo-op pit stop at Eilean Donan Castle. The A-87 links you over to Loch Ness, which you'll follow to Inverness. If you get in early enough, consider touring Culloden Battlefield this evening. Sleep in Inverness (1 night).

Day 6: See the Day 3 options for my Highlands Highlights Blitz, earlier.

10-Day (or More) Highlands Explorer Extravaganza

Using the six-day Highlands and Islands Loop as a basis, pick and choose from these possible modifications (listed in order of where they'd fit into the itinerary):

- Add an overnight in **Glencoe** to make more time for hiking there.
- Leaving the Isle of Skye, drive north along **Wester Ross** (the scenic northwest coast). Go as far as Ullapool, then cut back down to Inverness, or...
- Take another day or two (after spending the night in Ullapool) to carry on northward through remote and rugged scenery to the far reaches of Scotland—the famous **North Coast 500** (NC-500) driving route. Drive east along the coast all the way to John O'Groats; then either take the ferry from Scrabster across to Orkney, or shoot back down to Inverness on the A-9 (about 3 hours).
- Visit **Orkney** (2-night minimum). This can fit into the above plan after John O'Groats. Or, to cut back on the remote driving, simply zip up on the A-9 from Inverness (about 3 hours)— or fly up from Inverness, Edinburgh, or Aberdeen.
- On the way south from Inverness, follow the **Speyside whisky trail,** cut through the **Cairngorms,** visit **Balmoral Castle,** and sleep in **Ballater.** Between Balmoral and Edinburgh, consider visiting Glamis Castle (Queen Mum's childhood home), Dundee (great industrial museums), or Culross (scenic firth-side village).
- Add an overnight wherever you'd like to linger; the best options are the **Isle of Skye** (to allow more island explorations) or **Inverness** (to fit in more side trips).

GETTING AROUND THE HIGHLANDS
By Car

The Highlands are made for joyriding. There are a lot of miles, but they're scenic, the roads are good, and the traffic is light. The farther north you go, the more away-from-it-all you'll feel. Even on a sunny weekend, you can go miles without seeing another car. Don't wait too long to gas up—

Scottish Highland Games

Throughout the summer, Highland communities host traditional festivals of local sport and culture. These Highland Games (sometimes called Highland Gatherings) combine the best elements of a track meet and a county fair. They range from huge and glitzy (such as Braemar's world-famous games, which members of the royal family attend, or the Cowal Highland Gathering, Scotland's biggest) to humble and small-town. Some of the more modern games come with loud pop music and corporate sponsorship, but still manage to celebrate the Highland spirit.

Most Highland Games take place between mid-June and late August (usually on Saturdays, but occasionally on weekdays). The games are typically a one-day affair, kicking off around noon and winding down in the late afternoon. At smaller games, you'll pay a nominal admission fee (typically around £5-7). Events are rain or shine (so bring layers) and take place in a big park ringed by a running track, with the heavy events and Highland dancing stage at opposite ends of the infield. Surrounding the whole scene are junk-food stands, a few test-your-skill carnival games, and local charities raising funds by selling hamburgers, fried sausage sandwiches, baked goods, and bottles of beer and Irn-Bru. The emcee's running commentary is a delightful opportunity to just sit back and enjoy a lilting Scottish accent.

The day's events typically kick off with a **pipe band** parading through town—often led by the local clan chieftain—and ending with a lap around the field. Then the sporting events begin.

In the **heavy events**—or feats of Highland strength—brawny, kilted athletes test their ability to hurl various objects of awkward shapes and sizes as far as possible. In the weight throw, competitors spin like ballerinas before releasing a 28- or 56-pound ball on a chain. The hammer throw involves a similar technique with a 26-pound ball on a long stick, and the stone put (with a 20- to 25-pound ball) has been adopted in American sports as the shot put. In the "weight over the bar" event, Highlanders swing a 56-pound weight over a horizontal bar that begins at 10 feet high and ends at closer to 15 feet. (That's like tossing a 5-year-old child over a double-decker bus.) And, of course, there's the caber toss: Pick up a giant log (the caber), get a running start, and release it end-over-end with enough force to (ideally) make the caber flip all the way over and land at the 12 o'clock position. (Most competitors wind up closer to 6.)

Meanwhile, the **track events** run circles around the muscle: the 90-meter dash, the 1,600-meter, and so on. The hill race adds a Scottish spin: Combine a several-mile footrace with the ascent of a nearby summit. The hill racers begin with a lap in the stadium before disappearing for about an hour. Keep an eye on nearby hillsides to pick out their colorful jerseys bobbing up and down a distant peak. This custom supposedly began when an 11th-century king staged a competition to select his personal letter carrier. After about an hour—when you've forgotten all about them—the hill racers start trickling back into the stadium to cross the finish line.

The **Highland dancing** is a highlight. Accompanied by a lone piper, the dancers (in groups of two to four) toe their routines

with intense concentration. Dancers remain always on the balls of their feet, requiring excellent balance and stamina. While some men participate, most competitors are female—from wee lassies barely out of nappies, all the way to poised professionals. Common steps are the Highland fling (in which the goal is to keep the feet as close as possible to one spot), sword dances (in which the dancers step gingerly over crossed swords on the stage), and a variety of national dances.

Other events further enliven the festivities. The pipe band periodically assembles to play a few tunes, often while marching around the track (giving the runners a break). Larger games may have a massing of multiple pipe bands, or bagpipe and drumming competitions. You may also see re-enactments of medieval battles, herd-dog demonstrations, or dog shows (grooming and obedience). Haggis hurling—in which participants stand on a whisky barrel and attempt to throw a cooked haggis as far as possible—has caught on recently. And many small-town events end with the grand finale of a town-wide tug-of-war, during which everybody gets bruised, muddy, and hysterical.

If you're traveling to Scotland in the summer, check online schedules to see if you'll be near any Highland Games before locking in your itinerary. Rather than target the big, famous gatherings, I make a point of visiting the smaller clan games. A helpful website—listing dates for most but not all the games around Scotland—is www.shga.co.uk. For many travelers to Scotland, attending a Highland Games can be a trip-capping highlight. And, of course, many communities in the US and Canada also host their own Highland Games.

village gas stations are few and far between, and can close unexpectedly. Stay alert on single-lane roads, and slow down on blind corners. If you do encounter an oncoming vehicle, the driver closest to a pullout is expected to use it—even if they have to back up. Remember to always stay on the left side of the road—don't cross over to a pullout on the right, which confuses this carefully orchestrated system. (Rather, stay on the straight side and let the oncoming car use the pullout to pass you.)

By Public Transportation

Glasgow is the gateway to this region (so you'll most likely have to transfer there if coming from Edinburgh). **Trains** zip from Glasgow to Fort William, Oban, and Kyle of Lochalsh in the west; and up to Stirling, Pitlochry, and Inverness in the east. For more remote destinations (such as Glencoe), the bus is better.

Most **buses** are operated by Scottish Citylink. In peak season—when these buses fill up—it's smart to buy tickets even a few days ahead in advance: Book at Citylink.co.uk, call +44 871 216 3333, or stop by a bus station or TI.

Glasgow's Buchanan Station is the main Lowlands hub for reaching Highlands destinations. From Edinburgh, it's best to transfer in Glasgow (fastest by train, also possible by bus)—though there are direct buses from Edinburgh to Inverness, where you can connect to Highlands buses. Once in the Highlands, Inverness and Fort William serve as the main bus hubs.

Note that bus frequency can be substantially reduced—sometimes to zero—on Sundays and in the off-season (Oct-mid-May). Unless otherwise noted, I've listed bus information for summer weekdays. Always confirm schedules locally. These buses are particularly useful:

Connections from Glasgow: Buses **#976** and **#977** connect Glasgow with Oban (5/day, 3 hours).

Buses **#914/#915/#916** go from Glasgow to Fort William, stopping at Glencoe (8/day, 2.5 hours to Glencoe, 3 hours total to Fort William). From Fort William, some of these buses continue all the way up to Portree on the Isle of Skye (3/day, 7 hours for the full run).

Bus **#M10** connects Glasgow and Inverness (5/day, 3.5 hours; also stops in Pitlochry).

Connections from Edinburgh: Bus **#M90** runs from Edinburgh to Inverness (8/day, 4 hours; stops en route at Pitlochry, 2.5 hours).

Bus **#913** runs just once daily (in the morning) from Edinburgh into the Highlands, stopping at Glencoe (4 hours) and Fort William (4.5 hours); with a transfer, you can continue on to Oban (4.5 hours, change in Tyndrum) and Portree on the Isle of Skye (8 hours, change in Fort William). For additional options, take the train to Glasgow and transfer to bus from there.

Connections Within the Highlands: Bus **#918** goes from Oban to Fort William, stopping en route at Ballachulish near Glencoe (4/day, 1 hour to Ballachulish, 1.5 hours total to Fort William, no buses Sun).

Bus **#N44** (operated by Shiel Bus) is a cheaper alternative for connecting Glencoe to Fort William (about 8/day, fewer Sat-Sun, www.shielbuses.co.uk).

Bus **#919** connects Fort William with Inverness (6/day, 2 hours, fewer on Sat-Sun).

Bus **#917** connects Inverness with Portree, on the Isle of Skye (3-4/day, 3 hours).

OBAN & THE INNER HEBRIDES

Oban • Isles of Mull, Iona & Staffa •
Glasgow to Oban Drive

For a taste of Scotland's west coast, head to Oban, a port town that's equal parts endearing and functional. This busy little ferry and train terminus has no important sights, but makes up the difference in character, in scenery (with its low-impact panorama of overlapping islets and bobbing boats), and with one of Scotland's best distillery tours. Oban is also convenient: It's midway between the Lowland cities (Glasgow and Edinburgh) and the Highland riches of the north (Glencoe, Isle of Skye). And it's the "gateway to the isles," with handy ferry service to the Hebrides Islands.

If time is tight and serious island-hopping is beyond the scope of your itinerary, Oban is ideally situated for a busy and memorable full-day side trip to three of the most worthwhile Inner Hebrides: big, rugged Mull; pristine little Iona, where buoyant clouds float over its historic abbey; and Staffa, a remote, grassy islet inhabited only by seabirds. (The best of the Inner Hebrides—the Isle of Skye—is covered in its own chapter.) Sit back, let someone else do the driving, and enjoy a tour of the Inner Hebrides.

This chapter also outlines the most scenic route between Glasgow and Oban (along the bonnie, bonnie banks of Loch Lomond and through the town of Inveraray, with its fine castle), plus a detour through Kilmartin Glen, the prehistoric homeland of the Scottish people.

PLANNING YOUR TIME

If you're on a speedy blitz tour of Scotland, Oban is a strategic and pleasant place to spend the night. But you'll need two nights to enjoy Oban's main attraction: the side-trip to Mull, Iona, and Staffa. There are few actual sights in Oban itself, beyond the distillery tour, but—thanks to its manageable size, scenic waterfront setting, and great restaurants—the town is an enjoyable place to linger.

Oban

Oban (pronounced OH-bin) is a low-key resort. Its winding promenade is lined by gravel beaches, ice cream stands, fish-and-chips joints, a tourable distillery, and a good choice of restaurants. Everything in Oban is close together, and the town seems eager to please its many visitors: Wool and tweed are perpetually on sale, and posters announce a variety of day tours to Scotland's  wild and wildlife-strewn western islands. When the rain clears, sun-starved Scots sit on benches along the Esplanade, leaning back to catch some rays. Wind, boats, gulls, layers of islands, and the promise of a wide-open Atlantic beyond give Oban a rugged charm.

Orientation to Oban

Oban, with about 10,000 people, is where the train system of Scotland Cmeets the ferry system serving the Hebrides Islands. As "gateway to the isles," its center is not a square or market, but its harbor. Oban's business action, just a couple of streets deep, stretches along the harbor and its promenade.

TOURIST INFORMATION

Oban's TI, located at the North Pier, sells intercity bus tickets and can help you sort through your island-hopping day-trip options (generally open Mon-Sat 9:00-17:00, Sun until 16:00, from 10:00 off-season, in the stately red-sandstone Columba Hotel building at 3 North Pier, +44 1631 563 122, www.oban.org.uk).

ARRIVAL IN OBAN

The small **train station** is right on the pier, a short walk from the giant ferry terminal (ticket windows open Mon-Sat 5:00-20:30, Sun 10:45-18:00; no baggage storage). The **bus "station"** is just a couple of bus-stop canopies on the big roundabout in front of the

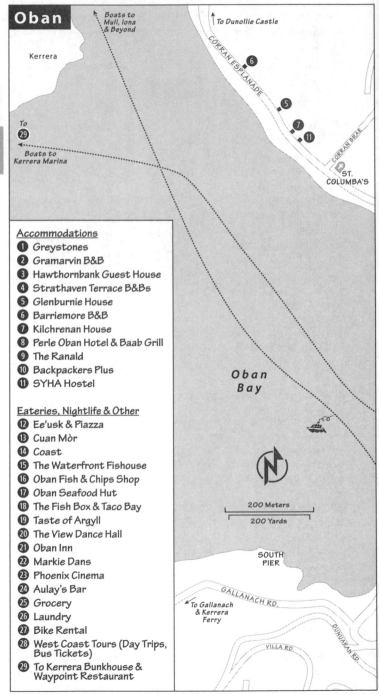

Oban

OBAN & INNER HEBRIDES

Kerrera

Boats to Mull, Iona & Beyond

To Dunollie Castle

CORRAN ESPLANADE

To 29

Boats to Kerrera Marina

CORRAN BRAE

ST. COLUMBA'S

Oban Bay

200 Meters

200 Yards

SOUTH PIER

GALLANACH RD.

To Gallanach & Kerrera Ferry

DUNUARAN RD.

VILLA RD.

Accommodations
1. Greystones
2. Gramarvin B&B
3. Hawthornbank Guest House
4. Strathaven Terrace B&Bs
5. Glenburnie House
6. Barriemore B&B
7. Kilchrenan House
8. Perle Oban Hotel & Baab Grill
9. The Ranald
10. Backpackers Plus
11. SYHA Hostel

Eateries, Nightlife & Other
12. Ee'usk & Piazza
13. Cuan Mòr
14. Coast
15. The Waterfront Fishouse
16. Oban Fish & Chips Shop
17. Oban Seafood Hut
18. The Fish Box & Taco Bay
19. Taste of Argyll
20. The View Dance Hall
21. Oban Inn
22. Markie Dans
23. Phoenix Cinema
24. Aulay's Bar
25. Grocery
26. Laundry
27. Bike Rental
28. West Coast Tours (Day Trips, Bus Tickets)
29. To Kerrera Bunkhouse & Waypoint Restaurant

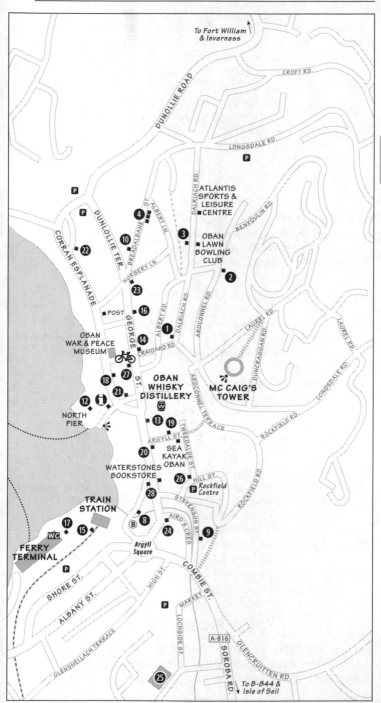

train station, marked by a stubby clock tower. Arriving either by train or bus, simply walk around the harbor (with the water on your left) and you'll be in the heart of town in a few minutes.

Drivers can get parking advice from their accommodations; most have free parking on site. If you're just dipping into town, there's a large pay parking lot near the ferry terminal. However, this lot can fill up on busy days, so don't count on it if you're rushing to catch a boat (leave time to find an alternative). Rockfield Centre, another pay lot a block off the harbor not far from the ferry (on Hill Street) may have space if you're in a pinch. There's street parking throughout town, but check signs carefully to make sure you're legal.

HELPFUL HINTS

Bookstore: Overlooking the harborfront, **Waterstones** is a well-stocked chain with maps and an excellent selection of books on Scotland (Mon-Sat 9:00-17:30, Sun 11:00-17:00, 12 George Street, +44 843 290 8529).

Laundry: You'll find **Oban Quality Laundry** tucked a block behind the main drag just off Stevenson Street (drop off by 12:00 for same-day service, no self-service; open Mon-Sat 9:00-15:00, closed Sun; +44 1631 563 554). The recommended **Backpackers Plus Hostel** (see "Sleeping in Oban") may also do laundry for nonguests.

Supermarket: The giant **Tesco** is a five-minute walk from the train station (Mon-Sat until 23:00, Sun until 20:00, walk through Argyll Square and look for entrance to large parking lot on right, Lochside Street).

Bike Rental: Get wheels at **Oban Cycles,** right on the main drag (£30/day, Tue-Sat 10:00-17:00, closed Sun-Mon, 87 George Street, +44 1631 566 033, www.obancyclescotland.com).

Bus and Island Tour Tickets: A block from the train station in the bright-red building along the harbor, **West Coast Tours** sells bus- and island-tour tickets (daily 8:30-17:30, 17 George Street, +44 1631 566 809, www.westcoasttours.co.uk).

Highland Games: Oban hosts its touristy Highland Games every August (www.obangames.com). Nearby Taynuilt, a 20-minute drive east, hosts their sweetly small-town Highland Games in mid-July (www.taynuilthighlandgames.com).

Tours from Oban

For the best day trip from Oban, tour the islands of Mull, Iona, and/or Staffa (offered daily Easter-Oct, described later)—or consider staying overnight on remote and beautiful Iona. With more time or other interests, consider one of many other options you'll see advertised.

Wildlife Tours

If you just want to go for a boat ride, the easiest option is the one-hour seal-watching tour (£15, various companies—look for signs at the harbor).

To really get a good look at Scottish coastal wildlife, several groups—including **Sealife Adventures** (https://sealife-adventures.com) and **SeaFari** (www.seafari.co.uk/oban)—run whale-watching tours that seek out rare minke whales, basking sharks, bottlenose dolphins, and porpoises. For an even more ambitious itinerary, the holy grail is the Treshnish Isles (out past Staffa), which brim with puffins, seals, and other sea critters.

Various companies run multi-day, overnight cruising trips around the islands, including **The Majestic Line** (www.themajesticline.co.uk) and **St. Hilda Sea Adventures** (www.sthildaseaadventures.co.uk)—book well ahead.

Sea Kayak Tours

If the weather is good and you'd like to get out on the water under your own power, **Sea Kayak Oban** rents gear and offers classes and guided tours for novice and experienced kayakers. A full-day tour costs £95 including equipment (office at 6 Argyll Street, +44 1631 565 310, www.seakayakoban.com).

Sights in Oban

▲The Burned-Out Sightseer's Visual Tour from the Pier

If the west-coast weather permits, get oriented to the town while taking a break: Head out to the North Pier, just past the TI, and find the benches that face back toward town (in front of the recommended Piazza restaurant). Take a seat and get to know Oban.

Scan the harborfront from left to right, surveying the mix of grand Victorian sandstone buildings and humbler modern storefronts. At the far-right end of town is the **ferry terminal** and—very likely—a huge ferry loading or unloading. Oban has always been on the way to somewhere, and today is no different. (A recent tourism slogan: Oban...it's closer than you think.) The townscape seems dominated by Caledonian-MacBrayne, Scotland's biggest ferry company. CalMac's 30 ships serve 24 destinations and transport over 4 million passengers a year. The town's port has long been a lifeline to the islands.

Hiding near the ferry terminal is the **train station.** With the arrival of the train in 1880, Oban became the unofficial capital of Scotland's west coast and a destination for tourists. Just to the left is the former Caledonian Hotel, the original terminus hotel (now the Perle Oban Hotel) that once served those train travelers.

Tourism aside, herring was the first big industry. A dozen boats still fish commercially—you'll see them tucked around the ferry terminal. The tourist board, in an attempt to entice tourists to linger longer, is trying to rebrand Oban as a "seafood capital" rather than just the "gateway to the isles." As the ocean's supply has become depleted, most local fish is farmed. There's still plenty of shellfish.

After fishing, big industries here historically included tobacco (imported from the American colonies), then whisky. At the left end of the embankment, find the building marked *The Oban Distillery.* It's rare to find a distillery in the middle of a town, but Oban grew up around this one. With the success of its whisky, the town enjoyed an invigorating confidence, optimism, and, in 1811, a royal charter. Touring Oban's distillery is the best activity in Oban (that doesn't involve heading to the islands).

Above the distillery, you can't miss the odd mini-Colosseum. This is **McCaig's Tower,** an employ-the-workers-and-build-me-a-fine-memorial project undertaken by an Oban tycoon in 1900. McCaig died before completing the structure, so his complete vision for it remains a mystery. This is an example of a "folly"—that uniquely British notion of an idiosyncratic structure erected by a colorful aristocrat. Building a folly was an in-your-face kind of extravagance many extremely wealthy people enjoyed even when surrounded by struggling working-class people (an urge that survives among some of the upper crust to this day). While the building itself is nothing to see up close, a 10-minute hike through a Victorian residential neighborhood leads you to a peaceful garden and a commanding view (nice at sunset).

Now turn and look out to sea, and imagine this: At the height of the Cold War, Oban played a critical role when the world's first two-way transatlantic telephone cable was laid from Gallanach Bay to Newfoundland in 1956—a milestone in global communication. This technology later provided the White House and the Kremlin with the "hotline" that was created after the Cuban Missile Crisis to avoid a nuclear conflagration.

▲▲Oban Whisky Distillery Tours

Founded in 1794, Oban Whisky Distillery produces more than 25,000 liters a week and exports much of that to the US. A free

exhibit (upstairs) gives a quick, whisky-centric history of Oban and Scotland. Oban whisky is moderately smoky ("peaty") and characterized by notes of sea salt, citrus, and honey.

The distillery offers serious and fragrant one-hour **tours** explaining the process from start to finish, with three smooth samples of their signature product—including one standard whisky, one exclusive one, and one straight from the cask. You'll also receive a whisky glass and a discount coupon for the shop. This is the handiest whisky tour you'll encounter—just a block off the harbor—and one of the best. Come 10 minutes before your tour starts to check out the exhibit upstairs. Then your guide will walk you through each step of the process: malting, mashing, fermentation, distillation, and maturation. Photos are not allowed inside.

Cost and Hours: Exhibit—free; tours—£22, limited to 16 people, departures about once per hour (10:30-15:23). This is a very popular tour and always fills up, so book far ahead on their website. (You can try dropping in to see if there are any cancellations, but it's unlikely). The shop is open daily 10:15-17:00, possibly later in summer (Stafford Street, +44 1631 572 004, www.obanwhisky. com).

Oban War & Peace Museum

Opened in 1995 on the 50th anniversary of Victory in Europe Day, this charming little museum focuses on Oban's experience during World War II. But it covers more than just war and peace. Photos show Oban through the years, and a 15-minute looped video gives a simple tour around the town and region. Volunteer staffers love to chat about the exhibit—or anything else on your mind.

Cost and Hours: Free, Sat-Thu 10:00-16:00, Fri until 14:00, maybe later in summer, next to Regent Hotel on the promenade, +44 1631 570 007, www.obanmuseum.org.uk.

Dunollie Castle and Museum

In a park just a mile up the coast, a ruined castle and an old house hold an intimate collection of clan family treasures. This spartan, stocky castle with 10-foot walls offers a commanding, windy view of the harbor—a strategic spot back in the days when transport was mainly by water. For more than a thousand years, clan chiefs ruled this region from this ancestral home of Clan MacDougall, but the castle was abandoned in 1746. The adjacent house, which dates from 1745, shows off the MacDougall clan's heritage with a handful of rooms filled with a humble yet fascinating trove of treasures. While the exhibit won't dazzle you, the family and clan pride in the display, their "willow garden," and the lovely walk from Oban make the visit fun.

Cost and Hours: £8; April-Oct Sun-Fri 10:00-16:00, closed

Nov-March and Sat year-round; last entry 45 minutes before closing; free one-hour tours Mon-Fri at 12:30 and 14:30; Sun bagpiping on the lawn at 12:30; +44 1631 570 550, www.dunollie.org.

Getting There: Head out of town—by foot or by car—along the harborfront promenade. At the war memorial (with inviting seaview benches), cross the street. A gate leads to a little lane, lined with historic and nature boards along the way to the castle.

ACTIVITIES IN OBAN

Atlantis Leisure Centre

This industrial-type sports center has a rock-climbing wall, tennis courts, indoor "soft play centre" (for kids under 5), and indoor swimming pool with a big water slide. The outdoor playground is free and open all the time (pool only-£4.80, no rental towels or suits, fees for other activities; open Mon-Fri 6:30-21:00, Sat 9:00-16:00, Sun 10:00-14:30; on the north end of Dalriach Road, +44 1631 566 800, www.atlantisleisure.co.uk).

Oban Lawn Bowling Club

The club has welcomed visitors since 1869. This elegant green is the scene of a wonderfully British spectacle of old men tiptoeing wishfully after their balls. It's fun to watch, and—if there's no match scheduled and the weather's dry—anyone can rent shoes and balls and actually play (£5/person; generally daily 10:00-12:00 & 14:00-16:00 or "however long the weather lasts"; just south of sports center on Dalriach Road, +44 1631 570 808).

ISLANDS NEAR OBAN

The isles of Mull, Iona, and Staffa are farther out, require a full day to visit, and are described later in this chapter. For a quicker glimpse at the Inner Hebrides, consider these two options.

Isle of Kerrera

Functioning like a giant breakwater, the Isle of Kerrera (KEH-reh-rah) makes Oban possible. Just offshore from Oban, this stark but very green island offers a quick, easy opportunity to get that romantic island experience. While it has no proper roads, it offers nice hikes, a ruined castle, and a few sheep farms. It's also a fine place to bike (ask for advice at Oban Cycles; see "Helpful Hints," earlier). You may see the Kerrera ferry filled with sheep heading for Oban's livestock market.

Getting There: You have two options for reaching the island. A boat operated by the Kerrera Marina goes from **Oban's North Pier** to the Kerrera Marina on the northern part of the island (£5 round-trip, roughly every hour, book ahead at +44 1631 565 333, www.kerreramarina.com).

A ferry departs from **Gallanach** (two miles south of Oban) and goes to the middle of the island. This is the best option if you want to hike to Kerrera's castle (passengers only, £3.40 round-trip, bikes free, runs 8:20-12:30 & 14:00-18:00, none off-season, 5-minute ride, +44 1475 650 397, www.calmac.co.uk). To reach Gallanach, drive south, following the coast road past the ferry terminal (parking available).

Sleeping and Eating on Kerrera: For lodging, your only option is the **$ Kerrera Bunkhouse,** a refurbished 18th-century stable that can sleep up to seven people in a small, cozy space (1 double and 5 single bunks, 2-night minimum, includes bedding and towels, open April-Sept but must book ahead, kitchen, +44 7951 964 231, www.kerrerabunkhouse.co.uk, info@kerrerabunkhouse.co.uk, Martin and Aideen). They also run a **tea garden** that serves meals (Thu-Mon 11:00-16:00, closed Tue-Wed and Oct-Easter). **$$$$ Waypoint Restaurant,** at the Kerrera Marina, has a laid-back patio and works hard to put out good-quality food; on a nice day, the open-air waterside setting is unbeatable (Wed-Fri 17:00-20:00, Sat from 14:00, Sun 14:00-17:00, bar for drinks open longer hours, closed Mon-Tue and in winter, reservations highly recommended, +44 1631 565 333, www.kerreramarina.com).

Isle of Seil

Enjoy a drive, a walk, some solitude, and the sea. Drive 12 miles south of Oban on the A-816 to the B-844 to the Isle of Seil (pronounced "seal"), connected to the mainland by a bridge (which, locals like to brag, "crosses the Atlantic"...well, maybe a small part of it).

Just over the bridge on the Isle of Seil is a pub called **Tigh-an-Truish** ("House of Trousers"). After the Jacobite rebellions, a new law forbade the wearing of kilts on the mainland. Highlanders on the island used this pub to change from kilts to trousers before they made the crossing. The pub serves great meals and good seafood dishes to those either in kilts or pants (pub generally open daily—call ahead, +44 1852 300 242).

Seven miles across the island, on a tiny second island and facing the open Atlantic, is **Easdale,** a historic, touristy, windblown little slate-mining town with a small folk museum (shuttle ferry goes the 300 yards). Wildlife/nature tours plus tours to Iona and Staffa also run from Easdale (www.seafari.co.uk).

Nightlife in Oban

Little Oban has a few options for entertaining its many visitors; ask at the TI, or try checking ObanWhatsOn.co.uk. Fun low-key activities may include open-mic, disco, or quiz theme nights in pubs; occasional Scottish folk shows; coffee meetings; and—if you're lucky—duck races. Here are a few other ways to entertain yourself while in town.

Music and Group Dancing: On many summer nights, you can climb the stairs to **The View,** a sprawling venue on the main drag for music and dancing. There's *ceilidh* (KAY-lee) dancing a couple of times per week, where you can learn some group danc-es to music performed by a folk band (includ-ing, usually, a piper). These group dances are a lot of fun—wallflowers and bad dancers are warmly welcomed, and the staff is happy to give you pointers (£10, generally May-Sept Mon & Thu at 20:00). They also host con-certs by folk and traditional bands (usually Fri-Sat at 22:00, check website for schedule, 34 George Street, +44 1631 569 599, www. obanview.com).

Traditional Music: Various pubs and hotels in town have live traditional music in the summer; the TI compiles these into its *Oban Music Trail* map—ask your B&B host or at the TI for the latest. Two possible venues are the **Oban Inn,** right at the corner of the harborfront near the TI; and **Markie Dans,** between the town center and the Esplanade B&Bs.

Cinema: True to its name, **The Phoenix Cinema** closed down but then was saved by the community. It's now volunteer-run and booming (140 George Street, +44 1631 562 905, www. obanphoenix.com).

Characteristic Pubs: With decor that shows off Oban's mari-time heritage, **Aulay's Bar** has two sides, each with a different per-sonality (I like the right-hand side). Having a drink here invari-ably comes with a good "blether" (conversation), and the gang is mostly local (daily 11:00-24:00, 8 Airds Crescent, just around the corner from the train station and ferry terminal). The **Oban Inn,** mentioned earlier, is also a fun and memorable place for a pint and possibly live music.

Sleeping in Oban

Oban's B&Bs offer a much better value than its hotels. Several places have recently gone to "no breakfast"—you'll be on your own to picnic-breakfast in your room, or find a café in town. (If you're heading to Mull in the morning, the on-ferry cafeteria serves a full breakfast menu.)

ABOVE THE TOWN CENTER

These places perch on the hill above the main waterfront zone—a short (but uphill) walk from all the action. Many rooms come with views and are priced accordingly.

$$$$ Greystones is an enticing splurge. It fills a big, stately, turreted mansion at the top of town with five spacious rooms that mix Victorian charm and sleek gray-and-white minimalism. Built as the private home for the director of Kimberley Diamond Mine, it later became a maternity hospital, and today Archie and Mo run it as a stylish and restful retreat. The breakfast room offers stunning views over Oban and the offshore isles (closed Nov-mid-Feb, 1 Dalriach Road, +44 1631 570 795, www.greystonesoban.com, info@greystonesoban.com).

$ Gramarvin B&B, an exceptional value, feels a little more homey and personal than the fancier places in Oban, and is more plush than the "cheap" ones. It has just two rooms and warm host Mary. Window seats in each room provide a lovely view over Oban, but be warned—the climb up from town and then up their stairs is steep (simple breakfast, cash only, 2-night minimum in summer preferred, on-street parking, Benvoulin Road, +44 1631 564 622, www.gramarvin.co.uk, mary@gramarvin.co.uk, Mary and Joe).

$ Hawthornbank Guest House fills a big Victorian sandstone house with seven traditional-feeling rooms. Half of the rooms face bay views, and the other half overlook the town's lawn bowling green (2-night minimum in summer, Dalriach Road, +44 1631 562 041, www.hawthornbank.co.uk, info@hawthornbank.co.uk, Ian and Jen).

ON STRATHAVEN TERRACE

The following B&Bs line up on a quiet, flowery street that's nicely located two blocks off the harbor, three blocks from the center, and a 10-minute walk from the train station. It's basic—rooms here are compact and don't have views, and none of these places offer breakfast. But the location is handy and prices are lower than the other places I list. These B&Bs generally have a two-night minimum in summer.

To get here by car, as you enter town from the north, turn left immediately after King's Knoll Hotel, and take your first right onto Breadalbane Street. ("Strathaven Terrace" is actually just the name for this row of houses on Breadalbane Street.) The alley behind the buildings has tight, free parking.

$ Rose Villa Guest House has five crisp, fresh, and cheery rooms (no breakfast, at #5, +44 1631 566 874, www.rosevillaoban. co.uk, info@rosevillaoban.co.uk, Stuart and Jacqueline).

$ Sandvilla B&B rents six pleasant, polished rooms (no

breakfast, at #4, +44 1631 564 483, www.holidayoban.co.uk, sandvilla@holidayoban.co.uk, Josephine and Robert).

$ Raniven Guest House has eight decent rooms and is a bit less personal, usually operating by self check-in (no breakfast, at #1, +44 1631 562 713, www.ranivenoban.com, bookings@ranivenoban.com, Liam).

ALONG THE ESPLANADE

These are a 10-minute walk from the center along the Corran Esplanade, which stretches north of town above a cobble beach. Rooms here are generally spacious and many have beautiful bay views. Walking from town, you'll reach them in this order: Kilchrenan, Glenburnie, and Barriemore.

$$$ Glenburnie House, a stately Victorian home, has an elegant breakfast room overlooking the bay. Its eight spacious, comfortable, classy rooms feel like plush living rooms. There's a tiny sunroom with a stuffed "hairy coo" head (no breakfast, closed Nov-Easter, +44 1631 562 089, www.glenburnie.co.uk, stay@glenburnie.co.uk, Graeme and Dan).

$$$ Barriemore B&B, at the very end of Oban's grand waterfront Esplanade, is a welcome refuge after a day of exploration. Its 14 well-appointed rooms come with robes, sherry, and other thoughtful touches. It has a nice front patio, spacious lounge, and glassed-in sun porch with a view of the water (no breakfast, family suite, closed Nov-March, +44 1631 566 356, www.barriemore.co.uk, info@barriemore.co.uk, Jan and Mark).

$$ Kilchrenan House, the turreted former retreat of a textile magnate, has 15 large rooms, most with bay views. The stunning rooms #5, #9, and #15 are worth the few extra pounds, while the "standard" rooms in the newer annex are a good value. This is a rare place in Oban that still serves a full cooked breakfast—including a different "breakfast special" every day (2-night minimum for some rooms, welcome drink of whisky or sherry, family rooms, closed Oct-March, +44 1631 562 663, www.kilchrenanhouse.co.uk, info@kilchrenanhouse.co.uk, Colin and Frances).

IN THE TOWN CENTER

A number of hotels are in the center of town along or near the main drag—but you'll pay for the convenience.

$$$$ Perle Oban Hotel is your luxury boutique splurge. Right across from the harbor, it has 59 super-sleek rooms with calming sea-color walls, decorative bath-tile floors, and rain showers (suites, bar with light bites, pay parking nearby, Station Square, +44 1631 700 301, www.perleoban.co.uk, stay@perleoban.co.uk).

$$$ The Ranald is a modern change of pace from the B&B scene. This narrow, 17-room, three-floor hotel has a budget-boutique vibe; they also rent 10 studio apartments on the same street (family rooms, bar, no elevator, street parking, a block behind the Royal Hotel at 41 Stevenson Street, +44 1631 562 887, https://theranaldhotel.com, info@theranaldhotel.com).

HOSTELS

¢ **Backpackers Plus** is central, laid-back, and fun. It fills part of a renovated old church with a sprawling public living room and a staff generous with travel tips. Check out the walls as you go up to the reception desk—they're covered with graffiti messages from guests (10-minute walk from station, on Breadalbane Street, +44 1631 567 189, www.backpackersplus.com, info@backpackersplus.com, Peter). They have two other locations nearby with private rooms.

¢ The official **SYHA hostel** is institutional but occupies a grand building on the waterfront Esplanade with smashing views of the harbor and islands from the lounges and dining rooms (all rooms en suite, private rooms available, also has family rooms and 8-bed apartment with kitchen, bike storage, +44 1631 562 025, www.hostellingscotland.org.uk, oban@hostellingscotland.org.uk).

Eating in Oban

Oban brags that it is the "seafood capital of Scotland," and indeed its sit-down restaurants are surprisingly high quality for such a small town. For something more casual, consider a fish-and-chips joint, fish tacos, or an easygoing café.

NICE, SIT-DOWN RESTAURANTS

These fill up in summer, especially on weekends. To ensure getting a table, you'll want to book ahead. The restaurants in this section are generally open daily 12:00-15:00 and 17:30-21:00.

$$$ Ee'usk (Scottish Gaelic for "fish") is a popular, stylish seafood place on the waterfront. It has a casual-chic, yacht-clubby atmosphere, with a bright and glassy interior and sweeping views on three sides—fun for watching the ferries come and go. They sometimes offer an early-bird special until 18:45, and their seafood platters are a hit. Reservations are recommended (no kids under age 12 at dinner, North Pier, +44 1631 565 666, www.eeusk.com, MacLeod family).

$$$ Cuan Mòr is a popular, casual restaurant that combines traditional Scottish food with modern flair—both in its crowd-pleasing cuisine and in its furnishings, made of wood, stone, and metal scavenged from the beaches of Scotland's west coast. Its harborside tables on the sidewalk are popular when it's warm (brewery in back, 60 George Street, +44 1631 565 078).

$$$$ Coast proudly serves fresh local fish, meat, and veggies in a mod pine-and-candlelight atmosphere. As everything is cooked to order and presented with care by husband-and-wife team Richard and Nicola—who try to combine traditional Scottish elements in innovative new ways—this is no place to dine and dash (two- and three-course "lite bite" specials, closed Sun for lunch, 104 George Street, +44 1631 569 900, www.coastoban.co.uk).

$$$ The Waterfront Fishouse perches above the busy ferry landing and Seafood Hut. It's easy to miss the ground-floor entrance, but the upstairs dining room is nicely contemporary. In other towns this size, this would be *the* seafood place; here in Oban, it's simply one more solid, well-regarded choice if others are full, or if you happen to walk by while you're hungry (early bird specials before 18:45; open Wed-Sun 12:00-14:15 & 17:30-21:00, closed Mon-Tue; No. 1 Railway Pier, +44 1631 567 415).

$$ Baab Grill brings a refreshing taste of the Eastern Mediterranean to Western Scotland. Besides the usual standbys (baba ghanoush, tabbouleh, moussaka) the menu includes some "fusion" dishes such as Scottish salmon with za'atar in a tahini sauce (attached to the Perle Oban Hotel, Station Road, +44 1631 707 130, www.baabgrill.co.uk).

SIMPLE PLACES FOR AN AFFORDABLE MEAL

$$ Oban Fish and Chips Shop—run by Lewis, Sammy, and their family—serves praiseworthy haddock and mussels among other tasty options in a cheery cabana-like dining room. You can bring your own wine for no charge (daily, sit-down restaurant closes at 19:30, takeaway available later, 116 George Street, +44 1631 569 828).

$$ Oban Seafood Hut, in a green shack facing the ferry dock, is a finger-licking festival of cheap and fresh seafood. John and Marion regularly get fresh deliveries from local fishermen—this is the best spot to pick up a seafood sandwich or a snack. They sell smaller bites (such as cold sandwiches), as well as some bigger cold platters and a few hot dishes (outdoor seating only, daily from 10:00 until the boat unloads from Mull around 18:00).

$ The Fish Box and Taco Bay feels like a glorified food truck, occupying a big, black container parked along an unromantic stretch of the harbor. But the food—fish tacos and other fried fish dishes—is fresh and good, and the seating up top is pleasant on a nice day (no indoor seating, daily 9:00-21:00, Corran Esplanade).

$$ Taste of Argyll—with the motto "from field to fork"—is a humble, simple little hole-in-the-wall that enjoys celebrating fresh local ingredients. They have all-day breakfasts, a burger bar, and other comfort food without the pretense—and the prices—

of Oban's fancier eateries (Mon-Wed 10:00-17:00, Thu-Sat until 21:00, Sun until 15:00, 9 Argyll Street, +44 1631 358 160).

$$ Piazza, next door to Ee'usk, is a casual, affordable, family-friendly place serving basic Italian dishes with a great harborfront location. They have some outdoor seats and big windows facing the sea (smart to reserve ahead July-Aug, +44 1631 563 628, www.piazzaoban.com).

Oban Connections

By Train: Trains link Oban to the nearest transportation hub in **Glasgow** (6/day, fewer on Sun, 3 hours); to get to **Edinburgh,** you'll transfer in Glasgow (roughly 6/day, 4.5 hours). To reach **Fort William** (a transit hub for the Highlands), you'll take the same Glasgow-bound train, but transfer in Crianlarich (3/day, 4 hours)—the direct bus is easier (see next). Train info: +44 845 748 4950, NationalRail.co.uk.

By Bus: Bus #918 passes through Ballachulish—a half-mile from **Glencoe**—on its way to **Fort William** (4/day, 1 hour to Ballachulish, 1.5 hours total to Fort William—but never runs on Sun). Take this bus to Fort William, then transfer to reach **Inverness** (4 hours) or **Portree** on the Isle of Skye (5 hours)—see page 74 for onward bus information. A different bus (#976 and #977) connects Oban with **Glasgow** (5/day, 3 hours), from where you can easily connect by bus or train to **Edinburgh** (figure 4.5 hours). Buses tend to fill up during the busy summer months—book well in advance (online at the Citylink website, or at the TI or West Coast Tours shop). Bus info and tickets: +44 871 266 3333, www.citylink.co.uk.

By Boat: Ferries fan out from Oban to the **southern Hebrides** (see information on the islands of Iona and Mull, later). Caledonian MacBrayne Ferry info: +44 800 066 5000, CalMac.co.uk.

ROUTE TIPS FOR DRIVERS
From Glasgow to Oban via Loch Lomond and Inveraray: For details on this photogenic route from Glasgow to the coast, see the "Glasgow to Oban Drive" at the end of this chapter.

From Oban to Glencoe and Fort William: It's an easy one-hour drive from Oban to Glencoe. From Oban, follow the coastal A-828 toward Fort William. After about 20 miles—as you leave the villages of Appin and Portnacroish—you'll see the photogenic **Castle Stalker** marooned on a lonely island (you can pull over at the Castle Stalker View Café for a good photo from just below its parking lot). At North Ballachulish, you'll reach a bridge spanning Loch Leven; rather than crossing the bridge, turn off and follow the A-82 into the Glencoe Valley for about 15 minutes. (For tips on the best views and hikes in Glencoe, see the next chapter.) After exploring the dramatic valley, make a U-turn and return through Glencoe village. To continue on to Fort William, backtrack to the bridge at North Ballachulish (great view from bridge) and cross it, following the A-82 north.

For a scenic shortcut directly back to Glasgow or Edinburgh, continue south on the A-82 after Glencoe via Rannoch Moor and Tyndrum. Crianlarich is where the road splits, and you'll either continue on the A-82 toward Loch Lomond and Glasgow or pick up the A-85 and follow signs for Stirling, then Edinburgh.

Isles of Mull, Iona, and Staffa

For the easiest one-day look at a good sample of the dramatic and historic Inner Hebrides (HEB-rid-eez) islands, take a tour from Oban to Mull, Iona, and Staffa. Though this trip is spectacular when it's sunny, it's worthwhile in any weather (though there's not much to do on Iona if it's pouring, and if rain or rough seas are expected, I'd skip the Staffa option). For an even more in-depth look at the Inner Hebrides, head north to Skye.

GETTING AROUND THE ISLANDS
Visiting Mull and Iona
To visit Mull and ultimately Iona, you'll take a huge ferry run by Caledonian MacBrayne (CalMac) from Oban to the town of Craignure on Mull (45 minutes). From there, you'll ride a bus or drive across Mull to its westernmost ferry terminal, called Fionnphort (1.25 hours), where you can catch the ferry to Iona (10 minutes) for several hours of free time. It's a long journey, but it's all incredibly scenic.

By Tour (Easiest): If you book a tour with **West Coast Tours,** all your ferry and bus transportation is taken care of. The Mull and Iona tour costs £45 and runs every day, all summer long (no tours Nov-Easter). Because tours can sell out, book in advance at www. westcoasttours.co.uk—several days ahead in July and August. Even at other times, it's smart to book a few days ahead—ideally, once you have a sense of the weather forecast. After booking, when you arrive in Oban—or, if arriving late, in the morning on your way to the ferry dock—go to the West Coast Tours office in person to pick up your tickets (you'll get a strip of paper tickets, one for each leg).

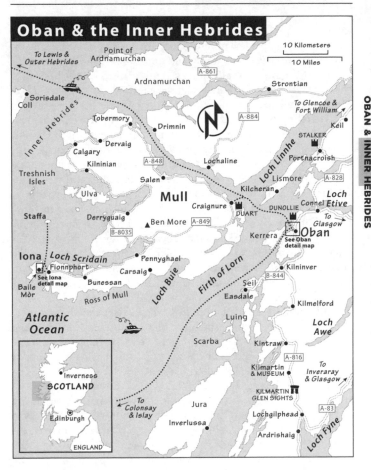

Oban & the Inner Hebrides

Tour Tips: You'll begin by walking on the **Oban-Mull** ferry that leaves from the Oban pier at 9:55 (as schedule can change from year to year, confirm times locally; board at least 20 minutes before departure). The best inside seats on the ferry—with the biggest windows—are in the sofa lounge on the "observation deck" (level 4) at the back end of the boat. (Follow signs for the toilets, and look for the big staircase to the top floor.) The ferry has a cafeteria with hot meals (including cooked breakfast items) and packaged sandwiches, a small snack bar on the top floor (hot drinks and basic sandwiches), and a gift/book shop. If it's a clear day, ask a local or a crew member to point out Ben Nevis, the tallest mountain in Britain. About 10 minutes before landing on Mull, on the left, you'll see the striking 13th-century Duart Castle—the seat of Clan MacLean.

Reaching Mull's port, called Craignure, walk-on passengers

disembark from deck 3, across from the bookshop (port side). It's worth queuing up a few minutes early and making a beeline outside to your **bus** for the entertaining and informative ride across the Isle of Mull. (The bus is usually full, and early arrivals get the best seats; the right/driver's side offers better sea views during the second half of the journey to Fionnphort, while the left side has fine views of Mull's rolling wilderness.) The driver spends the entire ride chattering away about life on Mull, slowing to point out wildlife, loudly complaining about each passing motorist who hasn't mastered the single-track road system, and sharing adages like, "If there's no flowers on the gorse, snogging's gone out of fashion." These hardworking locals make historical trivia fascinating—or at least fun.

At Fionnphort, you'll board a small, rocking **ferry to Iona,** landing in the village of Baile Mòr. You'll have about two hours to roam freely around the island. Then you'll reverse the route: Pay attention as your driver tells you which ferry to return on, and what time his bus will leave. There's little to no commentary on the way back, and the bus is coordinated with the ferry back to Oban (arrives a bit before 18:00).

By Public Transit: For an early start, fewer crowds, and more time on Iona (including spending the night—see "Sleeping and Eating on Iona")—or if you don't get a space on the tour—you can take the early ferry and public bus across Mull, paying individually per leg (Tue-Sat only; round-trip price: £7.80 for Oban-Mull ferry, £16 for public bus across Mull, £3.70 for Mull-Iona ferry).

Take the first boat of the day (departs about 7:25, buy ticket at Oban ferry terminal), then connect at Mull to bus #96 or #496 to Fionnphort (departs 8:24, 80 minutes, buy ticket from driver—cash or card, no tour narration, no guarantee you'll get to sit), then hop on the Iona ferry (roughly every 30 minutes, buy ticket from small trailer ferry office; if closed, purchase ticket from ferry worker at the dock; cash or card accepted; leaving Iona, do the same, as there's no ferry office). You'll have about four hours on Iona and need to return to Fionnphort in time for the bus back (15:18). It's important to confirm all of these times in Oban (just pop in to the West Coast Tours office).

By Car: You can do this trip on your own by driving your car onto the ferry to Mull (£29.40 round-trip for the car, plus passengers, www.calmac.co.uk), then driving across the island and walking on the ferry to Iona (no visitor cars are allowed on Iona). Space on the Oban-Mull ferry is limited, so book well in advance. Keep in mind that because of tight ferry timings, you'll wind up basically following the tour buses across Mull anyway, but you'll miss all the commentary.

By Taxi: Alan from **Mull Taxi** can get you around his home island and also offers day trips (+44 7760 426 351, www.mulltaxi. co.uk).

Visiting Staffa

With two extra hours, you can add a Staffa side trip to your Mull/ Iona visit (£78 total for the "Three Isles Tour" through **West Coast Tours** in Oban; or if you're getting to Fionnphort on your own, you can book the £30 Staffa portion directly via **Staffa Tours**—+44 7831 885 985, www.staffatours.com).

While Staffa is a thrill for nature lovers, it's far more appealing in good weather than in bad (and, given its popularity, you may have to book before you know for sure...so it can be a crapshoot). You'll begin the same as the Mull/Iona tour (ferry from Oban, then bus or drive across Mull). But then, upon arrival at Fionnphort, you'll board a much smaller boat bound for Staffa (35-minute trip, about an hour of free time on Staffa). From Staffa, you'll head to Iona for about two hours before returning to Mull. If you're on West Coast's Three Isle Tour, you can either depart Oban on the 9:55 ferry, arriving back to Oban around 20:21; or do the "early bird" tour, departing at 7:25 and returning a bit before 18:00.

For a more relaxed schedule, both **Staffa Tours** (listed above) and **Staffa Trips** (www.staffatrips.co.uk, +44 1681 700 358) offer other variations that include more time on Staffa.

Turus Mara offers nature/wildlife tours from Oban to just Staffa or Staffa and the small island of Ulva—skipping Iona (www. turusmara.com, +44 1688 400 242).

Picnic Tip: If you're taking a later departure to Staffa, be aware you won't have much access to food until you arrive on Iona in the midafternoon. It's smart to pack along a lunch (buy something near the Oban terminal before you board, or in the on-board ferry café).

Mull

The Isle of Mull, the second largest of the Inner Hebrides (after Skye), has nearly 300 scenic miles of coastline and castles and a 3,169-foot-high mountain, one of Scotland's Munros. Called **Ben More** ("Big Mountain" in Gaelic), it was once much bigger. At 10,000 feet tall, it made up the entire island of Mull— until a volcano erupted. Things are calmer now, and, similarly, Mull has a

noticeably laid-back population of only about 2,850 residents. My bus driver reported that there are no deaths from stress, and only a few from boredom.

With steep, fog-covered hillsides topped by cairns (piles of stones, sometimes indicating graves) and ancient standing stones and stone circles, Mull has a gloomy, otherworldly charm. It's sparsely populated and very scenic. Bring plenty of rain protection and wear layers in case the sun peeks through the clouds. As my driver said, Mull is a place of cold, wet, windy winters and mild, wet, windy summers.

As the road is almost entirely single-track, on your trip across Mull you'll get an unforgettable education in how to drive on British back roads. ("We don't drive on the left," my driver said. "We drive on what's left.") If you're driving, my driver made me promise to remind you: Always stay to the left at passing places, even if that means you're along the straight part of the road and the oncoming car (or bus) must use the turnout to get around you. In other words, don't cross over into the "other" lane's passing place in an attempt to be helpful...it isn't.

The Drive Across Mull: From where the Oban ferry docks at **Craignure,** to get to Fionnphort and boats to Iona or Staffa, you'll ride the bus (or drive) about 1.25 hours across the island. The road passes or traverses several picturesque 300-year-old stone bridges, built by the great Scottish engineer Thomas Telford. You'll drive by Loch Spelve (with a thriving mussel-farming operation), follow the Lussa River, go past an intense forestry operation (they replant trees every 30 years, rotating the harvest each year), then climb up over the empty and lonesome glen that defines the middle of the island.

Passing three lochs on your left, you'll begin to coast downhill to the southwestern lobe of Mull, following the trout-rich River Coladoir. You'll see loads of sheep as you drive through the village of **Pennyghael,** on the banks of Loch Scridain. As this sea loch opens up, you'll begin to see the hazy form of Staffa and the nearby Treshnish Isles (off on the right horizon). Going through the farming community of Bunessan, you're just around the corner from Fionnphort—and your next boat trip.

On the far side of Mull, the caravan of tour buses unloads at **Fionnphort** (FIH-nih-fort)—a tiny ferry landing with a small ferry-passenger building with a meager snack bar and a pay WC; a more enticing seafood bar is across the street. Parking is clearly marked for drivers.

The ferry to the island of **Iona** takes about 200 walk-on passengers. Bus riders should listen to your driver's instructions and follow the blue path to the dock to catch the first trip over (otherwise, it's a 30-minute wait; on extremely busy days, those who dillydally may not fit on the first ferry). On board, the ferry has tight little indoor lounges, crowded outdoor decks, and free WCs. After the 10-minute ride, you wash ashore on sleepy Iona, and the ferry mobs that crowded you on the boat seem to disappear up Baile Mòr's main road and into Iona's back lanes.

Iona

The tiny island of Iona, just 3 miles by 1.5 miles, is famous as the birthplace of Christianity in Scotland. If you're on the West Coast

Tours ferry-and-bus trip from Oban outlined earlier, you'll have about two hours here on your own before you retrace your steps (your bus driver will tell you which return ferry to take back to Mull).

A pristine quality of light and a thoughtful peace pervade the stark, (nearly) car-free island and its tiny community. With buoyant clouds bouncing playfully off distant bluffs, sparkling-white crescents of sand, eerily colorful water in its yawning bays, and lone tourists camped thoughtfully atop huge rocks just looking out to sea, Iona is a place that's perfect for meditation. To experience Iona, it's important to get out and take a little hike; you can follow some or all of my self-guided walk outlined below. And you can easily climb a peak—nothing's higher than 300 feet above the sea.

Orientation to Iona

The ferry arrives at the island's only real village, Baile Mòr, with shops, a restaurant/pub, a few accommodations, and no bank. (Bring cash—some businesses here don't accept credit cards.) The only taxi based on Iona is **Iona Taxi** (+44 7810 325 990, www.ionataxi.co.uk).

Leaving the ferry dock, on the left, look for free WCs. Up the road, also on the left, is the National Trust for Scotland "**Shelter**"—a small indoor exhibit offering a quick orientation to the island. Straight ahead and just a bit farther up the hill is a little **Spar** grocery (one of many places to get a takeaway lunch—others are noted under "Eating," later). Next door, the **Iona Craft Shop** sells good coffee drinks and rents bikes (£15/3 hours).

Iona has no real TI, though the **Welcome Center**—up near the Iona Abbey, at the end of my self-guided walk—is close enough. The official website www.isle-of-iona.net has good information about the island.

Open Days: Unless otherwise noted, everything I mention on Iona should be open every day during the window of time when tours from Oban are in town.

Iona Walk

Here's a basic self-guided route for exploring the village and points nearby on foot (since no private cars are allowed unless you're a resident or have a permit). With the standard two hours on Iona that a day trip allows, you will have time for a visit to the abbey and then a light stroll; or do the entire walk described below, but skip the abbey (unless you're speedy and have time for a quick visit on your way back).

Nunnery Ruins: From the ferry dock, head directly up the single paved road that passes through the village and up a small hill to visit one of Britain's best-preserved medieval nunneries (free).

Immediately after the nunnery, turn right on North Road. You'll curve up through the fields—passing the parish church.

Heritage Center: This little museum, tucked behind the church (watch for signs), is small but well done, with displays on local and natural history and a garden café (free but donation requested, closed Sun and off-season, +44 1681 700 576, www.ionaheritage.co.uk).

St. Oran's Chapel and Iona Abbey: Continue on North Road. After the road swings right, you'll pass the St. Columba Hotel and Larder, then see **St. Oran's Chapel,** in the graveyard of the Iona Abbey. This chapel is the oldest church building on the island. Inside you'll find a few grave slabs carved in the distinctive Iona School style, which was developed by local stone carvers in the 14th century. On these tall, skinny headstones, look for the depictions of medieval warrior aristocrats with huge swords. Many more of these carvings have been moved to the abbey, where you can see them in its cloister and museum.

It's free to see the graveyard and chapel; the ▲ **Iona Abbey** itself has an admission fee, but it's worth the cost just to sit in the stillness of its lovely, peaceful interior courtyard (£9.50, includes guided tour and/or audioguide; open daily in summer, closed Sun in winter; +44 1681 700 512, www.historicenvironment.scot—search for "Iona Abbey").

The abbey marks the site of Christianity's arrival in Scot-

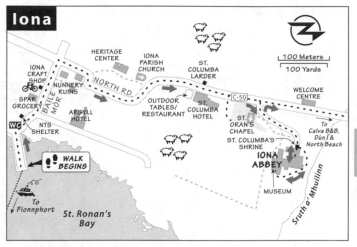

land. You'll see Celtic crosses, the original shrine of St. Columba, a big church slathered with medieval carvings, a tranquil cloister, and an excellent museum with surviving fragments of this site's fascinating layers of history. While the present abbey, nunnery, and graveyard go back to the 13th century, much of what you'll see was rebuilt in the 20th century. Be sure to read the "History of Iona" sidebar to prepare for your visit.

At the entrance building, pick up your included audioguide, and ask about the good 30-minute guided tours (4/day and worthwhile). Then head toward the church. You'll pass two faded **Celtic crosses** (and the base of a third); the originals are in the museum at the end of your visit. Some experts believe that Celtic crosses—with their distinctive shape so tied to Christianity on the British Isles—originated right here on Iona.

Facing the entrance to the church, you'll see the original **shrine to St. Columba** (a small chapel) on your left—a magnet for pilgrims.

Head inside the **church.** It feels like an active church—with hymnals neatly stacked in the pews—because it is, thanks to the Iona community. While much of this space has been rebuilt, take a moment to look around. Plenty of original medieval stone carving (especially the capitals of many columns) still survives. To see a particularly striking example, stand near the pulpit in the middle of the church and look back to the entrance. Partway up the left span of the pointed arch framing the transept, look for the eternally screaming face. While interpretations vary, this may have been a reminder for the priest not to leave out the fire-and-brimstone parts of his message. Some of the newer features of the church—including the base of the baptismal font near the entrance, and the main

History of Iona

St. Columba (521-597), an Irish scholar, soldier, priest, and founder of monasteries, got into a small war over the possession of an illegally copied psalm book. Victorious but sickened by the bloodshed, Columba left Ireland, vowing never to return. According to legend, the first bit of land out of sight of his homeland was Iona. He stopped here in 563 and established an abbey.

Columba's monastic community flourished, and Iona became the center of Celtic Christianity. Missionaries from Iona spread the gospel throughout Scotland and northern England, while scholarly monks established Iona as a center of art and learning. The Book of Kells—perhaps the finest piece of manuscript art from early medieval Europe—was probably made on Iona in the eighth century. The island was so important that it was the legendary burial place for ancient Scottish clan chieftains and kings (including Macbeth, of Shakespeare fame) and even some Scandinavian monarchs.

Slowly, the importance of Iona ebbed. Vikings massacred 68 monks in 806. Fearing more raids, the monks evacuated most of Iona's treasures to Ireland (including the Book of Kells, which is now in Dublin; there's a replica in the Iona Abbey museum). Much later, with the Reformation, the abbey was abandoned, and most of its finely carved crosses were destroyed. In the 17th century, locals used the abbey only as a handy quarry for other building projects.

Iona's population peaked at about 500 in the 1830s. In the 1840s, a potato famine hit, and in the 1850s, a third of the islanders emigrated to Canada or Australia. By 1900, the population was down to 210, and today it's only around 200.

But in our generation, a new religious community has given the abbey fresh life. The Iona Community is an ecumenical gathering of men and women who seek new ways of living the Gospel in today's world, with a focus on worship, peace and justice issues, and reconciliation (http://iona.org.uk).

altar—are carved from locally quarried Iona marble: white with green streaks. In the right/south transept is the tomb of George Campbell—the Eighth Duke of Argyll, who donated this property in 1900, allowing it to be restored.

When you're ready to continue, find the poorly marked door into the **cloister**. (As you face the altar, it's about halfway down the nave on the left, before the transept.) This space is filled with

harmonious light, additional finely carved capitals (these are modern re-creations), and—displayed along the walls—several more of the tall, narrow tombstones like the ones displayed in St. Oran's Chapel. On these, look for a couple of favorite motifs: the long, intimidating sword (indicating a warrior of the Highland clans) and the ship with billowing sails (a powerful symbol of this seafaring culture).

Around the far side of the cloister is the shop, and just beyond that is the door back outside. But before leaving the abbey grounds, don't overlook the easy-to-miss **museum.** (To find it, head outside, turn right, and walk around the far side of the abbey complex, toward the sea.) The modern, well-presented "Iona: Across Time" exhibit displays a remarkable collection of original stonework from the abbey—including what's left of the three Celtic crosses out front—all eloquently described.

Iona Community's Welcome Centre: Just beyond and across the road from the abbey is the Iona Community's Welcome Centre (free WCs), which runs the abbey with Historic Scotland and hosts modern-day pilgrims who come here to experience the birthplace of Scottish Christianity. (If you're staying longer, you could attend a worship service at the abbey—check the schedule here; +44 1681 700 404, www.iona.org.uk.) Its gift shop is packed with books on the island's important role in Christian history.

Views: Walk as far as you like beyond the abbey, following the only real road across the island. If you need a destination, one good choice is about a 10-minute walk past the welcome center, where you can find the footpath for **Dùn Ì** (the name for the bulbous, rocky hill that rises up in the middle of the island)—a steep but short climb with good views of the abbey looking back toward Mull.

North Beach: If you have plenty of time and a hankering to walk, back on the main road, carry on another 20-25 minutes to the end of the paved road, where you'll arrive at a gate leading through a sheep- and cow-strewn pasture to Iona's pristine white-sand beach. Dip your toes in the Atlantic and ponder what this Caribbean-like alcove is doing in Scotland. Be sure to allow at least 40 minutes to return to the ferry dock.

Sleeping on Iona

For a chance to really experience peaceful, idyllic Iona, spend a night or two (Scots bring their kids and stay on this tiny island for a week—reserve far in advance in the summer). To do so, you'll have to buy each leg of the ferry-bus-ferry (and return) trip separately (see "By Public Transit," earlier). These accommodations are listed roughly in the order you'll reach them as you climb the main road from the ferry dock. The first two hotels listed have restaurants that are open to the public for lunch, tea, and dinner and closed in winter (for more, see "Eating on Iona," below). For more accommodation options, see Isle-of-Iona.net/accommodation.

$$$ St. Columba Hotel, up near the Iona Abbey and situated in the middle of a peaceful garden with picnic tables, has 27 institutional rooms and spacious lodge-like common spaces—such as a big, cushy seaview lounge (closed Nov-March, +44 1681 700 304, www.stcolumba-hotel.co.uk, info@stcolumba-hotel.co.uk).

$$ Argyll Hotel, built in 1867, proudly overlooks the waterfront, with 17 cottage-like rooms and pleasingly creaky hallways lined with bookshelves. Of the two hotels, this one feels classier, with comfortable lounges with a piano and a fireplace, and a sunroom (+44 1681 700 334, www.argyllhoteliona.co.uk, reception@argyllhoteliona.co.uk).

$$ Calva B&B, a five-minute walk past the abbey, has three spacious rooms (second house on left past the abbey, look for sign in window and gnomes on porch, +44 1681 700 340—no email, just call to reserve; friendly Janetta and Ken).

Eating on Iona

For a little island, Iona has multiple options for lunch. Everything here is rated **$;** while some of the bigger restaurants are open for dinner, when prices are much higher, at lunchtime it's easy to find a simple (sandwich) lunch anywhere for less than £10. I've listed these roughly in the order you reach them, coming up from the ferry dock.

Argyll Hotel, down the little seaview side lane to the right as you head up from the ferry, has a fine dining room and some outdoor tables that are a good value at lunch.

Spar, the only grocery store on the island, is one place to grab a simple sandwich and snacks to go.

St. Columba Hotel also has a good restaurant, with a humdrum dining room and a beautiful lawn strewn with picnic tables.

St. Columba Larder—just above/across the street from the hotel—used to go by the name "The Low Door" (for reasons you'll understand as you enter). They sell coffee drinks, sweets, gourmet picnic fixings, and some prepared sandwiches you can enjoy at the picnic tables outside (no indoor seating).

Staffa

Those more interested in nature than in Christian history will enjoy the trip to the wildly scenic Isle of Staffa. Completely uninhabited (except for seabirds), Staffa is a knob of rock draped with a vibrant green carpet of turf. Remote and quiet, it feels like a Hebrides nature preserve.

Most day trips give you an hour on Staffa—barely enough time to see its two claims to fame: the basalt columns of Fingal's Cave and (in summer) a colony of puffins. To squeeze in both, be ready to hop off the boat and climb the staircase. Partway up to the left, you can walk around to the cave (about 7 minutes). Or continue up to the top, then turn right and walk across the spine of the grassy island (about 10-15 minutes) to the cove where the puffins gather. Be sure to get clear instructions from your captain on how and where to best watch the puffins. It's worth doing right.

▲▲Fingal's Cave

Staffa's shore is covered with bizarre, mostly hexagonal basalt columns that stick up at various heights. It's as if the earth were offering God his choice of thousands of six-sided cigarettes. (The island's name likely came from the Old Norse word for "stave"—the building timbers these columns resemble.) This is the other end of Northern Ireland's popular Giant's Causeway. You'll walk along the uneven surface of these columns, curling around the far side of the island, until you can actually step inside the gaping mouth of a cave—

Puffins

The Atlantic puffin *(Fratercula arctica)* is an adorably stout, tuxedo-clad seabird with a too-big orange beak and beady black eyes. Puffins live most of their lives on the open Atlantic, coming to land only to breed. They fly north to Scotland between mid-May and early June, raise their brood, then take off again in August. Puffins mate for life and typically lay just one egg each year, which the male and female take turns caring for. A baby puffin is called—wait for it—a puffling.

To feed their pufflings, puffins plunge as deep as 200 feet below the sea's surface to catch sand eels, herring, and other small fish. Their compact bodies, stubby wings, oil-sealed plumage, and webbed feet are ideal for navigating underwater. Famously, puffins can stuff several small fish into their beaks at once, thanks to their agile tongues and uniquely hinged beaks. This evolutionary trick lets puffins stock up before returning to the nest.

Squat, tiny-winged puffins have a distinctive way of flying. To take off, they either beat their wings like crazy (on sea) or essentially hurl themselves off a cliff (on land). Once aloft, they beat their wings furiously—up to 400 times per minute—to stay airborne. Coming in for a smooth landing on a rocky cliff is a challenge (and highly entertaining to watch): They choose a spot, swoop in at top speed on prevailing currents, then flutter their wings madly to brake as they try to touch down. At the moment of truth, the puffin decides whether to attempt to stick the landing; more often than not, he bails out and does another big circle on the currents...and tries again... and again...and again.

where floor-to-ceiling columns and crashing waves combine to create a powerful experience. Listening to the water and air flowing through this otherworldly space inspired Felix Mendelssohn to compose his overture *The Hebrides*.

While you're ogling the cave, consider this: Geologists claim these unique formations were created by volcanic eruptions more than 60 million years ago. As the surface of the lava flow quickly cooled, it contracted and crystallized into columns (resembling the caked mud at the bottom of a dried-up lakebed, but with deeper cracks). As the rock later settled and eroded, the columns broke off into the many stair-like steps that now honeycomb Staffa.

Of course, in actuality, these formations resulted from a heated rivalry between a Scottish giant named Fingal, who lived on Staffa, and an Ulster warrior named Finn MacCool, who lived across the sea on Ireland's Antrim Coast. Knowing that the giant was coming to spy on him, Finn had his wife dress him as a sleeping infant. The giant, shocked at the infant's size, fled back to Scotland in terror of whomever had sired this giant baby. Breathing a sigh of relief, Finn tore off the baby clothes and prudently knocked down the bridge.

▲▲Puffin Watching

A large colony of Atlantic puffins settles on Staffa each spring and summer during mating season (generally early May through early August). The puffins tend to scat-ter when the boat arrives. But after the boat pulls out and its passengers hike across the island, the very tame puffins' curiosity gets the better of them. First you'll see them flutter up from the offshore rocks, with their distinctive, bobbing flight. They'll zip and whirl around, and finally they'll start to land on the lip of the cove. Sit quietly, move slowly, and be patient, and soon they'll get close. (If any seagulls are nearby, shoo them away—puffins are undaunted by humans, who do them no harm, but they're terrified of predatory seagulls.)

In the waters around Staffa—on your way to and from the other islands—also keep an eye out for a variety of **marine life,** including seals, dolphins, porpoises, and the occasional minke whale, fin whale, or basking shark (a gigantic fish that hinges open its enormous jaw to drift-net plankton).

OBAN & INNER HEBRIDES

Glasgow to Oban Drive

The following drive outlines the best route from Glasgow to Oban, including the appealing town of Inveraray, with an optional detour to one of Scotland's most important prehistoric sites, Kilmartin Glen.

GLASGOW TO OBAN VIA INVERARAY

The drive from Glasgow (or Edinburgh) to Oban via Inveraray provides dreamy vistas and your first look at the dramatic landscapes of the Highlands, as well as historic sites and ample opportunity to stop for a picnic.

• *Leaving Glasgow on the A-82, you'll soon be driving along the west bank of...*

Loch Lomond

The first picnic turnout, at the town of Balloch, has good views of this famous lake, benches, a park, and a playground. You're driving over an isthmus between Loch Lomond and a sea loch

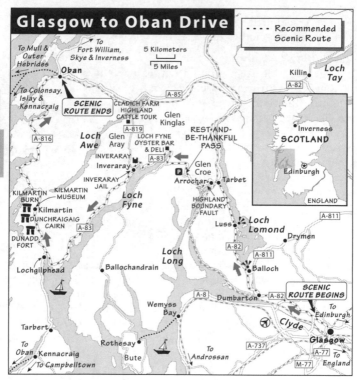

Glasgow to Oban Drive

- - - - Recommended
Scenic Route

(inlet). Farther along, Luss is a smaller village where you'll see more mountains. Halfway up the loch, you'll find the town of Tarbet—the Viking word for isthmus, a common name on Scottish maps. Imagine, a thousand years ago, Vikings dragging their ships across this narrow stretch of land to reach Loch Lomond.

• *At Tarbet, the road forks. The signs for Oban keep you on the direct route along A-82. For the scenic option that takes you past Loch Fyne to Inveraray (about 30 minutes longer to drive), keep left for the A-83 (toward Campbeltown).*

Highland Boundary Fault

You'll pass the village of Arrochar, then drive along the banks of Loch Long. The scenery crescendos as you pull away from the loch and twist up over the mountains and through a pine forest, getting your first glimpse of bald Highlands mountains—it's clear that you've just crossed the Highland Boundary Fault. Enjoy the waterfalls, and notice that the road signs are now in Gaelic as well as English. As you climb into more rugged territory—up the valley called Glen Croe—be mindful that the roads connecting the Lowlands with the Highlands (like the one down in the glen below) were originally a military project designed to facilitate government quelling of the Highland clans.

• *At the summit, watch for the large parking lot with picnic tables on your left (signed for* Argyll Forest Park*). Stretch your legs at what's aptly named...*

Rest-and-Be-Thankful Pass

The colorful name comes from the 19th century, when just reaching this summit was exhausting. At the top of the military road, just past the last picnic table, there's actually a stone (dated 1814) put there by the military with that phrase.

As you drive on, enjoy the dramatic green hills. You may see little bits of hillside highlighted by sunbeams. Each of these is known as a "soot" (Sun's Oot Over There). Look for soots as you drive farther north into the Highlands.

• *Continue twisting down the far side of the pass. You'll drive through Glen Kinglas and soon reach...*

Loch Fyne

This saltwater "sea loch" is famous for its shellfish (keep an eye out for oyster farms). In fact, Loch Fyne is the namesake of a popular UK restaurant chain with locations across the UK. **$$$$ Loch Fyne Oyster Bar and Deli,** in the big white building at the end of the loch, is the original. It's a famous stop for locals—an elegant seafood restaurant and oyster bar worth traveling for. If the restaurant is full, order from the bar menu (about the same as the restaurant) and grab more casual seating (daily 12:00-16:00, no reservations, +44 1499 600 482, www.lochfyne.com). Even if you're not eating, it's fun to peruse their salty deli (tasty treats to go, picnic tables outside, good coffee).

• *Looping around Loch Fyne, you approach Inveraray. As you get close, keep an eye on the right (when crossing the bridge, have your camera ready) for the dramatic...*

▲Inveraray Castle

This residence of the Duke of Argyll comes with a dramatic, turreted exterior (one of Scotland's most striking) and an interior that feels spacious, neatly tended, and lived in. Historically a stronghold of one of the more notorious branches of the Campbell clan,

The Irish Connection

The Romans called the people living in what is now Ireland the "Scoti" (meaning pirates). When the Scoti crossed the narrow Irish Sea and invaded the land of the Picts 1,500 years ago, that region became known as Scoti-land. Ireland and Scotland were never fully conquered by the Romans, and they retained similar clannish Celtic traits. Both share the same Gaelic branch of the linguistic tree.

On clear summer days, you can actually see Ireland—just 17 miles away—from the Scottish coastline. The closest bit to Scotland is the boomerang-shaped Rathlin Island, part of Northern Ireland. Rathlin is where Scottish leader Robert the Bruce retreated in 1307 after defeat at the hands of the English. Legend has it that he hid in a cave on the island, where he observed a spider patiently rebuilding its web each time a breeze knocked it down. Inspired by the spider's perseverance, Bruce gathered his Scottish forces once more and finally defeated the English at the decisive battle of Bannockburn.

Flush with confidence from his victory, Robert the Bruce decided to open a second front against the English...in Ireland. In 1315, he sent his brother Edward over to enlist their Celtic Irish cousins in an effort to thwart the English. After securing Ireland, Edward hoped to move on and enlist the Welsh, thus cornering England with their pan-Celtic nation. But Edward's timing was bad: Ireland was in the midst of famine. His Scottish troops had to live off the land and began to take food and supplies from the starving Irish. Some of Ireland's crops may have been intentionally destroyed to keep it from being used as a colonial "breadbasket" to feed English troops. The Scots quickly wore out their welcome, and Edward the Bruce was eventually killed in battle near Dundalk in 1318.

It's interesting to imagine how things might be different today if Scotland and Ireland had been permanently welded together as a nation 700 years ago. You'll notice the strong Scottish influence in Northern Ireland when you ask a local a question and he answers, "Aye, a wee bit." And in Glasgow—near Scotland's west coast, closest to Ireland—an Ireland-like division between royalist Protestants and republican Catholics survives today in the form of soccer team allegiances.  In big Scottish cities (like Glasgow and Edinburgh), you'll even see "orange parades" of protesters marching in solidarity with their Protestant Northern Irish cousins. The Irish—always quick to defuse tension with humor—joke that the Scots are just Irish people who couldn't swim home.

this castle is most appealing to those with Campbell connections or fans of *Downton Abbey*—this was "Duneagle Castle" (a.k.a. Uncle Shrimpy's pad) from the first Christmas special.

Cost and Hours: £14.50; Thu-Mon 10:00-17:45, closed Tue-Wed and Nov-March, last entry 45 minutes before closing; nice basement café, buy tickets at the car-park booth, +44 1499 302 551, www.inveraray-castle.com.

Visiting the Castle: Roam from room to room, reading the laminated descriptions and asking questions of the gregarious docents. The highlight is the Armoury Hall that fills the main atrium, where swords and rifles are painstakingly arrayed in starburst patterns. The rifles were actually used when the Campbells fought against the Jacobites at the Battle of Culloden in 1746.

Upstairs are more fine rooms, often displaying temporary exhibits. As with many such castles, the aristocratic clan still lives here (*private* signs mark rooms where the family resides). The room in the turret is like an Argyll family scrapbook; for example, see photos of the duke playing elephant polo—the ultimate aristocratic sport. The kids attend school in England, but spend a few months here each year; in the winter, the castle is closed to the public and they have the run of the place. The basement holds an old kitchen and a café, which has outdoor seating at the base of the fortress.

And what about the *Downton Abbey* connection? The Campbells seem content to move on; you'll find only a few scant reminders of the castle's moment of television fame—mostly down in the basement (ask the docents what there is to see).

After touring the interior, do a loop through the finely manicured gardens. The best views are at the far end from where you entered.

• *After visiting the castle, spend some time exploring...*

▲Inveraray Town

Nearly everybody stops at this lovely, seemingly made-for-tourists town on Loch Fyne. Browse the main street—lined with touristy shops and cafés all the way to the church at its top. As this is the geological and demographic border between the Highlands and the Lowlands, traditionally church services here were held in both Scots and Gaelic. Just before the church is Loch Fyne Whiskies with historic bottles on its ceiling.

There's free parking on the main street and plenty of pay-

and-display parking near the pier (public WCs at end of nearby pier).

The **Inveraray Jail** is the main sight in town—an overpriced, corny, but mildly educational former jail converted into a museum. This "living 19th-century prison" includes a courtroom where mannequins argue the fate of the accused. Then you'll head outside and explore the various cells of the outer courtyard. The playful guards may lock you up for a photo op, while they explain how Scotland reformed its prison system in 1839—you'll see both "before" and "after" cells in this complex (£13.50, includes 75-minute audioguide, open daily, +44 1499 302 381, www.inverarayjail.co.uk).

• *To continue directly to Oban from Inveraray (about an hour), leave town through the gate at the woolen mill and get on the A-819, which takes you through Glen Aray, past the turnoff for the Cladich Highland Cattle Farm Tour, then along the aptly named Loch Awe. A left turn on the A-85 takes you into Oban.*

But if you have a healthy interest in prehistoric sites, you can go to Oban by way of Kilmartin Glen (adds about 45 minutes of driving). To get there from Inveraray, head straight up Inveraray's main street and get on the waterfront A-83 (marked for Campbeltown*); after a half-hour, in Lochgilphead, turn right onto the A-816, which takes you through Kilmartin Glen and all the way up to Oban. (To avoid backtracking, be ready to stop at the prehistoric sites lining the A-816 between Lochgilphead and Kilmartin village.)*

OTHER SIGHTS BETWEEN GLASGOW AND OBAN
▲▲Cladich Farm Highland Cattle Tour

In rolling hills on the south shore of Loch Awe, 30 miles from Oban and 10 miles from Inveraray, Cladich Farm offers tours that get up close to some of their 100 head of Highland cattle. Queenie and Jon begin by showing you around the barn and explaining their operation. Then you'll board an ATV to head out into the hills for sweeping views over Loch Awe and the Cruachan mountain...and to find some cattle. The specifics of the tour can change with the weather, time of year, and your interests, but you'll always get up close and personal with some hairy coos—scratching them behind the ears, brushing their shaggy coat, and so on. This is a real, working farm (be prepared for cow pats, smells, and any kind of weather), but your hosts—who were both accountants in a previous life—include some classy touches. The tour, which takes about 2.5 hours, must be arranged in advance (£100/two people, ask for pricing for larger groups, usually at 10:00 and 14:30—reservations required; +44 7718 524 158, www.visitcladich.co.uk, highlandcattle@cladich-argyll.co.uk).

Sleeping at Cladich Farm: The property also includes a

comfortable, well-equipped **$$ Cladich House B&B,** with three rooms (+44 1838 200 845, mobile +44 7718 524 158, stay@ visitcladich.co.uk).

Kilmartin Glen

Except for the Orkney Islands, Scotland isn't as rich with pre-historic sites. But the ones in Kilmartin Glen, while faint, are some of Scotland's most accessible—and most important. This wide valley, imbued with some combination of spiritual and stra-tegic power, contains reminders of several millennia worth of in-habitants. Today it's a playground for those who enjoy tromping through grassy fields while daydreaming about who moved these giant stones here so many centuries ago. This isn't worth a long detour, unless you're fascinated by prehistory.

Four to five thousand years ago, Kilmartin Glen was inhab-ited by Neolithic people who left behind fragments of their giant, stony monuments. And 1,500 years

ago, this was the seat of the kings of the Scoti, who migrated here from Ireland around AD 500, giving rise to Scotland's own branch of Celtic culture. From this grassy valley, the Scoti kings ruled their empire, called Dalriada (also sometimes written Dál Riata), which encompassed much of Scotland's west coast, the Inner Heb-rides, and the northern part of Ire-land. The Scoti spoke Gaelic and were Christian; as they overtook the rest of the Highlands—eventually absorb-ing their rival Picts—theirs became a dominant culture, which is still evident in pockets of present-day Scotland. Today, Kilmartin Glen is scattered with burial cairns, standing stones, and a hill called Dunadd—the fortress of the Scoti kings.

Visiting Kilmartin Glen: Sites are scattered throughout the valley, including some key locations along or just off the A-816 south of Kilmartin village. If you're coming from Inveraray, you'll pass these *before* you reach the village and museum itself. Each one is explained by good informational signs.

Dunadd: This bulbous hill sits just west of the A-816, about four miles north of Lochgilphead and four miles south of Kilmartin village (watch for blue, low-profile *Dunadd Fort* signs). A fort had stood here since the time of Christ, but it was the Scoti kings—who made it their primary castle from the sixth to ninth centuries—that put Dunadd on the map. Park in the big lot at its base and hike through the faint outlines of terraces to the top, where you can enjoy sweeping views over all of Kilmartin Glen; this southern stretch is a marshland called "The Great Moss" (Moine Mhor). Look for carvings in the rock: early Celtic writing, the image of a boar, and a footprint (carved into a stone crisscrossed with fissures). This "footprint of fealty" (a replica) recalls the inauguration ceremony in which the king would place his foot into the footprint, symbolizing the marriage between the ruler and the land.

Dunchraigaig Cairn: About two miles farther north on the A-816, brown *Dunchraigaig* signs mark a parking lot where you can cross the road to the 4,000-year-old, 100-foot-in-diameter Dunchraigaig Cairn—the burial place for 10 Neolithic VIPs. Circle around to find the opening, where you can still crawl into a small recess. This is one of at least five such cairns that together created a mile-and-a-half-long "linear cemetery" up the middle of Kilmartin Glen.

From this cairn, you can walk five minutes to several more prehistoric structures: Follow signs through the gate, and walk to a farm field with **Ballymeanoch**—an avenue of two stone rows (with six surviving stones), a disheveled old cairn, and a stone circle.

Sites near Kilmartin Burn: About one more mile north on the A-816, just off the intersection with the B-8025 (toward *Tayvallich*), is the small Kilmartin Burn parking lot. From here, cross the stream to a field where the five **Nether Largie Standing Stones** have stood in a neat north-south line for 3,200 years. Were these stones designed as an astronomical observatory? Burial rituals or other religious ceremonies? Sporting events? Or just a handy place for sheep to scratch themselves? From here, you can hike the rest of the way through the field (about 10 minutes) to the **Nether Largie South Cairn** and the **Temple Wood Stone Circles** (which don't have their own parking). The larger, older of these circles dates to more than 5,000 years ago, and both were added onto and modified over the millennia.

Kilmartin Museum: This museum—likely to reopen in 2023 after a renovation—is in the center of Kilmartin village. The cute stone house has a ticket desk, bookshop, and café; the newly built museum plans to feature exhibits explaining this area's powerful history, with a few original artifacts and lots of re-creations (call to confirm details before visiting, +44 1546 510 278, www.kilmartin.org).

From the museum, you can look out across the fields to see **Glebe Cairn,** one of the five cairns of the "linear cemetery." Another one, the **Nether Largie North Cairn,** was reconstructed in the 1970s and can actually be entered (a half-mile south of the museum; ask for directions at museum).

Many more prehistoric sites fill Kilmartin Glen (more than 800 within a six-mile radius); the museum sells in-depth guidebooks for the curious, and can point you in the right direction for what you're interested in.

GLENCOE & FORT WILLIAM

Glencoe • Fort William • Road to the Isles

Scotland is a land of great natural wonders. And some of the most spectacular—and most accessible—are in the valley called Glencoe, just an hour north of Oban and on the way to Fort William, Loch Ness, Inverness, or the Isle of Skye. The evocative "Weeping Glen" of Glencoe aches with both history and natural beauty. Beyond that, Fort William anchors the southern end of the Caledonian Canal, offering a springboard to more Highlands scenery. This is where Britain's highest peak, Ben Nevis, keeps its head in the clouds, and where you'll find a valley made famous by a bonnie prince...and (later) by a steam train carrying a young wizard named Harry.

PLANNING YOUR TIME

On a quick visit, this area warrants just a few hours between Oban and either Inverness or Skye: Wander through Glencoe village, tour its modest museum, then drive up Glencoe valley for views before continuing north. But if you have only a day or two to linger in the Highlands, Glencoe is an ideal place to do it. Settle in for a night (or more) to make time for a more leisurely drive and to squeeze in a hike or two.

Beyond Glencoe, Fort William—a touristy and overrated transportation hub—is skippable, but can be a handy lunch stop. The "Road to the Isles," stretching west from Fort William to the coast, isn't worth a detour on its own, but is very handy for those connecting to the Isle of Skye. Along the way, the only stop worth more than a quick photo is Glenfinnan, with its powerful ties to Bonnie Prince Charlie and Jacobite history and its iconic viaduct.

Glencoe

This valley is the essence of the wild, powerful, and stark beauty of the Highlands. Along with its scenery, Glencoe offers a good dose

of bloody clan history: In 1692, government Redcoats (led by a local Campbell commander) came to the valley and were sheltered and fed for 12 days by the MacDonalds—whose leader had been late in swearing an oath to the British monarch. Then,

on the morning of February 13, the soldiers were ordered to rise up early and kill their sleeping hosts, violating the rules of Highland hospitality and earning the valley the nickname "The Weeping Glen." Thirty-eight men were killed outright; hundreds more fled through a blizzard, and some 40 additional villagers (mostly women and children) died from exposure. It's fitting that such an epic, dramatic incident—dubbed the Glencoe Massacre—should be set in this equally epic, dramatic valley, where the cliffsides seem to weep (with running streams) when it rains.

Aside from its tragic history, this place has captured the imaginations of both hikers and artists. Movies filmed here include everything from *Monty Python and the Holy Grail* to *Harry Potter and the Prisoner of Azkaban* and the James Bond film *Skyfall*, and Glencoe appears in the opening credits for the TV series *Outlander*. When filmmakers want a stunning, rugged backdrop; when hikers want a scenic challenge; and when Scots want to remember their hard-fought past...they think of Glencoe.

Orientation to Glencoe

The valley of Glencoe is an easy side trip just off the main A-828/A-82 road between Oban and points north (such as Fort William and Inverness). If you're coming from the north, the signage can be tricky—at the roundabout south of Fort William, follow signs to *Crianlarich* and *A-82*.

The most appealing town here is the sleepy one-street village of **Glencoe,** worth a stop for its folk museum and its status as the gateway to the valley. There's a free parking lot and pay WC at the entrance to town. The hub of activity, in the middle of town near the museum, is Glencoe's friendly and well-stocked grocery store (daily 8:00-19:00, closes earlier when it's slow).

The slightly larger and more modern town of **Ballachulish** (a

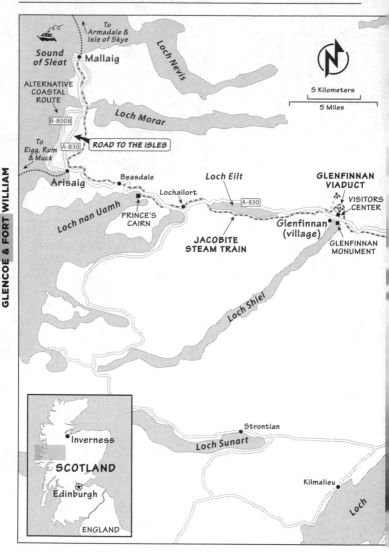

half-mile away) has more services, including a Co-op grocery store (daily 7:00-22:00), and more accommodations and restaurants.

In the loch just outside Glencoe (near Ballachulish), notice the **burial island**—where the souls of those who "take the low road" are piped home. Specifically, this was the final resting place of members of clan Stewart of Ballachulish, clan Cameron of Callart, and clan MacDonald of Glencoe. The next island was the Island of Discussion—where those in dispute went until they found agreement.

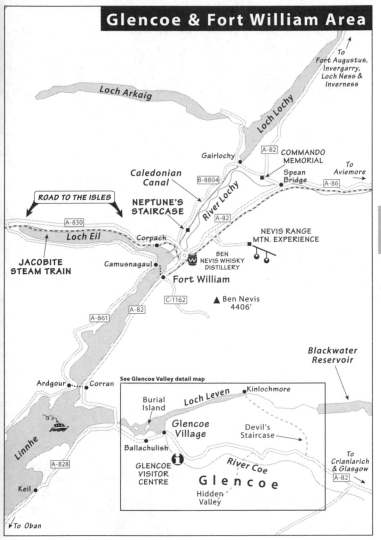

Glencoe & Fort William Area

TOURIST INFORMATION

There is no real TI in the area; the purported "information centre" inside Ballachulish's Quarry Centre café—sharing a parking lot with the Co-op grocery—stocks some brochures and sells souvenirs, but the staff is focused on café customers rather than answering travelers' questions. There is some good information on the area at https://discoverglencoe.scot.

For information on walks and hikes, the best resource is the **Glencoe Visitor Centre,** described later.

Harry Potter Sights

Harry Potter's story is set in a magical, largely fictional Britain, but you can visit real locations used in the film series. Glencoe was the main location for outdoor filming in *The Prisoner of Azkaban* and *The Half-Blood Prince,* and many shots of the Hogwarts grounds were filmed in the Fort William and Glencoe areas. The Hogwarts Express that carries Harry, Ron, and Hermione to school runs along the actual Jacobite Steam Train line (between Fort William and Mallaig).

In *The Prisoner of Azkaban* and *The Goblet of Fire,* Loch Shiel, Loch Eilt, and Loch Morar (near Fort William) were stand-ins for the Great Lake. And Steall Falls, at the base of Ben Nevis, is the locale for the Triwizard Tournament in *The Goblet of Fire.*

Bike Rental: At **Crank It Up Gear,** Davy rents road and mountain bikes, and can offer plenty of suggestions for where to pedal in the area (£30/day, just off the main street to the left near the start of town, 20 Lorn Drive, +44 7746 860 023, www. glencoebikehire.com, book ahead).

Sights in Glencoe

Glencoe Village

Glencoe village is just a line of houses sitting beneath the brooding mountains. The only real sight in town is the folk museum (de-

scribed later). But walking the main street gives a good glimpse of village Scotland. From the free parking lot at the entrance to town, go for a **stroll.** You'll pass several charming, small homes, but the town may feel a bit deserted. In a sign of the times, there used to be a dozen B&Bs in Glencoe, including

several charming two-room places right along this street; now they are down to just four, mostly in the surrounding hills—and many of the former B&Bs have been transformed into "self-catering" (read: Airbnbs) or housing for staff at the area's big hotels. You'll also pass the stony Episcopal church, the folk museum, the town's grocery store, and the village hall.

At the far end of the village, on the left just before the bridge, a Celtic cross **WWI** memorial stands on a little hill. Even this wee village lost 11 souls during that war—a reminder of Scotland's disproportionate contribution to Britain's war effort. You'll see memorials like this (usually either a Celtic cross or a soldier with bowed head) in virtually every town in Scotland.

If you were to cross the little bridge, you'd head up into Glencoe's wooded parklands, with some easy hikes (described later). But for one more landmark, turn right just before the bridge and walk about five minutes. Standing on a craggy bluff on your right is another memorial—this one to the **Glencoe Massacre,** which still haunts the memories of people here and throughout Scotland (described earlier).

▲Glencoe Folk Museum

This gathering of thatched-roof, early 18th-century croft houses is a volunteer-run community effort. It's jammed with local his-

tory, creating a huggable museum filled with humble exhibits gleaned from the town's old closets and attics. When one house was being rethatched, its owner found a cache of 200-year-old swords and pistols hidden there from the government Redcoats after the disastrous Battle of Culloden. You can listen to an interview with the late Arthur Smith, a local historian, about the valley and its story in the "Scottish Highlands" program available on my Rick Steves Audio Europe app.

Cost and Hours: £3; Tue-Sun 11:00-15:00, closed Mon and Nov-Easter; +44 1855 811 664, www.glencoemuseum.com.

Visiting the Museum: In the main building, you'll see those thatch-hidden swords, along with antique toys, boxes from old food products, sports paraphernalia (look for the crossed shinty sticks), a cabinet of curiosities, mountaineering gear, evocative old black-and-white photos, an exhibit on the slate quarry in nearby Ballachulish, and plenty of information on the MacDonald clan. Be sure to look for the museum's little door that leads out back, where additional, smaller buildings are filled with everyday items (furniture, farm tools, and so on) and exhibits on the Glencoe Massacre and a beloved Highland doctor. Out here, you'll also see the "coffin boat" that was used to transport the bodies of the departed to the burial isle in the loch.

Glencoe Visitor Centre

This modern facility, a mile past Glencoe village up the A-82 into the dramatic valley, is designed to resemble a *clachan*, or traditional Highland settlement. Inside is a big shop, a helpful information desk, a modest exhibit, a café, and some great views. Out back is an interesting reconstructed turf house.

Cost and Hours: Free entry but parking costs £4; daily 10:00-17:00, Nov-March until 16:00; café, +44 1855 811 307, www.nts. org.uk—search for "Glencoe."

Visiting the Center: You'll begin by working your way through the sprawling gift shop. Then, in the back part of the complex, you'll find an information desk that's your single best resource for advice (and maps or guidebooks) about local walks and hikes, several of which are outlined later in this chapter. A giant relief map of the area—clearly marked with various hiking paths—is ideal for understanding routes and difficulty levels before heading out. There's also a small, rotating exhibit, generally covering Glencoe's nature and mountaineering, as well as a short film about the Glencoe Massacre.

If you continue out back, you'll find a viewpoint with a smaller 3-D model of the hills for orientation. A short walk away is a thatched-roof **turf house** that was built from scratch in 2021, using 17th-century materials and methods. The views from here are superb. Step inside the turf house to hear sound effects and smell the peat smoke they use to help preserve the structure. (Free guided tours of the turf house typically run daily at 14:00.) An easy woodland walk starts nearby.

Glencoe Valley Drive

If you have a car, spend an hour or so following the A-82 through the valley, past the Glencoe Visitor Centre, up into the desolate moor beyond, and back again. You'll enjoy grand views, dramatic craggy hills, and, if you're lucky, a chance to hear a bagpiper in the wind: Roadside Highland buskers sometimes set up here on good-weather summer weekends. (If you play the recorder—and the piper's not swarmed with other tourists—ask to finger a tune while he does the hard work.)

Here's a brief explanation of the route. Along the way, I've pointed out sometimes easy-to-miss trailheads, in case you're up for a hike (hikes described in the next section).

From Glencoe Village to the End of the Valley: Leaving Glencoe village on the A-82, it's just a mile to the **Glencoe Visitor**

Centre (on the right, described earlier). Soon after, the road pulls out of the forested hills and gives you unobstructed views of the U-shaped valley.

About a mile after the visitor center, on the left, is a parking lot for **Signal Rock and An Torr,** a popular place for low-impact forested hikes. Just beyond, also on the left, is a one-lane road leading to the recommended **Clachaig Inn,** a classic hikers' pub. (The single-track road continues scenically, along the river then through the woods, all the way back to Glencoe village.) The hillsides above the inn were the setting for Hagrid's hut in the third Harry Potter movie.

Continuing along the A-82, you'll hit a straight stretch, passing a lake (Loch Achtriochtan), and then a small farm, both on the

right. After the farm, the valley narrows a bit as you cut through Glencoe Pass. Then, on the right, you'll pass two small parking lots. Pull into the second one for perhaps the best viewpoint of the entire valley, with point-blank views (directly ahead) of

the steep ridge-like mountains known as the **Three Sisters.** Hike about 100 feet away from the pullout to your own private bluff to enjoy the view alone—it makes a big difference. This is also the starting point for the challenging **Hidden Valley hike,** which leads between the first and second sisters.

As you continue, you'll pass a raging waterfall in a canyon— the Tears of the MacDonalds—on the right. After another mile or so—through more glorious waterfall scenery—watch on the left for the **Coffin Cairn,** which looks like a stone igloo (parking is just across the road if you want a photo op). Just after the cairn, look on the left for pullout parking for the **hike to The Study,** a viewpoint overlooking the road you just drove down.

After this pullout, you'll hit a straightaway for about a mile, followed by an S-curve. At the end of the curve, look for the pullout parking on the left, just before the stand of pine trees. This is the trailhead for the **Devil's Staircase** hike, high into the hills.

Continuing past here, you're nearing the end of the valley. The intimidating peak called the Great Shepherd of Etive (Stob Dearg, on the right) looms like a dour watchman, guarding the far end of the valley. Soon you'll pass the turnoff (on the right) for **Glen Etive,** an even more remote-feeling valley. (This was the setting for the final scenes of *Skyfall*. Yes, this is where James Bond grew up.) While you could detour up here for some bonus scenery, it just feels

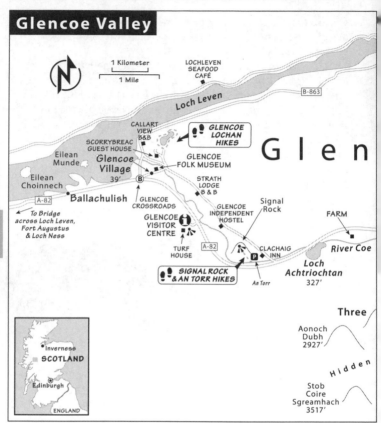

Glencoe Valley

1 Kilometer
1 Mile

LOCHLEVEN
SEAFOOD
CAFÉ

B-863

Loch Leven

CALLART
VIEW
B&B

GLENCOE
LOCHAN
HIKES

SCORRYBREAC
GUEST HOUSE

Glen

Eilean
Munde

Glencoe
Village
39'

GLENCOE
FOLK MUSEUM

Eilean
Choinnech

B

STRATH
LODGE
B & B

A-82 Ballachulish

GLENCOE
CROSSROADS

GLENCOE
INDEPENDENT
HOSTEL

Signal
Rock

FARM

To Bridge
across Loch Leven,
Fort Augustus
& Loch Ness

GLENCOE
VISITOR
CENTRE

River Coe

A-82

Loch
Achtriochan
327'

TURF
HOUSE

CLACHAIG
INN

P

SIGNAL ROCK
& AN TORR HIKES

An Torr

Three

Aonoch
Dubh
2927'

SCOTLAND

Inverness

Hidden

Edinburgh

Stob
Coire
Sgreamhach
3517'

ENGLAND

GLENCOE & FORT WILLIAM

empty—with peaty waterfalls flowing into a churning river—and is less striking than what you just drove through.

Continuing past the Glen Etive turnoff, the last sign of civilization (on the right) is the Glencoe Ski Centre. And from here, the terrain flattens out as you enter the vast **Rannoch Moor**—50 bleak square miles of heather, boulders, and barely enough decent land to graze a sheep. Robert Louis Stevenson called it the "Highland Desert."

You could keep driving as far as you like—but the moor looks pretty much the same from here on out. Turn around and head back through Glencoe...it's scenery you'll hardly mind seeing twice.

Hiking in Glencoe

Glencoe is made for hiking. Many routes are not particularly well marked, so it's essential to get very specific instructions (from the rangers at the Glencoe Visitor Centre, or other knowledgeable locals) and equip yourself with a good map (the *Ordnance Survey*

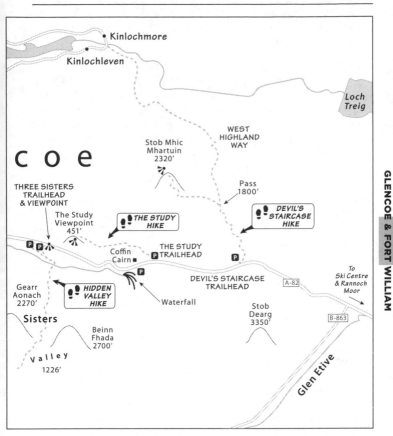

GLENCOE & FORT WILLIAM

Explorer Map #384, sold at the center). I've suggested a few of the most enticing walks and hikes. These vary from easy, level strolls to challenging climbs. Either way, wear proper footwear (even the easy trails can get swamped in wet weather) and carry rain gear—you never know when a storm will blow in.

I've listed these roughly in order of how close they are to Glencoe village, and given a rough sense of difficulty for each. Some of them (including the first two) are more forested, but the ones out in the open—which really let you feel immersed in the wonders of Glencoe—are even better.

While you can walk to the first two areas from Glencoe village, the rest are best for drivers. Some of these trailheads are tricky to find, which is why I've designed the driving commentary in the previous section to help you locate the hikes off the A-82.

Glencoe Lochan (Easy)

Perched on the forested hill above Glencoe village is an improbable slice of the Canadian Rockies. A century ago, this was the personal playground of Lord Strathcona, a local boy done good when he moved to Canada and eventually became a big Canadian Pacific Railway magnate. In 1894, he returned home with his Canadian wife and built the Glencoe House (which is now an exclusive, top-of-the-top hotel). His wife was homesick for the Rockies, so he had the grounds landscaped to represent the lakes, trees, and mountains of her home country. They even carved out a man-made lake (Glencoe Lochan), which looks like a piece of Alberta tucked under a craggy Scottish backdrop. (She was still homesick—they eventually returned to Canada.)

Today, the house and immediate surroundings are closed to visitors, but the rest of the area is open for exploration. Head to the end of Glencoe village, cross the bridge, and continue straight up (following signs for *Glencoe Lochan*)—it's a 20-minute uphill walk, or 5-minute drive (free parking), from the village center. Once there, a helpful orientation panel in the parking lot suggests three different, color-coded, one-mile walking loops—mostly around that beautiful lake, which reflects the hillsides of Glencoe.

From this area, a good trail network called the **Orbital Recreational Track** follows the river through the forest up the valley, all the way to the Clachaig Inn (about 45 minutes one-way). This links you to the Signal Rock and An Torr areas (described next). Eventually they hope to extend this trail system across the valley and back to the Glencoe Visitor Centre, which would allow a handy loop hike around the valley floor.

Signal Rock and An Torr (Easy to Moderate)

This forested area has nicely tended trails and gives you a better chance of spotting wildlife than the more desolate hikes described later. To explore this area, park at the well-marked lot just off the A-82 and go for a walk. A well-described panel at the trailhead narrates three options: easy yellow route to the Clachaig Inn; longer blue route to Signal Rock; and strenuous black route along the hillsides of An Torr. The Signal Rock route brings you to a panoramic point overlooking the valley—so named because a fire could be lit here to alert others in case of danger.

Hidden Valley (Challenging)

Three miles east of Glencoe village, this aptly named glen is tucked between two of the dramatic Three Sisters mountains. Also called the Lost Valley (Coire Gabhail in Gaelic), this was supposedly where the MacDonalds hid stolen cattle from their rivals, the Campbells (who later massacred them). This is the most challenging of the hikes I describe—it's strenuous and has stretches with uneven footing. Expect to scramble a bit over rocks, and to cross a river on stepping stones (which may be underwater after a heavy rain). As the rocks can be slippery when wet, skip this hike in bad weather. Figure about two-and-a-half to three hours round-trip (with an ascent of more than 1,000 feet).

Begin at the second parking lot at Glencoe Pass (on the right when coming from Glencoe), with views of the Three Sisters. You're aiming to head between the first and second Sisters (counting from the left). Hike down into the valley between the road and the mountains. Bear left, head down a metal staircase, and cross the bridge over the river. (Don't cross the bridge to the right of the parking lots—a common mistake.) Once across, you'll start the treacherous ascent up a narrow gorge. Some scrambling is required, and at one point a railing helps you find your way. The next tricky part is where you cross the river. You're looking for a pebbly beach and a large boulder; stepping stones lead across the river, and you'll see the path resume on the other side. But if the water level is high, the stones may be covered—though still passable with good shoes and steady footing. (Don't attempt to scramble over the treacherous slopes on the side of the river with the loose rocks called scree.) Once across the stepping stones, keep on the trail, hiking further up into the valley.

Much Easier Alternative: If you'd simply enjoy the feeling of walking deep in Glencoe valley—with peaks and waterfalls overhead—you can start down from the parking lot toward the Hidden Valley trail, and then simply stroll the old road along the valley floor as far as you want in either direction.

The Study (Easy to Moderate)

For a relatively easy, mostly level hike through the valley with a nice viewpoint at the end, consider walking to the flat rock called "The Study" and back. It takes about 45-60 minutes round-trip. The walk essentially parallels the main highway, but on the old road a bit higher up. You'll park just beyond the Three Sisters and the Coffin Cairn. From there, cut through the field of stone  and marshy turf to the old road—basically two gravel tire ruts—and follow them to your left. You'll hike above the modern road, passing several modest waterfalls, until you reach a big, flat rock with stunning views of the Three Sisters and the valley beyond. (Fellow hikers have marked the spot with a pile of stones.)

The Devil's Staircase (Strenuous but Straightforward)

About eight miles east of Glencoe village, near the end of the valley, you can hike this brief stretch of the West Highland Way. It was built by General Wade, the British strategist who came to Scotland after the 1715 Jacobite rebellion to help secure government rule here. Designed to connect Glencoe valley to the lochside town of Kinlochmore, to the north, it's named for its challenging switchbacks. While strenuous, it's easier to follow and has more comfortable footing than the Hidden Valley hike. Figure about 45-60 minutes up, and 30 minutes back down (add 45-60 minutes round-trip for the optional ascent to the summit of 2,320-foot Stob Mhic Mhartuin).

From the parking lot, a green sign points the way. Most hikers simply ascend to the **pass** at the top (an 800-foot gain), then come back down to Glencoe. It's a steep but straightforward hike up, on switchback trails.

From the pass (marked by a piled-stone cairn), you can return back down into the valley. Or, if you have stamina left, consider continuing higher—head up to the peak on the left, called **Stob Mhic Mhartuin.** The hike to the top (an additional gain of 500 feet) earns you even grander views over the entire valley.

For an even longer hike, it's possible to carry on down the other side of the staircase to **Kinlochmore** (about 2 hours' descent)—but your car will still be in Glencoe village. Consider this plan: Leave your car in Glencoe. Take a taxi to the trailhead. Hike across to Kinlochmore. From there you can take the #N44 bus back to Glencoe and your car, though be aware that the bus only runs a few times midday (see "Glencoe Connections," later).

Sleeping in Glencoe

Glencoe is an extremely low-key place to spend the night between Oban or Glasgow and the northern destinations. You'll join two kinds of guests: one-nighters just passing through and outdoorsy types settling in for several days of hiking.

IN GLENCOE VILLAGE

While the main street of Glencoe was once lined with charming B&Bs, only one remains—but it's a very nice choice.

$ Beechwood Cottage B&B is a shoes-off, slippers-on, whisky-honor-bar kind of place where Jackie rents three lovely rooms and Iain pursues his rock-garden dreams in the yard (look for the sign at the church on Main Street, +44 1855 811 062, www. beechwoodcottage.scot, stay@beechwoodcottage.scot).

JUST OUTSIDE TOWN

These options are close to both the village and the valley (for locations, see the "Glencoe Valley" map, earlier). Strath Lodge, Glencoe Independent Hostel, and Clachaig Inn are on the back road that runs through the forest parallel to the A-82 (best suited for drivers). Scorrybreac is on a hill above the village, and Callart View is along the flat road that winds past Loch Leven.

$$$ Strath Lodge, energetically run by Dawn and Lawrence, brings a fresh perspective to Glencoe's sometimes-stodgy accommodations scene. Their three spacious, luxurious-for-a-B&B rooms, in a modern, light-filled, lodge-like home, are partway down the road to the Clachaig Inn (2-night minimum, no kids under 16, +44 1855 811 820, www.strathlodgeglencoe.com, stay@ strathlodgeglencoe.com). Take the road up through the middle of Glencoe village, cross the bridge, and keep right following the river for a few minutes; it's on the right.

$$$ Clachaig Inn, which runs two popular pubs on site, also rents 23 rooms, all with private bath. It's a family-friendly place surrounded by a dramatic setting that works well for hikers seeking a comfy mountain inn (2-night minimum on weekends, +44 1855 811 252, 3 miles from Glencoe, www.clachaig.com, frontdesk@ clachaig.com). Follow the directions for the Strath Lodge, and drive another three miles past the campgrounds and hostels—the Clachaig Inn is on the right.

$$ Glencoe Independent Hostel has a variety of snazzy, self-contained units with kitchenettes—either in "eco-cabins" or in "caravans" (permanently parked trailers). They also have cheap, basic dorm beds in a rehabbed crofter farm building, and more in a newer "alpine bunkhouse" with its own shared kitchen. This is a good choice if you're looking for either a bargain-basement sleep or a private, self-catering option that's close to nature (2-night minimum preferred for cabins, +44 1855 811 906, www.glencoehostel. co.uk, info@glencoehostel.co.uk, energetic Keith). It's a few minutes farther up the road beyond Strath Lodge.

$$ Scorrybreac Guest House enjoys a secluded forest setting and privileged position next to the restored Glencoe House (now a luxury hotel). From here, walks around the Glencoe Lochan wooded lake park are easy, and it's about a 10-minute walk down into the village. Emma and Graham rent four homey rooms and serve a daily breakfast special that goes beyond the usual offerings (2-3 nights preferred in peak season, +44 1855 811 354, www. scorrybreacglencoe.com, stay@scorrybreacglencoe.com). After crossing the bridge at the end of the village, head left up the hill and follow signs.

$ Callart View B&B offers four rooms, quilted-home comfort, and a peaceful spot overlooking Loch Leven, less than a mile outside the village and close to the wooded trails of Glencoe Lochan. You'll be spoiled by Lynn's homemade shortbread (family room, self-catering cottages, sack lunches available, +44 1855 811 259, www.callart-view.co.uk, callartview@hotmail.com, Lynn and Geoff). Turn off from the main road for Glencoe village but instead of turning right into the village, keep left and drive less than a mile along the loch.

IN BALLACHULISH

$ St. Munda's Manse sounds rather grand—because Colin and Mary renovated a lovely old stone house that once belonged to the church down the road. Now they offer two bright rooms that manage to feel both modern and classic, in a quiet location above Ballachulish village (cash only, +44 1855 811 966, www.bedandbreakfastglencoe.com, hello@stmundasmanse.com). See their website for driving directions.

$ Fern Villa Guest House has five classic, cozy, tidy rooms in a big, traditional old stone house midway up the village, plus a lounge with a fireplace for cold nights (Loanfern, +44 1855 811 393, https://fernvilla.scot, ghfernvilla@gmail.com, David and Catherine).

$ Strathassynt Guest House sits in the center of Ballachulish, across from the recommended Laroch Bar & Bistro. Katya will make you pancakes for breakfast, and the six bedrooms are a good value (family rooms, closed Nov-Jan, +44 1855 811 261, www.strathassynt.com, info@strathassynt.com, Neil and Katya).

Eating in Glencoe

Choices around Glencoe are slim—this isn't the place for fine dining. But the following options offer decent food a short walk or drive away. For evening fun, take a walk or ask your B&B host where to find music and dancing.

In Glencoe: The only real restaurant is **$$$ The Glencoe Gathering,** with a busy dining area and a large outdoor deck. The menu has a variety of seafood, burgers, pizza, and pasta. While the food is nothing special, it will fill you up after a day in the mountains (daily 8:00-20:00, at junction of A-82 and Glencoe village, +44 1855 811 265). In the parking lot out back, their **$$ Red Shed Pizza** shack sells takeaway, wood-fired pizzas, which you can enjoy at one of the picnic tables.

$ Glencoe Café, also in the village, is just right for soups and sandwiches, and Deirdre's homemade baked goods—especially the carrot loaf—are irresistible (soup-and-panini lunch combo; Fri-Wed 11:00-16:00, last orders at 15:15, closed Thu; +44 1855 811 168, Alan).

Near Glencoe: Set in a stunning valley a few miles from Glencoe village, **$$ Clachaig Inn** serves solid pub grub all day long to a clientele that's half locals and half tourists. This unpretentious and very popular social hub features billiards, live music, and a wide range of whiskies and hand-pulled ales. There are two areas, sharing the same menu: The Bidean Lounge feels a bit like an upscale ski lodge, while the Boots Bar has a spit-and-sawdust, pub-around-an-open-fire atmosphere (open daily for lunch and dinner, music Sat from 21:00, Sun open-mic folk music also at 21:00, see hotel listing earlier for driving directions, +44 1855 811 252, no reservations).

If you need to grab lunch on your way to a hike, the **$ Glencoe Visitors Centre** has a decent café (see listing earlier, daily 10:00-17:00, Nov-March until 16:00).

In Ballachulish: Aiming to bring some sophistication to this rugged corner of Scotland, **$$$ The Laroch Bar & Bistro** has both a low-key pub section and a proper restaurant sharing the same menu (Tue-Sat 12:00-15:00 & 18:00-21:00, closed Sun-Mon, +44 1855 811 940, www.thelarochrestaurantandbar.co.uk). Drive three minutes from Glencoe into Ballachulish village, and you'll see it on the left, next to the town shinty pitch. A basic **$ Quarriers' Kitchen** fish-and-chips joint is next door (daily 16:00-20:00).

Across the Loch: The only "destination" restaurant between here and Fort William is **$$$ Lochleven Seafood Café**—across the loch from Glencoe. It requires an extremely scenic 15-minute drive, but it's worth it for the views and for the food: good, unfussy dishes of mussels, clams, scallops, langoustine, and fish, along with both seafood and landfood specials. It has two indoor areas and outdoor tables, all with views looking out over the loch to the steep hills beyond; it's worth booking ahead before making the drive (Thu-Mon 12:00-15:00 & 17:45-20:45, closed Tue-Wed, +44 1855 821 048, www.lochlevenseafoodcafe.co.uk).

Glencoe Connections

Buses don't actually drive down the main road through Glencoe village, but they stop nearby at a place called **"Glencoe Crossroads"** (a short walk into the village center). They also stop in the town of **Ballachulish,** which is just a half-mile away (or a £3 taxi ride). Tell the bus driver where you're going ("Glencoe village") and ask to be let off as close as possible.

Citylink buses #914/#915/#916 stop at Glencoe Crossroads

and Ballachulish, heading north to **Fort William** (8/day, 30 minutes) or south to **Glasgow** (3 hours). Another option is Shiel bus #N44, which runs from either Glencoe Crossroads or Ballachulish to **Fort William** (about 8/day, fewer Sat-Sun). From Ballachulish, you can take Citylink bus #918 to **Oban** (4/day, 1 hour).

To reach **Inverness** or **Portree** on the Isle of Skye, transfer in Fort William. To reach **Edinburgh,** there's one direct bus each afternoon (#913, 4 hours); otherwise, transfer in Glasgow.

Bus info: Citylink +44 871 266 3333, Citylink.co.uk; Shiel Buses +44 1967 431 272, ShielBuses.co.uk.

Fort William

Fort William—after Inverness, the second-biggest town in the Highlands (pop. 10,000)—is Glencoe's opposite. While Glencoe is a humble one-street village, appealing to hikers and nature lovers, Fort William's glammed-up, car-free main drag feels like one big Scottish shopping mall (with souvenir stands and outdoor stores touting perpetual "70 percent off" sales). The town is clogged with a United Nations of tourists trying to get out of  the rain. Big bus tours drive through Glencoe...but they sleep in Fort William.

While Glencoe touches the Scottish soul of the Highlands, Fort William was a steely and intimidating headquarters of the British counter-insurgency movement—in many ways designed to crush that same Highland spirit. After the English Civil War (early 1650s), Oliver Cromwell built a fort here to control his rebellious Scottish subjects. This was beefed up (and named for King William III) in 1690. And following the Jacobite uprising in 1715, King George I dispatched General George Wade to coordinate and fortify the crown's Highland defenses against further Jacobite dissenters. Fort William was the first of a chain of intimidating bastions (along with Fort Augustus on Loch Ness, and Fort George near Inverness) stretching the length of the Great Glen. But Fort William's namesake fortress is long gone, leaving precious little tangible evidence (except a tiny bit of rampart in a park near the train station) to help today's visitors imagine its militaristic past.

With the opening of the Caledonian Canal in 1822, the first curious tourists arrived. Many more followed with the arrival of

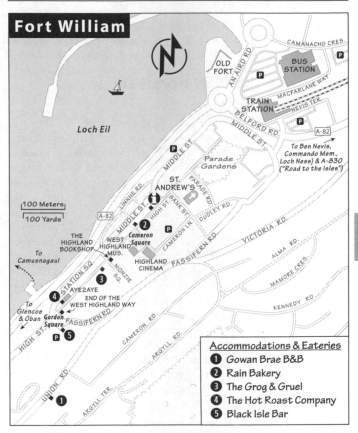

Accommodations & Eateries
1. Gowan Brae B&B
2. Rain Bakery
3. The Grog & Gruel
4. The Hot Roast Company
5. Black Isle Bar

the train in 1894, and grand hotels were built. Today, sitting at the foot of Ben Nevis, the tallest peak in Britain, Fort William is considered the outdoors capital of the United Kingdom.

Orientation to Fort William

Given its strategic position—between Glencoe and Oban in the south, Inverness in the east, and the Isle of Skye in the west—you're likely to pass through Fort William at some point during your Highlands explorations. And, while "just passing through" is the perfect plan here, Fort William can provide a good opportunity to stock up on whatever you need (last supermarket before Inverness), grab lunch, and get any questions answered at the TI.

Arrival in Fort William: You'll find pay parking lots flanking the main pedestrian zone, High Street. The train and bus stations sit side by side just north of the old town center, where you'll also find a handy pay parking lot.

Tourist Information: The TI is near the north end of the car-free main drag (daily 9:00-17:00, likely open later in summer, 15 High Street, +44 1397 701 801, www.visitscotland.com).

Sights in Fort William

Fort William's High Street

Enjoy a half-hour stroll up and down the length of Fort William's main street for lots of Scottish clichés and great people-watching. The heart of this strip runs from **St. Andrew's Church** (the pointy spire near the TI, with WCs nearby) south several blocks to Gordon Square. Along the way, you'll pass a variety of shops: outdoor outfitters; tacky "tartan tat" souvenir shops; charity stores; whisky shops; lowbrow pubs and fish-and-chips joints; and a few good eateries (described later, under "Sleeping and Eating in Fort William").

Halfway along the street is **Cameron Square,** with the West Highland Museum (described next) on its right side. Dominating the square is the big, modern (yet tasteful) Highland Cinema, which shows first-run movies as well as a short film of Highland scenery from the air—either one a tempting activity if you need to get out of the rain (https://highlandcinema.co.uk).

Keep window-shopping your way down the street. You'll pass the great **Highland Bookshop** (on the left at #60). Near the far end, look for the **Aye2Aye** storefront (on the right at #125), which favors a new referendum on Scottish independence.

The main drag culminates at **Gordon Square** (in front of the Travelodge). Here a marker represents the end of the **West Highland Way**—a challenging 95-mile hiking path that begins in Glasgow. You may see happy but exhausted hikers celebrating here (likely ready to unwind at the big, recommended Black Isle Bar, just behind). Notice the map of the walk's main landmarks etched into the square's paving stones.

▲West Highland Museum

Fort William's only real sight is its humble but well-presented museum. It's a fine opportunity to escape the elements, and—if you take the time to linger over the many interesting exhibits—genuinely insightful about local history and Highland life.

Cost and Hours: Free, £3 suggested donation, may charge extra for special exhibits; Mon-Fri 10:00-16:30, Sat 10:30-13:30, closed Sun—but may be open later and on Sun in July-Aug; Nov-April until 15:30; midway down the main street on Cameron Square, +44 1397 702 169, www.westhighlandmuseum.org.uk.

Visiting the Museum: Follow the suggested one-way route through exhibits on two floors. You'll begin by learning about the WWII green beret commandos, who were trained in secrecy near here (see "Commando Memorial" listing, later). Then you'll see the historic Governor's Room, decorated with the original paneling from the room in which the order for the Glencoe Massacre was signed. The ground floor also holds exhibits on natural history (lots of stuffed birds and other critters), mountaineering (old equipment), and archaeology (stone and metal tools).

Upstairs, you'll see a selection of old tartans and a salacious exhibit about Queen Victoria and John Brown (her Highlander attendant...and, possibly, suitor). The Jacobite exhibit gives a concise timeline of that complicated history, from Charles I to Bonnie Prince Charlie, and displays a selection of items emblazoned with the prince's bonnie face—including a clandestine portrait that you can only see by looking in a cylindrical mirror. Finally, the Highland Life exhibit collects a hodgepodge of tools, musical instruments (some fine old harps that were later replaced by the much louder bagpipes as the battlefield instrument of choice), and other bric-a-brac.

NEAR FORT WILLIAM
Ben Nevis

From Fort William, take a peek at Britain's highest peak, Ben Nevis (4,406 feet). Thousands walk to its summit each year. On a clear day, you can admire it from a distance. Scotland's only mountain cable cars—at the **Nevis Range Mountain Experience**—can take you to a not-very-lofty 2,150-foot perch on the slopes of Aonach Mòr for a closer look (£25, 15-minute ride, generally open daily but closed in high winds and winter—call ahead, signposted on the A-82 north of Fort William, café at bottom and restaurant at top, +44 1397 705 825, www.nevisrange.co.uk). The cable car also provides access to trails particularly popular with mountain bikers.

▲Commando Memorial

This powerful bronze ensemble of three stoic WWII commandos, standing in an evocative mountain setting, is one of Britain's most beloved war memorials. During World War II, Winston Churchill decided that Britain needed an elite military corps. He created the British Commandos, famous for wearing green berets (an accessory—and name—later borrowed by elite fighting forces in the US and other countries). The British Commandos trained in the Lochaber region near Fort William, in the windy shadow of Ben Nevis. Many

later died in combat, and this memorial—built in 1952—remembers those fallen British heroes.

Nearby is the Garden of Remembrance, honoring British Commandos who died in more recent conflicts, from the Falkland Islands to Afghanistan. It's also a popular place to spread Scottish military ashes. Taken together, these sights are a touching reminder that the US is not alone in its distant wars. Every nation has its share of honored heroes willing to sacrifice for what they believe to be the greater good.

Getting There: The memorial is about nine miles outside of Fort William, on the way to Inverness (just outside Spean Bridge); see "Route Tips for Drivers" later in this section.

Sleeping and Eating in Fort William

Sleeping: The Hobbit-cute **$ Gowan Brae B&B** ("Hill of the Big Daisy") has an antique-filled dining room and two rooms with loch or garden views (cash only, 2-night minimum, on Union Road—a 5-minute walk up the hill above High Street, +44 1397 704 399, www.gowanbrae.co.uk, gowan_brae@btinternet.com, Jim and Ann Clark).

Eating: These places are on traffic-free High Street. I've listed them in the order you'll pass them, heading south from the TI. **$ Rain Bakery** serves breakfast, brunch, and lunch (soup and sandwiches) in a mellow, trendy atmosphere (closed Sun-Mon, 41 High Street, +44 1397 701 011). **$$ The Grog & Gruel** serves real ales, good pub grub, and Tex-Mex and Cajun dishes, with some unusual choices such as burgers made from boar and haggis or Highland venison. There's also a variety of "grog dogs" (daily for lunch and dinner, 66 High Street, +44 1397 705 078). **$ Hot Roast Company** sells beef, turkey, ham, or pork sandwiches topped with some tasty extras, along with soup, salad, and coleslaw (lunch only, closed Sun, 127 High Street, +44 1397 700 606). **$$ Black Isle Bar,** an outpost of the Inverness-based brewery, is popular for its microbrews and wood-fired pizzas (daily for lunch and dinner, on Gordon Square at the south end of the main drag, +44 1397 7008 76).

Fort William Connections

Fort William is a major transit hub for the Highlands, so you'll likely change buses here at some point during your trip.

From Fort William by Bus to: Glencoe or **Ballachulish** (all Glasgow-bound buses—#914, #915, and #916; 8/day, 30 minutes; also Shiel bus #N44, hourly, fewer on Sun), **Oban** (bus #918, 4/day, 1.5 hours), **Portree** on the Isle of Skye (buses #914, #915, and #916,

3/day, 3 hours), **Inverness** (bus #919, 6/day, 2 hours, fewer Sat-Sun), **Glasgow** (#914/#915/#916, 8/day direct, 3 hours). To reach **Edinburgh,** there's a direct bus once each afternoon in the summer (#913, 4.5 hours); otherwise, take the bus to Glasgow, then transfer to a train or bus (figure 5 hours total). Citylink: +44 871 266 3333, Citylink.co.uk; Shiel Bus: +44 1397 700 700, ShielBuses.co.uk.

From Fort William by Train to: **Glasgow** (4/day, 4 hours), **Mallaig** and ferry to Isle of Skye (4/day, 1.5 hours). Also see the listing for the Jacobite Steam Train on page 78.

ROUTE TIPS FOR DRIVERS

From Fort William to Loch Ness and Inverness: Head north out of Fort William on the A-82. After about eight miles, in the village of Spean Bridge, take the left fork (staying on the A-82). About a mile later, on the left, keep an eye out for the **Commando Memorial** (described earlier and worth a quick stop). From here, the A-82 sweeps north and follows the Caledonian Canal, passing through **Fort Augustus** (a good lunch stop, with its worthwhile Caledonian Canal Centre), and then follows the north side of Loch Ness on its way to Inverness. Along the way, the A-82 passes **Urquhart Castle** and the **Loch Ness Centre & Exhibition** in Drumnadrochit (described in the Inverness & Loch Ness chapter).

From Oban to Fort William via Glencoe: See page 31 in the Oban chapter.

From Fort William to the Isle of Skye: You have two options: Head west on the A-830 through **Glenfinnan,** then catch the ferry from Mallaig to Armadale on the Isle of Skye (this "Road to the Isles" area is described in the next section). Or, head north on the A-82 to Invergarry, and turn left (west) on the A-87, which you'll follow (past **Eilean Donan Castle**) to Kyle of Lochalsh and the **Skye Bridge** to the island. Consider using one route one way, and the other on the return trip.

The Road to the Isles

Between Fort William and the Isle of Skye lies a rugged landscape with close ties to the Jacobite rebellions. It was here that Bonnie Prince Charlie first set foot on Scottish soil in 1745, in his attempt to regain the British throne for his father. The settlement of Glenfinnan, about 30 minutes west of Fort William, is where he first raised the Stuart family standard—and an army of Highlanders. Farther west, the landscape grows even more rugged, offering offshore glimpses of the Hebrides. It's all tied together by a pretty, meandering road—laid out by the great Scottish civil engineer

Thomas Telford—that's evocatively (and aptly) named "The Road to the Isles." While these sights aren't worth going out of your way to see, they're ideal for those heading to the Isle of Skye (via the Mallaig-Armadale ferry), or for those who'd enjoy taking the so-called "Harry Potter train" through a Hogwartian landscape.

If you're driving, be sure you allow enough time to make it to Mallaig at least 20 minutes before the Skye ferry departs (figure at least 90 minutes of driving time from Fort William to the ferry, not including stops). In summer it's smart to reserve a spot on the ferry a few days before, either online or by phone. For more tips on the Mallaig-Armadale ferry, see "Getting to the Isle of Skye" on page 82.

Sights on the Road to the Isles

I've connected these sights with some commentary for those driving from Fort William to Mallaig for the Skye ferry. (If you're interested in the Jacobite Steam Train instead, see the sidebar.) In addition to the sights at Glenfinnan, this route is graced with plenty of loch-and-mountain views and, near the end, passes along a beautiful stretch of coast with some fine sandy beaches.

• *From Fort William, head north on the A-82 (signed* Inverness and Mallaig*). At the big roundabout (where you'll see the tempting Ben Nevis Whisky Distillery with a visitors center), turn left onto the A-830 (marked for* Mallaig and Glenfinnan*). You'll pass a big sign listing the next Skye ferry departure. Just after, you'll cross a bridge; look up and to the right to see Neptune's Staircase. There's a park-like viewing zone on the right.*

Neptune's Staircase

This network of eight stair-step locks, designed by Thomas Telford in the early 19th century, offers a handy look at the ingenious locks of the Caledonian Canal. For more on this remarkable engineering accomplishment—which combined natural lochs with man-made locks and canals to connect Scotland's east and west coasts—see the sidebar on page 150. Engineers might want to pull over just after the bridge (well marked) to stroll around

the locks for a closer look, but the rest of us can pretty much get the gist from the road.

• *Continue west on the A-830 for another 14 miles, much of it along Loch Eil. Soon you'll reach a big parking lot and visitors center at...*

▲Glenfinnan

In the summer of 1745, Bonnie Prince Charlie—grandson of James II of England, who was kicked off the British throne in 1688—arrived at Glenfinnan...and waited. He had journeyed a long way to this point, sailing from France by way of the Scottish Isle of Eriskay and finally making landfall at Loch nan Uamh (just west of here). For the first time in his life, he set foot on his ancestral homeland... the land he hoped that, with his help, his father would soon rule. But to reclaim the thrones of England and Scotland for the Stuart line, the fresh-faced, 24-year-old prince would need the support of the Highlanders. And here at Glenfinnan, he held his breath at the moment of truth. Would the Highland clans come to his aid?

As Charlie waited, gradually he began to hear the drone of bagpipes filtering through the forest. And then, the clan chiefs appeared: MacDonalds. Camerons. MacDonnells. McPhees. They had been holding back—watching and waiting, to make sure they weren't the only ones. Before long, the prince felt confident that he'd reached a clan quorum. And so, here at Glenfinnan, on August 19, 1745, Bonnie Prince Charlie raised his royal standard—officially kicking off the armed Jacobite rebellion that came to be known as "The Forty-Five." Two days later, Charlie and his 1,500 clansmen compatriots headed south to fight for control of Scotland. (Glenfinnan is also the place where Bonnie Prince Charlie retreated, just eight months later, after his crushing defeat at Culloden.)

Today Glenfinnan, which still echoes with history, is a wide spot in the road with a big visitors center and two landmarks: a monument to Bonnie Prince Charlie's raising of the standard, and a railroad viaduct made famous by the Hogwarts Express.

Visiting Glenfinnan: Start at the **visitors center** (free; daily 10:00-17:00, Oct-March until 16:00; café, WCs, +44 1397 722 250, www.nts.org.uk). The small but enlightening **Jacobite Exhibit**

The Jacobite Steam Train

The West Highland Railway Line (they don't actually call it the "Hogwarts Express") chugs 42 miles from Fort William west to the ferry port at Mallaig. Although one of the steam engines and some of the coaches were used in the films, don't expect a Harry Potter theme ride. However, you can expect beautiful scenery. Along the way, the train stops for 20 minutes at Glenfinnan Station (just after the Glenfinnan Viaduct), and then gives you 1.75 hours (more time than you really need) to poke around the port town of Mallaig before heading back to Fort William.

Cost and Hours: Same-day round-trip ("day return") prices are £52 for adults and £30 for kids (16 and under); more for plusher first class—some of which have elegant tables. The entire journey takes about six hours (a bit over 2 hours each way on the train, plus some stretch-your-legs time in Mallaig). Trains make the journey twice daily (departs Fort William at 10:15 and 12:50—except Sat, when the afternoon train departs at 14:40; morning train runs April-Oct, afternoon train runs only May-Sept; +44 844 850 3131, https://westcoastrailways. co.uk/jacobite).

Booking Tickets: You must book ahead online or by phone—you cannot buy tickets for this train at ticket offices. This is a hugely popular trip, and seats often sell out, especially in summer; booking months in advance is your best bet. A limited number of seats may be available each day on a first-come, first-served basis (cash only, buy from conductor at coach D). Rail passes are not accepted.

Cheaper Alternative: The 84-mile round-trip from Fort William takes the better part of a day to show you the same scenery twice. Modern "Sprinter" trains follow the same line and accept rail passes. Consider taking the steam train one-way to Mallaig, then speeding back on a regular train to avoid the long Mallaig layover and slow return ("Sprinter" train: £14.50 one-way between Fort William and Mallaig, 4/day, 1.5 hours, to ensure a seat in peak season book ahead, +44 3457 484 950, www.nationalrail.co.uk).

Skye Connection: You can use either the steam train or the Sprinter to reach the Isle of Skye: Take the train to Mallaig, walk onto the ferry to Armadale (on Skye), then catch a bus in Armadale to your destination on Skye (bus #52, www. stagecoachbus.com).

inside the visitors center explains the story of Bonnie Prince Charlie and "The Forty-Five." You can pay £5 at the visitors center for a ticket to climb the 62 stairs to the top of the **monument** (limited hours).

The **Glenfinnan Viaduct,** with 416 yards of raised track over 21 supporting arches, is worth seeing—especially if you can time

your visit for when the
steam **train** goes chugging
over the tracks, trailing a
giant white plume. Times
vary so confirm by phone
or online before you plan
a trip around it; current
times are also posted in-
side the visitors center (in
the summer, you'll likely

see the train go by Sun-Fri at 10:45, 13:20, 15:15, and 18:00; or Sat
at 10:45, 15:10, 15:15, and 19:45; different times off-season).

There are various ways to get a better view of the viaduct. Most
straightforward is to hike 10 minutes up the **hill** next to the visitors
center—find the well-marked, steep switchback path. From the
viewpoint, you'll enjoy sweeping (if distant) views of the viaduct
in one direction, and the monument and banks of Loch Shiel in
the other. The other options involve heading to the big, adjacent
parking lot, then walking toward the viaduct. It's a nice, scenic
walk across a bridge, then along a gurgling river. You can find a
vantage point from here; walk all the way up until you're actually
right under the viaduct (takes about 20 minutes each way); or carry
on to the other side of the viaduct and climb the hill behind it for
an even more dramatic view (allow plenty of time to get to the top).

The **Glenfinnan Monument** sits across the road, between
the visitors center and the loch. Capped with a stirring statue of a
kilted "Unknown Highlander," it commemorates the Jacobites who
perished in the Forty-Five. While it's possible to climb to the top
(see above), it's plenty evocative just to see it from below. A couple
of half-mile nature walks, on boardwalks and through the woods,
also begin from this area—look for signs.

• *Carrying on west along the A-830, the scenery crescendos and grows
more rugged: bald, mossy mountains; bushy trees; shaggy ferns. The road
plays hopscotch with the train line, crossing to and fro. Keep an eye out
for humble and sweet, middle-of-nowhere train stations that are little
more than lonely platforms.*

*Shortly you'll begin to catch glimpses of silver sand beaches at the
heads of the rocky lochs. (If catching a ferry, figure 50 minutes' drive
from Glenfinnan to Mallaig.) Fans of Bonnie Prince Charlie with some
time to spare should consider the next stop, 13 miles west of Glenfinnan.*

The Prince's Cairn
Just after the road passes under a small railway viaduct and begins
to travel alongside a sea loch, look for a small sign on the right.
Park in the waterside pullout just beyond, on the left. From here

you can walk a few minutes back along the main road, then follow signs down through the woods to the Prince's Cairn.

Perched above bonnie Loch nan Uamh, this cairn memorializes the spot from where Prince Charlie sailed for France after his failed uprising. (To find the cairn, from the pullout, hug the roadside guardrail and backtrack a hundred yards to the short trail.) The haystack-shaped cairn is made of local stone and marked by a memorial plaque. Imagine the day, September 20, 1746, when a French frigate spirited away the weary prince and his followers. He would never set foot in Scotland again.

• *Continuing west you'll soon reach the village of...*

Arisaig

While there's not much to see in this village, it has an interesting history. Gaelic for "safe place," Arisaig has provided shelter for many seafarers—including the real Long John Silver (Robert Louis Stevenson was inspired by tales from his father, who was an engineer who built lighthouses here). In the 20th century, remote Arisaig was a secret training ground for WWII-era spies. The "Special Operations Executive" prepared brave men and women here for clandestine operations in Nazi-occupied Europe.

• *Around Arisaig, signs for the Alternative Coastal Route direct you to the B-8008, which parallels the A-830 highway the rest of the way (7 miles) to Mallaig. If you've got ample time, consider taking these back roads for a more scenic approach to the end of the road. Either way, you'll end up at...*

Mallaig

This small, hardworking port town makes most of its income these days as a transit hub where the Jacobite Steam Train meets the Isle of Skye ferry (to Armadale). Mallaig has a certain salty charm and is enjoyable for a stroll; in fact, at midday, when Jacobite Steam Train passengers have no choice but to kill some time here, you'll see them doing just that. There's a big parking lot with pay WCs along the main road into town, which essentially drives straight onto the ferry dock. To the right runs the little main street, past the train station and Co-op grocery store to a small marina area. There are several takeaway fish-and-chips places along here, popular with steam-trainers on their own for lunch.

Consider walking a few minutes past the core of town, and past a busy shipyard (where you may see old boats being restored), to the marina area. Overlooking the marina, near a modern crannog building, is **$ The Bakehouse,** selling good sandwiches and sweet rolls (Tue-Sat 9:00-15:00, closed Sun-Mon, Old Quay, +44 1687 462 808).

ISLE OF SKYE

Portree • Touring the Isle of Skye

The rugged, remote-feeling Isle of Skye has a reputation for unpredictable weather ("Skye" comes from the Old Norse for "The Misty Isle"). But it also offers some of Scotland's best scenery, and it rarely fails to charm its many visitors. Narrow, twisty roads wind around Skye in the shadows of craggy, black, bald mountains, and the coastline is ruffled with peninsulas and sea lochs (inlets).

Skye is the largest of the Inner Hebrides, and Scotland's second-biggest island overall (over 600 square miles), but it's still manageable: You're never more than five miles from the sea. The island has only about 13,000 residents; roughly a quarter live in the main village, Portree. The mountain-like Cuillin Hills separate the northern part of the island (Portree, Trotternish, Dunvegan) from the south (Skye Bridge, Kyleakin, Sleat Peninsula).

Set up camp in Portree, Skye's charming, low-key tourism hub. Then dive into Skye's attractions. Drive around the appealing Trotternish Peninsula, enjoying Scotland's scenic beauty: sparsely populated rolling fields, stony homes, stark vistas of jagged rock formations, and the mysterious Outer Hebrides looming on the horizon. Go for a hike in (or near) the dramatic Cuillin Hills, sample a peaty dram of whisky, and walk across a desolate bluff to a lighthouse at the end of the world. Learn about the clan history of Skye, and visit your choice of clan castles: the MacLeods' base at Dunvegan, the MacDonalds' ruins near Armadale, and—nearby but not on Skye—the postcard-perfect Eilean Donan fortress, previously a Mackenzie stronghold but today held by the Macraes. Or just settle in, slow down, and enjoy island life.

One thing to be aware of: Skye is no secret. This lovely island has been discovered. A burgeoning destination for gourmands, it has multiple Michelin-listed restaurants, and prices are as high here as anywhere outside of Edinburgh. The island is struggling with some growing pains. Places are short-staffed; service can be a bit flaky; and hotels and restaurants book up far in advance, especially (but not exclusively) in the peak months of July and August. Come prepared to share Skye, get a head start on booking your accommodations, and do some restaurant scouting (and reserving) well before your trip...and you'll be ahead of the game.

PLANNING YOUR TIME

With two weeks in Scotland, Skye merits two nights, allowing a full day to hit its highlights: Trotternish Peninsula loop, Dunvegan Castle, the Fairy Pools hike (or another hike in the Cuillin Hills), and the Talisker Distillery tour. Mountaineers need extra time for hiking and hillwalking. Because it takes time to reach, Skye is skippable if you only have a few days in Scotland—instead, focus on the more accessible Highlands sights (Oban and its nearby islands, and Glencoe).

Situated between Oban/Glencoe and Loch Ness/Inverness, Skye fits neatly into a Highlands itinerary. To avoid seeing the same scenery twice, it works well to drive the "Road to the Isles" from Fort William to Mallaig, then take the ferry to Skye; later, leave Skye via the Skye Bridge and follow the A-87 east toward Loch Ness and Inverness, stopping at Eilean Donan Castle en route; or vice versa. With (much) more time, take the very long and scenic North Coast 500 route north from Skye, up Wester Ross and across Scotland's north coast, then down to Inverness (see the Northern Scotland chapter).

GETTING TO THE ISLE OF SKYE

By Car: Your easiest bet is the slick, free **Skye Bridge** that crosses from Kyle of Lochalsh on the mainland to Kyleakin on Skye (for more on the bridge, see "South Skye" on page 113).

The island can also be reached by **car ferry.** The major ferry line connects the mainland town of Mallaig (west of Fort William along "The Road to the Isles"—see page 75) to Armadale on Skye (£16/car with 2 people, reservations required, April-late Oct 9/day each way, off-season very limited Sat-Sun connections, must check in at least 20 minutes before sailing or your place will be sold and you will not get on, can be canceled in rough weather, 30-minute trip, operated by Caledonian Mac-Brayne, +44 1475 650 397, www.calmac.co.uk).

There's yet another route, which is favored by romantics who are in no hurry whatsoever: A tiny, six-car, proudly local **"turn-table" ferry** crosses the short gap between Glenelg on the mainland and Kylerhea on Skye, allowing for a more scenic route that avoids the obvious tourist path (runs frequently Easter-Oct, www.skyeferry.co.uk). Take this only if you'd get a thrill out of riding the world's only manually operated turntable ferry.

By Bus: Skye is connected to the outside world by Scottish Citylink buses (www.citylink.co.uk), which use Portree as their Skye hub. From Portree, buses connect to **Inverness** (bus #917, 3-4/day, 3 hours) and **Glasgow** (buses #915 and #916, 3/day, 7.5 hours, also stop at **Fort William** and **Glencoe**). For **Edinburgh,** you'll transfer in either Inverness, Fort William, or Glasgow (5/day, 8-9 hours total). For connections within the Isle of Skye, see later.

More complicated **train-plus-bus** connections are possible for the determined: Take the train from Edinburgh or Glasgow to Fort William; transfer to the "Sprinter" train to Mallaig (4/day, 1.5 hours); take the ferry across to Armadale; then catch Stagecoach bus #52 to Portree (1 hour). Alternatively, you can take the train from Edinburgh or Glasgow to Inverness, take another train to Kyle of Lochalsh, then catch a bus to Portree.

GETTING AROUND THE ISLE OF SKYE
By Car

Once on Skye, you'll need a car to thoroughly enjoy the island. (Even if you're doing the rest of your trip by public transportation, a car rental is worthwhile here to make maximum use of your time; car-rental options are listed under "Orientation to Portree," later.) The roads here are simple and well signposted, but a good map can be helpful for exploring. Sample driving times: Kyleakin and Skye Bridge to Portree—45 minutes; Portree to Dunvegan—30 minutes; Portree to the tip of Trotternish Peninsula and back again—2 hours (more with sightseeing stops); Portree to Armadale/ferry to Mallaig—1 hour; Portree to Talisker Distillery—40 minutes.

By Public Bus

Getting around Skye can be frustrating by bus (slow and limited). Portree is the hub for bus traffic. Most buses within Skye are operated by Stagecoach (www.stagecoachbus.com; buy individual tickets or, for longer journeys, consider the £7.70 all-day Dayrider ticket or the £26.30 weeklong Megarider ticket; buy tickets onboard, cash or card). From Portree, you can loop around the **Trotternish Peninsula** on bus #57A (counterclockwise route) or bus #57C (clockwise route; Mon-Sat 4/day in each direction, very infrequent

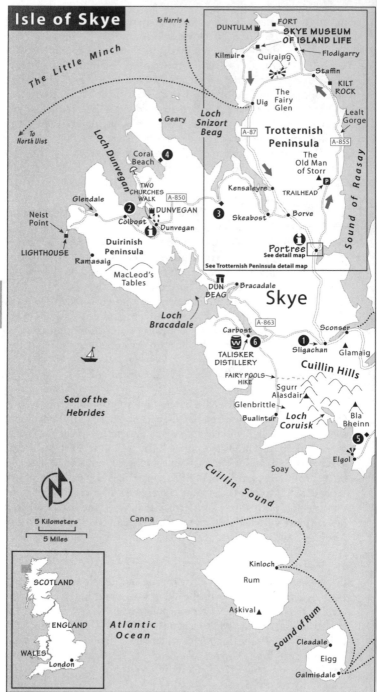

Isle of Skye

To Harris

The Little Minch

To North Uist

Loch Dunvegan

Geary

Coral Beach 4

TWO CHURCHES WALK

Glendale

2 DUNVEGAN

Colbost Dunvegan

Neist Point

LIGHTHOUSE

Ramasaig

Duirinish Peninsula

MacLeod's Tables

Loch Snizort Beag

DUNTULM FORT

SKYE MUSEUM OF ISLAND LIFE

Kilmuir Quiraing Flodigarry

Staffin KILT ROCK

The Fairy Glen

Uig Lealt Gorge

A-87 Trotternish Peninsula A-855

The Old Man of Storr

Kensaleyre TRAILHEAD P

3 Skeabost Borve

Portree See detail map

See Trotternish Peninsula detail map

Sound of Raasay

Skye

DUN BEAG Bracadale

Loch Bracadale

Carbost 6

TALISKER DISTILLERY

FAIRY POOLS HIKE

Glenbrittle

Bualintur

A-863

Sconser

Sligachan 1 Glamaig

Cuillin Hills

Sgurr Alasdair

Loch Coruisk

Bla Bheinn

5

Elgol

Sea of the Hebrides

Soay

Cuillin Sound

5 Kilometers

5 Miles

N

SCOTLAND

ENGLAND

WALES

London

Atlantic Ocean

Canna

Kinloch

Rum

Askival

Sound of Rum

Cleadale

Eigg

Galmisdale

ISLE OF SKYE

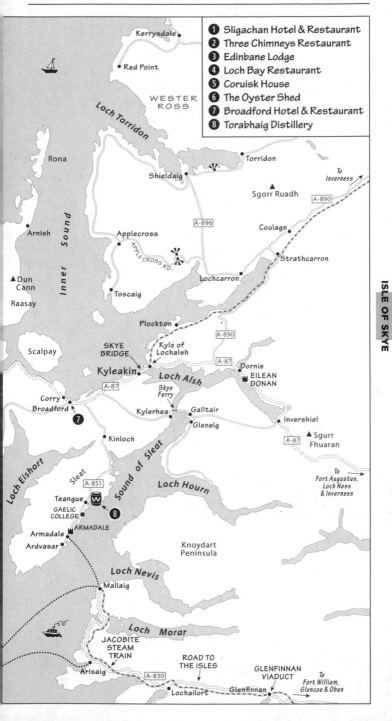

1. Sligachan Hotel & Restaurant
2. Three Chimneys Restaurant
3. Edinbane Lodge
4. Loch Bay Restaurant
5. Coruisk House
6. The Oyster Shed
7. Broadford Hotel & Restaurant
8. Torabhaig Distillery

ISLE OF SKYE

on Sun). Bus #56 connects Portree and **Dunvegan Castle** (2/day, none on Sun, 40 minutes).

A few longer-distance buses are operated by Citylink (so they are not covered by the Stagecoach tickets described above). For example, Buses #915, #916, or #917 connect Portree to **Kyleakin** (7/day, 1 hour) before continuing a few minutes farther to **Eilean Donan Castle** (get off at Dornie and walk 5 minutes), then on to Fort William or Inverness (www.citylink.co.uk).

By Tour

Several operations on the island take visitors to hard-to-reach spots. Figure about £55-60 per person to join an all-day island tour (about 8 hours). Compare the offerings at the following companies, which use smaller 8- or 16-seat minibuses: **Skye Scenic Tours** (+44 1478 617 006, www.skyescenictours.com), **Tour Skye** (+44 1478 613 514, www.tourskye.com), **SkyeBus** (+44 1470 532 428, www.realscottishjourneys.com), and **Skye Minibus Tours** (+44 1470 521 448, www.skye-minibus-tours.co.uk). As these can sell out, it's smart to book ahead for high season.

Michelle Rhodes—formerly from Skye but now based near Loch Ness—offers all-day guided drives around the island, tailored to your interests. Her specialty: clan battles, fairies, myths, and legends (£180/person, includes all admissions, michellelorrainerhodes@gmail.com).

Other Activities: Sea kayaking is popular; it's based on the southern end of the island (www.southskyeseakayak.co.uk or www.highlandexperiences.com). For more adrenaline-pumping activities—such as coasteering, canyoning, and gorge walking—check your options at **Skye Adventure** (www.skyeadventure.com).

By Taxi

For private rides around the island, consider **Don's Taxis** (+44 1478 613 100, https://donstaxis.vpweb.co.uk) or **BW's Taxi** (+44 1478 612 865, www.skye-taxi-tours.co.uk).

Portree

Skye's main attraction is its natural beauty, not its villages. But of those villages, the best home base is Portree (pore-TREE), Skye's largest settlement, transportation hub, and tourism center—ideally located for exploring Skye's quintessential sights on the Trotternish Peninsula loop drive.

Portree is nestled deep in its protective, pastel harbor; overlapping peninsulas just offshore guard it from battering west coast storms. Most of today's Portree dates from its early 19th-century boom time as a kelp-gathering and herring-fishing center.

As the most popular town on Scotland's most popular island, Portree is absolutely jammed with visitors in the summer. There are lots of hotels and B&Bs and an abundance of good restaurants—all of which book up well in advance. To avoid disappointment, have your room booked months ahead, and restaurants weeks ahead.

Orientation to Portree

Although Portree doesn't have any real sights, it does boast a gorgeous harbor area and—in the streets above—all of the necessary tourist services: a good TI, fine B&Bs, great restaurants, a small supermarket, a launderette, and so on. The main business zone of this functional town of about 3,000 residents is in the tight grid of lanes on the bluff just above the harbor, anchored by Portree's tidy main square, Somerled Square. From here, buses fan out across the island and to the mainland. B&Bs line the roads leading out of town.

Tourist Information: Portree's helpful TI is a block off the main square (daily 9:00-17:00, just below Bridge Road, +44 1478 612 992, www.visitscotland.com).

Opening Hours Warning: The opening times for Portree's restaurants and other tourist services can be unpredictable. This little town has suffered major staffing shortages in recent years, which may persist through your visit. The hours I list may be shorter or longer than what you find on your visit. Before making a special trip somewhere, call ahead or confirm hours online.

HELPFUL HINTS

WCs: Public WCs are across the street and down a block from the TI, across from the hostel.

Laundry: There's a **self-service launderette** below the Independent Hostel, just off the main square (usually 11:00-21:00, last load at 20:00, The Green, +44 1478 613 737).

Car Rental: To make the most of your time on Skye, rent a car (figure around £60/day; smart to book well in advance). The rental lineup changes from year to year, but in Portree, try **Morrison** (+44 1478 612 688, www.morrisoncarrental.com).

ISLE OF SKYE

DriveSkye is based in the southern part of the island, in Armadale. They're strategically located for this clever open-jaw plan: You could take the train along the "Road to the Isles" to Mallaig and cross on the ferry to Armadale, where you can pick up your rental car for your time on Skye. Then you can pay extra to drop it off across the Skye Bridge in Kyle of Lochalsh and take the train to Inverness (+44 1471 844 361, www.driveskye.com, rent@driveskye.com).

Parking: For a quick visit, the easiest choice is the small parking strip right on Somerled Square (£1/hour, 2-hour limit, free 18:00-8:00). For a longer stay and lower rates, you can head down to the "Bayfield" parking lot down below, at water level (watch for signs on the right as you enter town; £1/2 hours, £3/5 hours, £4/24 hours, free 20:00-8:00)—after parking, just head up the stairs to the TI. There's also a small pay lot called "The Green" next to the TI (same prices as Somerled Square).

Sights in Portree

There's not a turnstile in town, but Portree is fun to explore. Below I've described the village's three areas: the main square and "downtown," the harborfront, and the hill above the harbor.

Somerled Square and the Town Center

Get oriented to Portree on the broad **main square,** with its mercat cross, bus stops, parking lot, and highest concentration of public benches. The square is named for Somerled (Old Norse for "Summer Wanderer"), the 12th-century ruler who kicked off the MacDonald clan dynasty and first united Scotland's western islands into the so-called Lordship of the Isles.

It seems every small Scottish town has both a mercat cross and a WWI memorial—and in Portree, they're combined into one. A **mercat cross** indicated the right for a town to host a market, and was the community gathering point for celebrations, public shamings, and executions. The **WWI memorial** is a reminder of the disproportionate loss of life that Scotland suffered in the Great War. In the case of wee Portree, a band of 28 Gaelic-speaking brothers went to war...and eight came back. (Ten were killed in a single night of fighting.)

Much of present-day Portree was the vision of Sir James MacDonald, who pushed to develop the town in the late 18th century. City leaders commissioned the impressive

Portree

To Uig, Dunvegan & Grocery

PLAY FIELDS

To Staffin, Portrush Peninsula & 12

To Scorrybreac Trail & 6

SCHOOL

Somerled Square

THE GREEN

Harbor

MEALL HOUSE

ROYAL HOTEL

SKYE GATHERING HALL

Main Parking Lot

PORTREE MEDICAL CENTRE

APOTHECARY TOWER

"The Lump"

Loch Portree

HIGHLAND GATHERING BOWL

To Sligachan & Kyle of Lochalsh

200 Meters

200 Yards

ISLE OF SKYE

Accommodations

1. The Portree Hotel & West Highland Bar
2. Rosedale Hotel
3. Pink House
4. The Bosville; Dulse & Brose
5. To Marmalade Hotel
6. To Cuillin Hills Hotel/Rest.
7. High Beech House
8. Easdale B&B
9. Youth Hostel
10. Independent Hostel & Launderette
11. To Greenacres Guest House, The Gables, Almondbank Guest House & LAS Theatre
12. To Ballintoy B&B; Riverside B&B

Eateries & Other

13. Scorrybreac
14. The Isles Inn
15. Birch
16. Caberfeidh Bar
17. Café Arriba, The Chippy, Taste of India & Relish Deli
18. Caledonian Café
19. Sea Breezes
20. Harbour Fish & Chips
21. Fat Panda
22. Grocery
23. Prince of India

engineer Thomas Telford (famous for his many great canals, locks, and bridges) to help design the village's harbor and the roads connecting it to the rest of the island.

Wentworth Street, running from this square to the harbor, is the main shopping drag. Several English-sounding streets in Portree (Wentworth, Bosville, Douglas, Beaumont) are named for aristocratic families that the MacDonalds married into, helping to keep the clan financially afloat. Window-shop your way two blocks along Wentworth Street. Turn right on Bank Street. The **Royal Hotel,** built on the site of MacNab's Inn, is where Bonnie Prince Charlie bid farewell to Flora MacDonald following his crushing defeat at Culloden, then set sail, never again to return to Scotland.

Quay Street leads down the hill to...

▲▲Portree Harbor

Portree's most pleasant space (unless you've got food the seagulls want) is its harbor, where colorful homes look out over bobbing boats and the surrounding peninsulas. As one of the most protected natural harbors on the west coast, it's the reason that Portree emerged as Skye's leading town. Find a scenic perch at the corner of the harbor and take it all in.

While tourism is today's main industry, Portree first boomed in the mid-18th century thanks to kelp. Seaweed was gathered here, sun-dried, and burned in kilns to create an ashy-blue substance that was rich in soda, an essential ingredient in the production of glass and soap. But with the defeat of Napoleon at Waterloo, international sources of kelp opened up, causing this local industry to crash. This economic downturn coincided with a potato famine (similar to the one across the sea in Ireland), and by the mid-1800s, many locals were setting sail from this harbor to seek a better life in North America. But Portree soldiered on, bolstered by its prime location for fishing—especially for herring. By the early 20th century, a nationwide herring boom had again buoyed Portree's economy, with hundreds of fishing boats crowding its harbor.

Notice the stone building with the sealed-off door at the base of the stairs leading up into town. This was the former **ice house,** which was in operation until the 1970s. The winch at the peak of the building was used to haul big blocks of ice into an enormous subterranean cellar, to preserve Atlantic salmon throughout the summer.

Survey the harbor, enjoying the **pastel homes**—which come with lots of local gossip. Rumor has it that these used to be more uniform, until a proud gay couple decided to paint their house pink (it's now a hotel annex). What used to be a blue-and-white house next door (now an all-blue hotel) belonged to a fan of the West Ham United soccer team. Soon the other homeowners followed suit, each choosing their own color.

Speaking of bright colors, look for the **traffic-cone-orange**

boat floating in the harbor. This belongs to the Royal National Lifeboat Institution (RNLI), Britain's charity-funded answer to the US Coast Guard.

You may notice the busy **fish-and-chips joint,** with its customers standing guardedly against the nearby walls and vicious seagulls perched on rooftops ready to swoop down at the first sight of battered cod.

Go for a stroll along the Telford-built pier. Along here, a couple of different companies offer 1.5-hour excursions out to the sea-eagle nests and around the bay, including by RIB—high-speed rigid inflatable boat (ask the captains at the port, or inquire at the TI). At the far end of the pier is a gas station with huge, underwater tanks for fueling visiting boats. When big cruise ships are in port, they drop the hook and tender their passengers in to this pier.

Ascending "The Lump" (Hill Above the Harbor)

For a different perspective on Portree—and one that gets you away from the tourists—hike up the bluff at the south end of the harbor. From the Royal Hotel, head up Bank Street.

After a few steps, you'll spot the white **Meall House** on your left—supposedly Portree's oldest surviving home (c. 1800) and once the sheriff's office and jail. Today it's a center for the Gaelic cultural organization Fèisean nan Gàidheal, which celebrates the Celtic tongue that survives about as well here on Portree as anywhere in Scotland. Hiding behind the Meall House, along the harborview path, is the stepped-gable **Skye Gathering Hall** (from 1879). This is where Portree's upper crust throws big, fancy, invitation-only balls on the days before and after Skye's Highland Games. The rest of the year, it hosts cultural events and—on occasion—a fun little market with a mix of crafts and flea-market-type items.

Back on Bank Street, continue uphill. Soon you'll approach the **Portree Medical Centre**—one of just two hospitals on the entire Isle of Skye. (Is it just me, or do those parking spots each come with a graveyard cross?)

Just before the hospital's parking lot, watch on the left for the uphill lane through the trees. Use this to hike on up to the top of the hill that locals call "The Lump" (or, for those with more local pride, "Fancy Hill"). Emerging into the clearing, you'll reach a huge, flat **bowl** that was blasted out of solid rock to hold 5,000 people during Skye's annual Highland Gathering.

Isle of Skye (side tab)

In addition to the typical Highland dancing, footraces, and feats of strength, Skye's games have a unique event: From this spot, runners climb downhill, swim across Loch Portree, ascend the hill on the adjacent peninsula, then swim back again.

Walk left, toward the harbor, then head left again onto a path leading away from the bowl; you'll run into the crenellated **apothecary tower.** It was built in 1834, not as a castle fortification but to alert approaching sailors that a pharmacist was open for business in Portree. This tower was literally blown over by gale-force winds in a 1991 storm, but has since been rebuilt. It's usually open if you'd like to climb to the top for views over the harbor and the region—on a clear day, you can see all the way to the Old Man of Storr (see page 101).

Walks and Hikes near Portree

The Portree TI can offer advice about hikes in the area; if either of the below options interests you, get details there before you head out.

Scorrybreac Path: This popular choice doesn't require a car. To get to the trailhead—three-quarters of a mile from Somerled Square—walk north out of Portree on Mill Road, veer right onto Scorrybreac Road when you're just leaving town (following the sign for *Budhmor*), then follow the coastline to the start of the hiking trail, marked by signs. From here, you'll walk along the base of a bluff with fine views back on Portree's colorful harborfront. The loop back into town takes about an hour.

Old Man of Storr: Drivers can tackle the more ambitious hike up to this rocky formation. You'll drive about 15 minutes north of town (following the start of my Trotternish Peninsula Driving Tour) and park at the Old Man of Storr trailhead. Green trail signs lead you through a gate and up along a well-trod gravel path through a felled woodland. Once you've reached the top of the first bluff, take the right fork, and continue all the way up to the pinnacle. Plan on about two hours round-trip. (If you don't mind a longer drive, a better hike is at **The Quiraing**—see page 103.)

Nightlife in Portree

Portree goes to bed pretty early, but in high season a couple venues offer live music most evenings. The **West Highland Bar,** attached to the recommended Portree Hotel, has music on weekends. The **Isles Inn** (one of my recommended restaurants) hosts bands several nights a week in summer, usually starting around 21:30. Also check what's on at the **LAS Theatre,** in the Isle of Skye Candle Company Visitors Centre at the edge of town; in addition to movies—tempting on a rainy day—they often have live music and other performances (Viewfield Road, www.lasportrigh.co.uk).

Sleeping in Portree

Portree is crowded with hikers and tourists in July and August, and can be fully booked between April and September. To have the best range of choices, reserve your room months in advance—as far ahead as you can. You may need to check with several places. The B&Bs I list are just a representative sampling; Portree has dozens upon dozens of small B&Bs, so if you're late to the game, try searching around online or on Airbnb. If looking last-minute, try the Facebook group "Skye Rooms," where hotels, B&Bs, and short-term apartments with late cancelations and random openings list their availability for the next day. Travelers looking for accommodations can also post their desired dates.

When comparison-shopping online, look out for price gouging. An en suite double room at a solid, midrange, comfortable, friendly B&B within walking distance of town should run in the neighborhood of £100-120. Similar places in the same areas add a few extra amenities (fully stocked mini-fridges, for example) and charge double those rates, or more. These may be worthwhile if you're desperate and deep-pocketed. But what you get for the added expense is hard to justify for those on a tight budget.

BIGGER HOTELS

These places are all run by the same owners, offering plenty of beds, professional service, and higher prices.

On Somerled Square: $$$$ The Portree Hotel is your functional, impersonal town-center accommodation, with 24 small but modern rooms on three floors and no elevator (family rooms, bar/restaurant, no parking—must use public lots, +44 1478 612 511, www.theportreehotel.com, contact@theportreehotel.com).

On the Harbor: $$$ Rosedale Hotel fills three former fishermen's houses with mazelike hallways and 17 rooms—some modern, some more traditional (full cooked breakfast, family room and a few small, no-view, cheaper doubles available; no elevator and lots of stairs; restaurant and bar, parking lot down the road; Beaumont Crescent, +44 1478 613 131, www.rosedalehotelskye.co.uk, reservations@rosedalehotelskye.co.uk). They also run the annex **$$$ Pink House,** around the side of the harbor, with nine seaview rooms (continental breakfast, closed Nov-Feb, large family rooms, Quay Street, +44 1478 612 263, www.pinkhouseportree.

ISLE OF SKYE

co.uk, info@pinkhouseportree.co.uk). Note that both of these have rooms facing the harborfront walkway, which offer views but very little privacy.

Other Hotels: If things are booked up, you can try checking at some bigger, more expensive hotels in town. These two share the same owner: **$$$$ The Bosville,** with 20 rooms right in the heart of Portree; and **$$$$ Marmalade Hotel,** with 32 rooms a short walk above the town center (www.perlehotels.com). And **$$$$ Cuillin Hills Hotel** has 39 rooms around the harbor—a short drive away—on a nice lawn overlooking town (www.cuillinhills-hotel-skye.co.uk). While pricey, each of these offers a high level of modern predictability and professionalism.

CHARACTERISTIC PLACES IN TOWN

$$ High Beech House wows guests with stupendous views from its breakfast room, overlooking the whole bay around Portree. Its two cozy rooms are a short walk up the hill above town, still central but with a peaceful and secluded vibe (2-night minimum preferred, driveway parking, Coolin Drive, +44 7767 216 205, www.highbeechhouse.co.uk, info@highbeechhouse.co.uk, Jonathan and Pauline).

$ Easdale B&B is an old-school place with two rooms, a bright breakfast room with nice views, and a large, traditional lounge set just above the busy main road (cash only, continental breakfast, no kids, closed Oct-March, Bridge Road, +44 1478 613 244—call to reserve; spunky, plainspoken, and happily computer-free Chrissie).

¢ Portree Youth Hostel, run by Hostelling Scotland (SYHA), is a modern-feeling, institutional, cinderblock-and-metal building with 50 beds in 16 rooms (cash only, private and family rooms available, continental breakfast extra, kitchen, laundry, +44 1478 612 231, www.hostellingscotland.org.uk, portree@hostellingscotland.org.uk).

¢ Portree Independent Hostel, in the unmissable yellow building just off the main square, has 60 beds and equally bold colors inside (cash only, one twin room and several 4-person rooms, no breakfast, kitchen, laundry, +44 1478 613 737, www.hostelskye.co.uk, skyehostel@yahoo.co.uk).

JUST OUTSIDE TOWN

For a better value and far more choices, head a bit out of town. These options are all a longish walk or a very short drive into the heart of Portree.

South of Portree, off Viewfield Road

Viewfield Road, stretching south from Portree, is B&B central.

All offer convenient parking and are within walking distance of town (figure 10-20 minutes). Some are on smaller side lanes that stretch down toward the water, but all are well marked from the main road.

$$ Greenacres Guest House feels estate-like and borderline formal, with fine china on the table, fountain and manicured hedges in the garden, a glassed-in sunroom, and a patio with some of the best views in the area. The four rooms have different color schemes and styles, and some feature Ewen's handmade headboards, built from wood recycled from an old school (cash only, closed Oct-Easter, about a 20-minute walk from town at 11 Viewfield Road, , +44 1478 612 605, https://greenacres-skye.co.uk, greenacreskye@aol.com, Marie and Ewen).

$$ The Gables, run by Margaret, has three rooms next door to Greenacres, including two with great water views (family room, Viewfield Road, +44 1478 613 184, www.gablesportree.com, mdgables@btinternet.com).

$ Almondbank Guest House, just below the main road, has four homey, traditional rooms. Two have grand views over the water, for no extra charge, and one has a private bathroom down the hall (Viewfield Road, +44 1478 612 696, jan@jans.co.uk, Effie).

North of Portree

These places are a 15-minute walk from town on Staffin Road, toward the Trotternish Peninsula.

$ Ballintoy Bed and Breakfast, an excellent value set back from the road and surrounded by a large field, has three immaculate ground-floor rooms accessorized with fun pops of color and artwork (family room, 2-night minimum preferred, continental breakfast, Staffin Road, +44 1478 611 719, www.ballintoy-skye.co.uk, ballintoyskye@gmail.com, Gillian and Gavin).

$ Riverside B&B is a shoes-off-tidy home with three fresh rooms—two with Cuillin Hills views—in a big house perched above the road out of town (Staffin Road, +44 1478 612 117, www.riversideskye.co.uk, Jane and Fred).

BETWEEN PORTREE AND KYLEAKIN

$$$$ Sligachan Hotel (pronounced SLIG-a-hin), perched at a crossroads in the scenic middle of nowhere (yet handy for road-tripping sightseers) is a compound of sleeping and eating options that is a local institution and a haven for hikers. The hotel's 20 rooms are comfortable, if a bit dated and simple for the price, while the nearby campground and bunkhouse offer a budget alternative. The setting—surrounded by the mighty Cuillin Hills—is remarkably scenic (closed Dec-Jan, on the A-87 between Kyleakin and Portree in Sligachan, hotel and campground +44 1478 650 204, bunkhouse +44 1478 650 458, www.sligachan.co.uk, reservations@ sligachan.co.uk). For location, see the map on page 84.

Eating in Portree

Always reserve ahead for dinner here; these places can book up weeks ahead in peak season. (Lunch at the nicer places is also worth prebooking.) Portree's eateries tend to close early (21:00 or 22:00).

UP IN TOWN

$$$$ Scorrybreac is Portree's best splurge, offering a delightful array of well-presented international dishes that draw from local ingredients and traditions. The cozy, modern, unpretentious dining room with eight tables fills up quickly, so reservations are a must (set multicourse menus only, Wed-Sat 17:00-21:00, closed Sun-Tue, 7 Bosville Terrace, +44 1478 612 069, www.scorrybreac.com).

$$$ Dulse & Brose is refined but unpretentious, with wooden bookshelves along the wall and old wooden benches (comfier than they sound). It offers a small menu of well-executed fish, beef, fowl, and veggie dishes, mostly using Scottish ingredients (Sat-Wed 17:00-22:00, closed Thu-Fri, Bosville Terrace, +44 1478 612 846, http://bosvillehotel.co.uk).

$$ The Isles Inn is a happening place, popular with hikers, with two halves serving the same menu—a brighter high-energy dining area and the darker pub—or you can sit at the bar. Offering a fun energy and warm service, they dish up simple, honest food one notch above pub grub. They have popular burgers, and their big slabs of salmon or haddock are served with fresh vegetables (daily 12:00-15:00 & 17:00-21:30, no reservations, facing Somerled Square, +44 1478 612 129).

$$ Birch is a wonderful little café that would be at home in hipster Glasgow or Edinburgh, but instead it's tucked on a quiet side street in the heart of Portree. The minimalist interior, looking out to a mural of the Cuillin Hills across the street, is inviting. The brief menu is thoughtfully curated, with brunch and lunch dishes that provide a welcome, foodie break from most places in town (for example, open-face sandwiches with avocado or poached eggs). Their coffee drinks and pastries are also excellent (Tue-Sat 8:00-17:00, Sun 10:00-16:00, closed Mon, Bayfield Road, www. birch-skye.co).

$$ Caberfeidh Bar, hipper than the Portree norm, is a cocktail bar and pizza joint offering wood-fired pizzas with both predictable and adventurous toppings. The name is Scots Gaelic for "Stag's Antlers"—an important symbol of Clan Mackenzie (Tue-Sat 15:00-21:00, closed Sun-Mon, facing the parking lot on Somerled Square, +44 1478 613 794).

$$ Café Arriba is a fun and welcoming space offering refreshingly eclectic flavors in this small Scottish town. With a menu that includes local specialties, burgers, and Italian, this youthful, colorful, easygoing eatery's hit-or-miss cuisine is worth trying. Drop in to see what's on the blackboard menu today (lots of vegetarian options, Tue-Sun 9:00-16:00, closed Mon, Quay Brae, +44 1478 611 830).

$$ Caledonian Café, a few steps off the main square, is a busy, popular hometown diner serving good crank-'em-out food to an appreciative local crowd. It's family-friendly, with a good selection of burgers and fish-and-chips (daily 9:00-21:00, Wentworth Street, +44 1478 612 553). Their homemade ice cream from the stand in front is a nice way to finish your meal.

DINING BY THE WATER

Portree's little harbor has a scattering of good eateries but none have actual waterfront seating. My hunch: It's because of the mean seagulls that hang out here.

$$$ Sea Breezes is a basic, salty, no-nonsense eatery, with plain decor and a seafood-focused menu (Tue-Sat 12:30-14:00 & 17:30-21:30, closed Sun-Mon and Nov-Easter, +44 1478 612 016).

$$$$ Cuillin Hills Hotel Restaurant is in a big, classy old-world hotel set on a lawn high above the water, a five-minute drive from the town center. It has a peaceful and formal dining room, a commanding view, delightful service, and tasty food. Reserve well ahead (daily 12:00-14:00 & 18:00-21:30, Coolin Hills Gardens, +44 1478 612 003, www.cuillinhills-hotel-skye.co.uk).

EATING CHEAPER

Fish-and-Chips: Portree has two chippies, both cash only: **$ The Harbour Fish & Chips Shop** is delightfully located on the charming harbor with good fish that's cheap and in big portions (daily 11:00-21:00, later in summer). The downside: Aggressive seagulls drive diners up against the wall. It's funny to watch. For a more relaxing meal, **$ The Chippy** sells very basic fish-and-chips and burgers, just up the harbor lane (on Bank Street) with peaceful-if-grungy tables and no seagulls.

Other Takeaways in Town: $$ Fat Panda Asian restaurant on Bayfield Road is satisfying (closed Tue). **$ Relish** is a deli serving good, fresh sandwiches (eat in or to go, Mon-Sat 8:30-17:00, Sun 10:00-14:00, end of Wentworth Street). And the **Co-op** grocery has a small selection of sandwiches and other prepared foods (daily 7:00-22:00). There's also a larger Co-op supermarket on the way out of town, on the road toward Uig and Dunvegan Castle.

When Other Places Are Full: If you can't get into any of the above, and you don't want to do takeout, consider Portree's two Indian restaurants (**Prince of India** on Bayfield Road and **Taste of India** on Bank Street), or see if they can squeeze you in at the **Portree Hotel**'s restaurant.

EATING ELSEWHERE ON THE ISLE OF SKYE

In Sligachan: The **Sligachan Hotel** (described earlier) is a grand and rustic old hotel in an extremely scenic setting, nestled in the Cuillin Hills. Popular with campers and hikers, it's also family-friendly, with a zip line for kids in the playground. There are two eateries here: The more refined **$$$ Harta Restaurant** offers "casual dining with fine food" (nightly 17:30-21:00). On the other side of the complex, the big, open-feeling **$$ Seumas Bar** serves microbrews and mountaineer-pleasing grub, plus a Scotsman-pleasing range of more than 400 whiskies (daily 12:00-22:30, food served until 20:30, closed Oct-Feb; on the A-87 between Kyleakin and Portree, +44 1478 650 204). There's also a microbrewery on site (separate owners).

In Colbost, near Dunvegan: About a 15-minute drive west of Dunvegan (about 45 minutes each way from Portree), the **$$$$ Three Chimneys Restaurant** is out on a deserted road with just sheep for neighbors. This place is known throughout Scotland as a magnet for gourmands; now well established, it was the original "destination" restaurant on the island. Its 16 tables fill an old three-chimney croft house, with a stone-and-timbers decor that artfully melds old and new—a perfect complement to the modern Scottish cuisine. It's cozy, classy, candlelit, and a bit dressy (do your best), but not stuffy. Reservations are essential (set multicourse menus only, daily 12:00-13:15 & 18:30-21:00, shorter hours off-season, +44 1470 511 258, www.threechimneys.co.uk). They also rent six swanky, pricey **$$$$** suites next door.

Other Foodie Splurges: Beyond the Three Chimneys, Skye has a variety of newish, well-regarded gourmet hotspots scattered around the island. If you're serious about dining well (at high prices), research these choices—and always book far ahead: **$$$$ Edinbane Lodge** is about a 25-minute drive west of Portree, on the way to Dunvegan Castle (www.edinbanelodge.com). **$$$$ Loch Bay Restaurant**—where chef Michael Smith, formerly of the Three Chimneys, has earned a Michelin star—is a 10-minute detour from the Portree-Dunvegan road (about 35 minutes from Portree) on the Waternish Peninsula (www.lochbay-restaurant.co.uk). And **$$$$ Coruisk House** is down in the southern part of the island, near Elgol, about an hour's drive south of Portree (www.coruiskhouse.com). **$$$$ Scorrybreac,** right in the heart of Portree and described earlier, is also in this category.

Touring the Isle of Skye

There is a well-trodden tourist path around Skye, and it's clearly the most memorable way for someone with a car to spend the day. The three big sights are the Trotternish Peninsula (to the north of Portree), with its memorable Skye Museum of Island Life; Dunvegan Castle (to the east); and Talisker Distillery (to the south).

Planning Your Time: It's possible—but rushed—to see all three in one day. (The challenge: The Skye Museum of Island Life closes at 17:00.) Start with the first distillery tour at 10:00, tour the castle, and circle the peninsula to get to the museum by about 16:30. This will rush the wonderful natural sights along the peninsula, but it might be worth it if time is short and you want to experience it all. While you could drive directly from Dunvegan Castle to the Skye Museum of Island Life and then tour the Trotternish Peninsula in a clockwise direction, it's far more scenic to drive it in a counterclockwise route as proposed here. Summer days are long, and the light can be wonderful in the early evening for the scenic west coast of the Trotternish Peninsula.

Another option is to skip the distillery, do the castle first, and then take a leisurely tour of the peninsula. With two days, you can do it all at a more comfortable pace.

TROTTERNISH PENINSULA LOOP DRIVE

This inviting peninsula north of Portree is packed with windswept castaway views, unique geological formations, a few offbeat sights, and some of Scotland's most dramatic scenery. The following loop tour starts and ends in Portree, circling the peninsula counterclock-

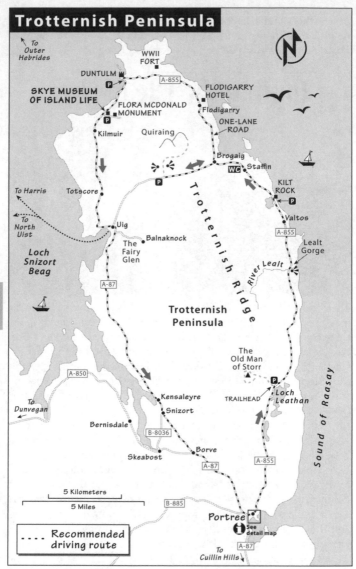

Trotternish Peninsula

To Outer Hebrides

WWII FORT

DUNTULM

A-855

SKYE MUSEUM OF ISLAND LIFE

FLODIGARRY HOTEL

FLORA MCDONALD MONUMENT

Flodigarry

ONE-LANE ROAD

Kilmuir

Quiraing

To Harris

Totscore

Brogaig

WC Staffin

KILT ROCK

P

To North Uist

Uig

Balnaknock

Valtos

A-855

The Fairy Glen

Lealt Gorge

Loch Snizort Beag

A-87

River Lealt

Trotternish Ridge

Trotternish Peninsula

A-850

The Old Man of Storr

Kensaleyre

TRAILHEAD

P

Loch Leathan

Sound of Raasay

To Dunvegan

Snizort

Bernisdale

B-8036

Borve

Skeabost

A-87

A-855

5 Kilometers

5 Miles

Portree

i See detail map

B-885

Recommended driving route

To Cuillin Hills

A-87

ISLE OF SKYE

wise (see the "Trotternish Peninsula" map, above). Along the way, you'll explore a gaggle of old-fashioned stone homes, learn about Skye's ancient farming lifestyles, and pay homage to a brave woman who rescued a bonnie prince. In good weather, a spin around Trotternish is the best activity Skye offers and is worth ▲▲▲.

Planning Your Drive: With minimal stops, this self-guided drive takes about two hours—but it deserves half a day or more.

Note that during several stretches, you'll be driving on a paved one-lane road; use the occasional "passing places" to pull over and allow oncoming traffic or faster cars to go by.

• *Head north of Portree on the A-855, following signs for* Staffin. *About three miles out of town, you'll begin to enjoy some impressive views of the Trotternish Ridge. You'll be passing peat bogs and may notice stretches where peat has been cut from the fields by the roadside. As you pass the small loch on your right, straight ahead is the distinctive rock tower called the…*

Old Man of Storr

This 160-foot-tall tapered slab of basalt stands proudly apart from the rest of the Storr (as the mountain is called). The unusual landscape of the Trotternish Peninsula is due to massive landslides (the largest in Britain). This block slid down the cliff about 6,500 years ago and landed on its end, where it has slowly been whittled by weather into a pinnacle. An icon of Skye, the Old Man of Storr has been featured in many films—from *Flash Gordon* to *Prometheus.* The lochs on your right supply drinking water for the town of Portree and have been linked together to spin the turbines at a nearby hydroelectric plant that once provided all of Skye's electricity.

ISLE OF SKYE

If you'd like to tackle the two-hour hike to the Old Man, there's a pay parking lot directly below the formation (pay with coins or card; for details on the hike, see "Walks and Hikes near Portree," earlier).

• *After passing the Old Man, enjoy the scenery on your right, overlooking nearby islands and the mainland.*

As you drive, you'll notice that Skye seems to have more sheep than people. During the Highland Clearances of the early 19th century, many human residents were forced to move off the island to make room for more livestock. The people who remain are some of the most ardently Gaelic Scots in Scotland. While only about one percent of all Scottish people speak Gaelic (pronounced "gallic"), one-third of Skye residents are fluent. A generation ago, it was illegal to teach Gaelic in schools; today, Skye offers its residents the opportunity to enroll in Gaelic-only education, from primary school to college (Sabhal Mòr Ostaig, on Skye's Sleat Peninsula, is the world's only college with courses taught entirely in Scottish Gaelic; see page 116).

• *About four miles after the Old Man parking lot, you'll pass a sign for the* River Lealt. *Immediately after, the turnoff on the right is an optional stop at the...*

Lealt Gorge

Where the River Lealt tumbles toward the sea, it carves out a long and scenic gorge. A viewing platform juts out over the gorge, over-looking a protected, pebbly cove and some dramatic rock formations. The formations on the left, which look like stacked rocks, are the opposite: They've been weathered by centuries of battering storms, which have peeled back any vegetation and ground the stones to their smooth state. Peering down to the beach,  you'll see a smokestack and some other ruins of a plant that once processed diatomite—a crumbly, clay-like substance made from algae fossils, which has hundreds of industrial uses. This factory, which closed in 1960, is a reminder of a time when tourism wasn't the island's main source of income. When this was functioning, no roads connected this point to Portree, so the factory's waterfront location made it possible to ship the diatomite far and wide.

• *Continue along the road. Just after the village of Valtos (about 2 miles after the Lealt Gorge viewpoint), you'll reach a loch (left), next to a parking lot (right). Park at the well-marked Kilt Rock viewpoint to check out...*

▲Kilt Rock

So named because of its resemblance to a Scotsman's tartan, this 200-foot-tall sea cliff has a layer of volcanic rock with vertical lava columns that look like pleats (known as columnar jointing), sitting atop a layer of horizontal sedimentary rock. The dramatic formations in the opposite direction are just as amazing.

• *Continuing north, as you approach the village of* **Staffin***, you'll begin to see interesting rock formations high on the hill to your left.*

Staffin's name, like that of the isle of Staffa, comes from Old Norse and means "the place of staves" (or "pillars")—both boast dramatic basalt rock columns. If you need a public WC, partway through town, watch on the left for the Staffin Community Hall (marked *Talla Stafainn,* sharing a building with a grocer). Or

ISLE OF SKYE

for a coffee or lunch break, you could visit (on the right) the **Columba 1400 Centre,** a Christian-run retreat for struggling teens from big cities. They run a nice cafeteria and shop to support their work (Mon-Sat 10:00-20:00, closed Sun, handy WCs for customers, +44 1478 611 400).

• Just after you leave Staffin, watch for signs on the left to turn off and head up to the quintessential Isle of Skye viewpoint—a rock formation called...

▲▲The Quiraing

You'll get fine views of this jagged northern end of the Trotternish Ridge (locals pronounce it "kerrANG") as you drive up. Land-slides caused the dramatic scenery in this area, and each rock formation has a name, such as "The Needle" or "The Prison."

At the summit of this road, you'll reach a parking area (which gets very busy in high season). Even a short walk to a nearby bluff—to get away from the cars and alone with the wind and the island wonder—is rewarding. And there are several exciting longer hikes from here for a closer look at the formations. If you've got the time, energy, and weather for a rewarding hike, here's your chance. You can follow the trail toward the bluff, and at the fork, decide to stay level (to the base of the formations) or veer off to the left and switch back up (to the top of the plateau). Both paths are faintly visible from the parking area. Once up top, your reward is a view of the secluded green plateau called "The Table," another landslide block, which isn't visible from the road.

• You could continue on this road all the way to Uig, at the other end of the peninsula. But it's more interesting to backtrack, then turn left onto the main road (A-855, now a one-lane road), to reach the...

Tip of Trotternish

A few miles north, after the village of Flodigarry, you'll pass the **Flodigarry Hotel,** with a cottage on the premises that was once home to Bonnie Prince Charlie's protector, Flora MacDonald (the cottage is now part of the hotel and not open to the public).

Soon after, at the top of a ridge ahead, you'll see the remains of an old **fort** from World War II, when the Atlantic was monitored for U-boats from this position.

Farther down the road, at the tip of the peninsula, you'll pass (on the right) the crumbling remains of another fort, this one much older: **Duntulm Castle** (free, roadside parking, 5-minute walk from road), which was the first stronghold on Skye of the influential MacDonald clan. It was from here that the MacDonalds fought many fierce battles against Clan MacLeod (for more on these clan battles, see "The Feuding Clans of Skye" sidebar later in this chapter). The castle was abandoned around 1730 for Armadale Castle on the southern end of Skye. While the castle ruins are fenced off, travelers venture in at their own risk. In the distance beyond, you can see the **Outer Hebrides**—the most rugged, remote, and Gaelic part of Scotland. The strait between Skye and these islands is called "The Minch."

• *A mile after the castle, watch for the turnoff on the left to the excellent...*

▲▲Skye Museum of Island Life

This fine little stand of seven thatched stone huts, organized into a family-run museum, explains how a typical Skye family lived a century and a half ago.

Cost and Hours: £5, Mon-Sat 10:00-17:00, closed Sun and Oct-Easter, +44 1470 552 206, www.skyemuseum.co.uk, run by Margaret, Dinah, Hector, and their team. Though there are ample posted explanations, the £1 guidebook is worth buying.

Visiting the Museum: The three huts closest to the sea are original (more than 200 years old). Most interesting is The Old Croft House, which was the residence of the Graham family until 1957. Inside you'll find three rooms: kitchen (with peat-burning fire), parents' "master bedroom," and a bedroom for the 10 kids. All are fully furnished and endearingly cluttered with historic bric-a-brac. Nearby, The Old Byre (Barn) displays farm implements, and the Old Ceilidh House (a gathering place for the entire community) contains dense but very informative displays about crofting (the traditional tenant-farmer lifestyle on Skye), the Gaelic poet Màiri Mhòr nan Òran, Bonnie Prince Charlie and Flora MacDonald, and old tales from the area.

The four other huts, reconstructed in this location, house exhibits about weaving; the village smithy; fishing, tilling, and peat harvesting; a local shop/post office—this isolated community's lifeline to the outside world; and more. As you explore, admire the smart architecture of these humble but deceptively well-planned structures. Rocks hanging from the roof keep the thatch from blowing away, and the streamlined shape of the structure embedded in the ground encourages strong winds to deflect around the hut rather than hit it head-on.

• *After touring the museum, drive or walk out to the very end of the small road that leads past the parking lot, to a lonesome cemetery. Let yourself in through the gate to reach the tallest Celtic cross at the far end, which is the...*

Monument to Flora MacDonald

This fine old cemetery, with mossy and evocative old tombs to ponder, features a tall cross dedicated to the local heroine who rescued the beloved Jacobite hero Bonnie Prince Charlie at his darkest hour. (After the original was chipped away by 19th-century souvenir seekers, this more modern replacement was placed here.) After his loss at Culloden, and with a hefty price on his head, Charlie retreated to the Outer Hebrides. But the Hanover dynasty, which controlled the islands, was closing in. Flora MacDonald rescued the prince, disguised him as her Irish maid, Betty Burke, and sailed him to safety on Skye. (Charlie pulled off the ruse thanks to  his soft, feminine features—hence the nickname "Bonnie," which means "beautiful" or "handsome.")

His flight inspired a popular Scottish folk song, "The Skye Boat Song": "Speed bonnie boat like a bird on the wing, / Onward, the sailors cry. / Carry the lad that's born to be king / Over the sea to Skye." You may recognize the tune as the theme to *Outlander*.

• *Return to the main road and proceed about six miles around the peninsula. Soon after what was once a loch (now a giant depression), you'll drop down over the town of Uig ("OO-eeg"), the departure point for ferries to the Outer Hebrides (North Uist and Harris islands, 3/day) and a handy spot for services (cafés, a gas station, pottery shop, Isle of Skye Brewing Co. brewery and bottle shop, and WC).*

Continue past Uig, climbing the hill across the bay. To take a brief detour to enjoy some hidden scenery, consider a visit to the Fairy Glen. To find it, just after passing the big Uig Hotel, take a very hard left, marked for Sheadar and Balnaknock. Follow this one-lane road about a mile through the countryside. You'll emerge into an otherworldly little valley. Wind through the valley to just past the tiny lake and park below the towering Fairy Castle rock (pay parking, cash or card).

▲The Fairy Glen

Whether or not you believe in fairies, it's easy to imagine why locals claim that they live here. With evocatively undulating terrain—ruffled, conical hills called "fairy towers" reflected in glassy ponds, rising up from an otherwise flat and dull countryside—it's a magical place. There's little to see on a quick drive-by, but hikers enjoy exploring these hills, discovering little caves, weathered stone fences, and delightful views. As you explore, keep an eye out for "Skye landmines" (sheep droppings). Hardy hikers enjoy clambering 10 minutes up to the top of the tallest rock tower, the "Fairy Castle." (By the way, the sheep are actually fairies until a human enters the valley.)

• *Head back the way you came and continue uphill on the main road (A-87), with views down over Uig's port. Looking back at Uig, you can see a good example of Skye's traditional farming system—crofting.*

Historically, arable land on the island was divided into plots. If you look across to the hills above Uig, you can see strips of demarcated land running up from the

water—these are crofts. Crofts were generally owned by landlords (mostly English aristocrats or Scottish clan chiefs, and later the Scottish government) and rented to tenant farmers. The crofters lived and worked under very difficult conditions and were lucky if they could produce enough potatoes and livestock to feed their families. Rights to farm the croft were passed down from father to eldest son over generations, but always under the auspices of a wealthy landlord.

• *But you live in a more affluent and equitable world, and more Scottish memories await to be created here on Skye. From here, you can continue along the main road, A-87, south toward Portree (and possibly continue from there to the Cuillin Hills). Or you can take the shortcut road just after Kensaleyre (B-8036) and head west on the A-850 to Dunvegan and its castle. All your Skye options are described in the following pages.*

NORTHWEST SKYE
▲▲Dunvegan Castle

Perched on a rock overlooking a sea loch, Dunvegan Castle is the residence of the MacLeod (pronounced "McCloud") clan. One

of Skye's preeminent clans, the MacLeods often clashed with their traditional rivals, the MacDonalds, whose castle is on the southern tip of the island (see "The Feuding Clans of Skye" sidebar, later). The MacLeods claim that Dunvegan is the oldest continuously inhabited castle in Scotland. The current (and 30th) clan chief, Hugh Magnus MacLeod, is a film producer who divides his time between London and the castle, where his noble efforts are aimed at preserving Dunvegan for future generations. Worth ▲▲▲ to people named MacLeod, the castle offers an interesting look at Scotland's antiquated clan system, provides insight into rural Scottish aristocratic lifestyles, and has fine gardens that are a delight to explore.

Cost and Hours: £14, daily 10:00-17:30, closed mid-Oct-March, café in parking lot, +44 1470 521 206, www.dunvegancastle. com.

Getting There: It's near the small town of Dunvegan in the northwestern part of the island, well signposted from the A-850 (free parking). From Portree, bus #56 takes you right to the castle's parking lot.

Visiting the Castle: From the parking lot, cross the road, buy your ticket (you may have to wait in line), enter through the big gates, and walk five minutes through the gardens to the castle entrance. Follow the one-way route through the interior, borrowing laminated descriptions in many rooms—and don't hesitate to ask the helpful docents if you have any questions. You'll start upstairs and then make your way to the ground floor.

Up the main staircase and left down the main hallway, you'll reach the **bedroom,** in the "Fairy Tower." On the elegant canopy bed, look for the clan's seal and motto, carved into the headboard. The words "Hold Fast," which you'll see displayed throughout the castle, recall an incident where a MacLeod chieftain saved a man from being gored by a bull by literally taking the bull by the horns and wrestling it to the ground.

Beyond the bedroom, you'll ogle several more rooms, including the **dining room.** Here and throughout the castle, portraits of clan chieftains and the MacLeod family seem to be constantly looking down on you. The **library's** shelves are crammed with rich, leather-bound books.

Then you're routed back across the top of the stairs to the right wing, with the most interesting rooms. The 14th-century **drawing room** is the oldest part of the castle—it served as the great hall of the medieval fortress. But today it's a far cry from its gloomy, stony, Gothic-vaulted original state. In the 18th century, a clan chief's new bride requested that it be brightened up and modernized, so they added a drop ceiling, painted plaster walls, and hardwoods over the stone floor. The only clue to its original bulkiness is how thick the walls are (notice that the window bays are nine feet thick). In the drawing room, look for the tattered silk remains of the **Fairy Flag,** a mysterious swatch with about a dozen different legends attached to it (explained by the posted description).

Leaving the drawing room, notice the entrance to the

ISLE OF SKYE

dungeon—a holdover from that stout medieval fortress. Squeeze inside the dungeon and peer down into the deep pit. (Hey, is that a MacDonald rotting down there?)

At the end of this wing is the **north room,** a mini-museum of the clan's most prestigious artifacts (Fairy Flag aside). In the display case in the corner, find Rory Mor's Horn—made from a horn of the subdued bull that gave the clan its motto. Traditionally, this horn would be filled with nearly a half-gallon of claret (Bordeaux wine), which a potential heir had to drink in one gulp to prove himself fit for the role. See the photo of the previous clan chief, in 1956, draining the horn in under two minutes.

Other artifacts include bagpipes and several relics related to Bonnie Prince Charlie (including his vest—framed on the wall). In the center glass case, near a lock of Charlie's hair, is a portrait of Flora MacDonald and some items that belonged to her.

Hiding in the small glass cabinet (look for the puffin) is perhaps the most fascinating exhibit in the castle. The MacLeods owned the rugged and remote St. Kilda islands (40 miles into the Atlantic, the most distant bit of the British Isles). They collected rent from the hardscrabble St. Kilda community of 100 or so (who were finally evacuated in 1930). Inside the cabinet, you'll see a puffin trap, a door latch carved out of driftwood, and a little wooden boat that the islanders would insert a letter into and simply toss into the sea—trusting the prevailing currents to deliver it ("message in a bottle"-style) to correspondents on the mainland.

From here a staircase leads to the **ground floor,** with a few more exhibits. In the darkened room, a glass case holds the Claymore Sword—one of two surviving swords made of extremely heavy Scottish iron rather than steel. Dating from the late 15th or early 16th century, this unique weapon is the bazooka of swords—designed not for dexterous fencing, but for one big kill-'em-all swing. You'll also peek into what would have been the servants' quarters, and watch a very dry 12-minute video about the castle and the MacLeods, solemnly narrated by the 29th chief of the clan (showing an entirely different side of the man who chugged a half-gallon of wine in his youth).

Between the castle and the parking lot are five acres of plush **gardens** to stroll through while pondering the fading clan system. Circling down to the sea loch, you'll enjoy grand views back up to the castle (and see a dock selling 30-minute boat rides on Loch Dunvegan to visit a seal colony on a nearby island). Higher up and tucked away are

some of the finer, hidden parts of the gardens: the walled garden, the woodland walk up to the water garden (with a thundering waterfall and a gurgling stream), and the wide-open round garden.

The flaunting of inherited wealth and influence in some English castles rubs me the wrong way. But here, I had the opposite feeling: sympathy and compassion for a proud way of life that's dissolving with the rising tide of modernity. You have to admire the way they "hold fast" to this antiquated system (in the same way the Gaelic tongue is kept alive). Paying admission here feels more like donating to charity than padding the pockets of a wealthy family. In fact, watered-down MacLeods and MacDonalds from America, eager to reconnect with their Scottish roots, help keep the Scottish clan system alive.

The Giant Angus MacAskill Museum

This oddball museum fills a humble roadside barn in the town of Dunvegan. Peter Angus MacAskill (whose son, Danny, is a YouTube star for his extreme mountain biking on Skye) is happy to tell the story of his very distant cousin, "The Giant"—all seven feet, nine inches of him—who teamed up with Tom Thumb to travel around the US in the circus and make Barnum and Bailey lots of money until he died in 1863 (£2, daily 10:00-18:00, closed off-season).

Hikes and Walks Near Dunvegan

While neither of these easy walks are worth lingering for (or missing other sights on the island), they're fun to consider if you have some time and energy to burn while you're in the area.

Duirinish Standing Stone and Two Churches Walk: As you approach Dunvegan on the road from Portree, watch on the right for the ruins of St. Mary's Church and its kirkyard—and, on a knob of land just above and beyond, the dramatic outline of the Duirinish Standing Stone. You can pull over at the little roadside parking lot, where a green sign outlines the 45-minute **Two Churches Walk,** an easy and satisfying hillwalk that takes you from here almost to Dunvegan Castle, before circling back and depositing you at the Duirinish Parish Church, just around the corner. In addition to (or instead of) that walk, you can huff up the hill to get a closer look at the **Duirinish Standing Stone.** While this may appear to be some ancient artifact of a bygone civilization, it was actually erected here in 2000—to celebrate the millennium.

Coral Beach: For another popular walk—especially on a nice day—drive north about four miles (past Dunvegan Castle) to the end of the road and a crowded parking lot. From there, walk about a mile through farmland to Coral Beach—an arcing bay with crystal-clear water and bleached-white algae underfoot (not actually "coral").

▲Dun Beag Broch (Fort)

If driving between Talisker distillery and Dunvegan on A-863, you'll pass Skye's best-preserved Iron Age fort. This 2,000-year-old round stone tower caps a hill a 10-minute walk above its parking lot (just north of the village of Struan). The walk rewards you with an unforgettable chance to be alone in an ancient stone structure with a commanding view. With all the stones scattered around Dun Beag, you can imagine it standing four times

as tall—perhaps with three wood-framed floors inside protecting an entire community with their animals in times of threat—back before Julius Caesar sailed to Britannia.

▲Neist Point and Lighthouse

To get a truly edge-of-the-world feeling, consider an adventure on the back lanes of the Duirinish Peninsula, west of Dunvegan. This trip is best for hardy drivers looking to explore the most remote corner of Skye and undertake a moderately strenuous hike to a lighthouse. Although it looks close on the map, give this trip 30 minutes each way from Dunvegan, plus at least 30 minutes to hike from the parking lot to the lighthouse (with a steep uphill return). After hiking around the cliff, the lighthouse springs into view, with the Outer Hebrides beyond.

Getting There: Head west from Dunvegan, following signs for *Glendale.* You'll cross a moor, then twist around the Dunvegan sea loch, before heading overland and passing through rugged, desolate hamlets that seem like the setting for a BBC sitcom about backwater Britain. After passing through Glendale, carefully track *Neist Point* signs until you reach an end-of-the-road parking lot.

Eating: It's efficient and fun to combine this trek with lunch or dinner at the pricey, recommended **Three Chimneys Restaurant,** on the road to Neist Point at Colbost (reservations essential; see page 98).

WESTERN SKYE
▲▲Talisker Distillery

Talisker, a Skye institution, has been distilling here since 1830 and takes its tours seriously. This venerable whisky distillery is situated at the base of a hill with 14 springs, and at the edge of a sea loch—making it easier to ship ingredients in and whisky out. On summer days, the distillery swarms with visitors: You'll sniff both peated and unpeated grains; see the big mash tuns, washbacks, and stills;

and sample a wee dram at the end. Island whisky tends to be smokier than mainland whisky due to the amount of peat smoke used during malting. Talisker workers describe theirs as "medium smoky," with peppery, floral, and vanilla notes.

Tours and Tastings: This is a popular spot, and tours and tastings are limited. Check their website to confirm tour times and book a spot well in advance during busy times. If you're making the trip out here, you might as well spring for the £20, one-hour distillery tour with three tastings—but these sell out faster. The other option is the £15, 30-minute "Made by the Sea" experience, which includes a multimedia show and three tastings, but no tour. For aficionados, they offer a more expensive cask draw and tasting (daily 10:00-17:00, Jan-Feb until 16:30, along the loch in Carbost, about a 45-minute drive from Portree, +44 1478 614 308, www.malts.com).

Nearby: Note that the **Fairy Pools Hike**—an easy walk that includes some of the best Cuillin Hills views on the island—starts from near Talisker Distillery (see page 110).

Eating near Talisker: A fun "budget foodie" eating option is just up the road past the distillery. **$$ The Oyster Shed** may sound like a faux-rustic name for some fancy restaurant—but it actually is a giant shed that sells a short menu of fresh seafood dishes for lunch. Options may include pan-fried scallops; smoked salmon, trout, or kippers and chips; lobster; and, of course, oysters. There's no seating, but a covered lean-to area on the side of the shed is where a United Nations of tourists huddles around stand-up tables, shucking and slurping oysters (Mon-Sat 11:00-17:00, closed Sun; to get here, carry on the road past the distillery and start up the hill, then watch for the turnoff to the let where the road switchbacks sharply to the right; +44 7751 025 074).

CENTRAL SKYE
▲▲Cuillin Hills

These dramatic, rocky "hills" (which look more like mountains to me) stretch along the southern coast of the island, dominating Skye's landscape. Unusually craggy and alpine for Scotland, the Cuillin ("cool-in") seem to rise directly from the deep. You'll see them from just about anywhere on the southern two-thirds of the island, but no roads actually take you through the heart of the Cuillin—that's reserved for hikers and climbers, who love this area. To get the best views with a car, consider these options.

Sligachan: The road from the Skye Bridge to Portree is the easiest way to appreciate the Cuillin (you'll almost certainly drive along here at some point during your visit). These mountains are all that's left of a long-vanished volcano. As you approach, you'll see that there are three separate ranges (from right to left): red, gray, and black. The steep and challenging Black Cuillin is the most popular for serious climbers; the granite Red Cuillin ridge is more rounded.

The crossroads of Sligachan has an old triple-arched stone Telford bridge—one of Skye's iconic views—and a landmark hotel (see "Between Portree and Kyleakin" on page 95). The village is nestled at the foothills of the Cuillin, and is a popular launchpad for mountain fun. The 2,500-foot-tall cone-shaped hill looming over Sligachan, named Glamaig ("Greedy Lady"), is the site of an annual 4.5-mile hill race in July: Speed hikers begin at the door of the Sligachan Hotel, race to the summit, run around a bagpiper, and scramble back down to the hotel. The record: 44 minutes (30 minutes up, 13 minutes down, 1 minute dancing a jig up top). A Gurkha from Nepal did it in near record time...barefoot. The Sligachan Hotel feels like a virtual mountaineering museum with great old photos and artifacts throughout its ground floor (especially behind the reception desk). You're welcome to browse around.

Fairy Pools Hike: Perhaps the best easy way to get some Cuillin views—and a sturdy but manageable hike—is to follow the popular trail to the Fairy Pools. This is relatively near Talisker Distillery (in the southwestern part of the island).

To reach the hike from the A-863 between Sligachan and Dunvegan, follow signs to *Carbost*. Just before reaching the village of Carbost, watch for signs and a turn-off on the left to *Glenbrittle*. Follow this one-track road through the rolling hills, getting closer and closer to the Cuillin peaks. The well-marked *Fairy Pools* turnoff will be on your right. There's a large, expensive (£5) parking lot with WCs. From here, you can easily follow the well-tended trail down across the field and toward the rounded peaks. (While signs suggest a 9.5-mile, 4- to 5-hour loop, most people simply hike 30 minutes to the pools and back; it's mostly level.)

Very soon you'll reach a gurgling river, which you'll follow toward its source in the mountains. Because the path is entirely through open fields, you enjoy scenery the entire time (and you can't get lost). Soon the river begins to pool at the base of each waterfall, creating a series of picturesque pools. Although footing can be treacherous, many hikers climb down across the rocks to swim and sunbathe. This is a fun place to linger (bring a picnic, if not a swimsuit). As I overheard one visitor say, "Despite the fact that it's so cold, it's so invitin'!"

Elgol: For the best view of the Cuillin, locals swear by the drive from Broadford (on the Portree-Kyleakin road) to Elgol, at the tip of a small peninsula that faces the Black Cuillin head-on. While it's just 12 miles as the crow flies from Sligachan, give it a half-hour each way to drive to the tip (mostly on single-track roads). For even more scenery, take a boat excursion from Elgol into Loch Coruisk, a sea loch surrounded by the Cuillin (April-Oct, departures several times a day, fewer Sun and off-season, generally 3 hours round-trip including 1.5 hours free time on the shore of the loch).

SOUTH SKYE
Kyleakin

Kyleakin (kih-LAH-kin), the last town in Skye before the Skye Bridge, used to be a big tourist hub...until the bridge connecting

it to the mainland enabled easier travel to Portree and other areas deeper in the island. Today this unassuming little village, with a ruined castle (Castle Moil), a cluster of lonesome fishing boats, and a forgotten ferry slip, is worth a quick look but little more.

Broadford: Birthplace of Drambuie

Up the road from Kyleakin, in the wide spot in the road called Broadford, you'll drive past the **Broadford Hotel.** It was at this hotel that a secret elixir—supposedly once concocted for Bonnie Prince Charlie—was re-created by hotelier James Ross after finding the recipe in his father's belongings. Now known as Drambuie, the popular liqueur—which caught on in the 19th century—is made with Scotch whisky, heather honey, and spices. With its wide variety of Drambuie drinks, the Broadford's Spinaker Lounge is the place to try it. (The hotel also has a good **$$$** restaurant if the timing is right for a meal; +44 1471 822 204, www.broadfordhotel. co.uk.)

Skye Bridge
Connecting Kyleakin on Skye with Kyle of Lochalsh on the mainland, the Skye Bridge was Europe's most expensive toll bridge per foot when it opened to great controversy in 1995 amid concerns that it would damage B&B business in the towns it connects, and disrupt native otter habitat. Here's the Skye natives' take on things: A generation ago, Lowlanders (city folk) began selling their urban homes and buying cheap property on Skye. Natives had grown to enjoy the slow-paced lifestyle that came with living life according to the whim of the ferry, but these new transplants found their commute into civilization too frustrating by boat. They demanded a bridge be built. Finally a deal was struck to privately fund the bridge, but the toll wasn't established before construction began. So when the bridge opened—and the ferry line it replaced closed—locals were shocked to be charged upward of £5 per car each way to go to the mainland. A few years ago, the bridge was bought by the Scottish government, the fare was abolished, and the Skye natives were somewhat appeased. There's no denying that the bridge has been a boon for Skye tourism, making a quick visit to the island possible without having to wait for a ferry.

SKYE'S SLEAT PENINSULA
Clan Donald Center and Armadale Castle
Facing the sea just outside Armadale is the ruined castle of Clan Donald, also known as the MacDonalds (Mac/Mc = "son of"), at

one time the most powerful clan in the Scottish Highlands and Hebrides. Today it is the "spiritual home of clan Donald," a sprawling site with castle ruins, woodland walks, manicured gardens, and the Museum of the Isles. While interesting to historians—and riveting for people named MacDonald—given that there's not much of the actual castle to see, it's not worth a long detour for anyone else. Because it's right along the main road near the Armadale-Mallaig ferry, it can be an enjoyable place to kill some time while waiting for your boat.

Cost and Hours: £12, April-Oct Wed-Sun 9:30-17:30, closed Mon-Tue, closed in winter, 2 minutes north of the Armadale ferry landing, +44 1471 844 305, www.armadalecastle.com.

Background: Armadale Castle—more of a mansion than a fortress—was built in 1790, during the relatively peaceful, post-Jacobite age when life at the MacDonalds' traditional home, Duntulm Castle at the tip of the Trotternish Peninsula, had become too

The Feuding Clans of Skye

Skye is one of the best places to get a taste of Scotland's colorful, violent history of clan clashes. As the largest of the Inner Hebrides Islands, with easy nautical connections to Scotland's west coast and much of northern Ireland, it's logical that Skye was home to two powerful rival clans: the MacDonalds and the MacLeods.

The MacDonalds (a.k.a. **"Clan Donald"**), with their base at Duntulm Castle, were the dominant clan of the Hebrides, likely with Irish and Norse bloodlines. In the 12th century, the MacDonalds' ancestral ruler Somerled unified the disparate islands and western Highlands into a "Lordship of the Isles" that lasted for centuries. Throughout this period, they struggled to maintain control against rival clans—starting with the MacLeods.

Clan MacLeod, with its castle at Dunvegan, controlled the western half of Skye. Another branch of the MacLeods was based on the Isle of Lewis, holding down the fort in the Outer Hebrides. The MacLeods' ancestor, Olav the Black, had been defeated by Somerled, pulling their territory in to the Lordship of the Isles. But over the centuries, the MacLeods frequently challenged the authority of the MacDonalds, clashing in countless minor skirmishes as well as major clan battles in 1411, 1480, and 1578.

Adding to the volatile mix was **Clan Mackenzie,** which controlled much of the northern Highlands from their base at Eilean Donan Castle. The Mackenzies waged battle against the MacDonalds in 1491 and again in 1497.

· The epic 1578 clash featured a series of grievous offenses. First, the MacLeods invaded the MacDonald-controlled Isle of Eigg, and, upon finding the islanders huddled in a cave for protection, set a roaring fire at the mouth of the cave—killing virtually the entire population. In retaliation, the MacDonalds barred the door of a church on the MacLeod-controlled Isle of Uist and burned all the worshippers alive. In the ensuing battle, the furious MacLeods massacred the MacDonalds and buried the dead on a turf dike—earning the conflict the name "Battle of the Spoiling Dike."

The final clan battle on Skye began with a strategic marriage designed to broker a peace between the warring clans. Donald MacDonald married Margaret MacLeod, following a tradition called a "handfast," in which the groom was allowed a "trial period" of one year and one day with his new bride. After Margaret injured her eye, Donald decided to "return" her. Adding insult to injury, he sent her back to Dunvegan Castle on a one-eyed horse, led by a one-eyed man with a one-eyed dog. And so began two years of brutal warfare between the clans (the War of the One-Eyed Woman). In 1601, the Battle of Coire Na Creiche decimated both sides, but the MacDonalds emerged victorious. It would be the last of the great clan battles between the MacDonalds and the MacLeods, and it's said to be the final battle fought in Scotland using only medieval weapons (swords and arrows), not guns.

rugged and inconvenient. Today the Armadale Castle ruins (which you can view, but not enter) anchor a sprawling visitors center that celebrates the MacDonald way of life.

Visiting the Castle: At the free parking lot is a big shop and café with free WCs. Buy your ticket inside, then head into the sprawling grounds and bear left to walk about five minutes to the **Museum of the Isles.** This modern museum tells the history of Scotland and Skye through the lens of its most influential clan. While it has only a few artifacts, the museum is well presented and uses replicas to evoke various periods of Skye's history (for the full story, borrow the free 1.5-hour audioguide). You'll begin with the geology of the island and early civilizations (with a replica stone circle), and continue through the Kingdom of the Isles and the rise and fall of the Highland clan system. It finishes with an exhibit on emigration, including the causes and effects of many Skye natives moving to the New World.

After touring the museum, follow signs (and use the free map) to navigate the rest of the gardens. You'll also have a chance to see the ruins of Armadale Castle.

Nearby: Heading north on the A-851 from the Clan Donald Centre, keep an eye out for **Sabhal Mòr Ostaig** (a big complex of white buildings on the point). Skye is very proud to host this college, with coursework taught entirely in Scottish Gaelic. Named "the big barn" after its origins, its mission is to further the Gaelic language (spoken today by about 60,000 people).

Torabhaig Distillery

While Talisker is Skye's classic distillery to tour, this newer option—opened in 2017 at a traditional-feeling, 19th-century farmstead—is convenient for those traveling along the Sleat Peninsula (it's right along the road to the Mallaig ferry and Armadale Castle). Given its newness, this is not the place for aficionados to expect mature whisky. But knowing they're the "new kids on the block," they hustle to put on good tours.

Cost and Hours: £10 distillery tours, check online for details and to book, shop generally open in summer Mon-Fri 10:00-17:00, Sat-Sun until 15:00, +44 1471 833 447, www.torabhaig.com.

ON THE MAINLAND, NEAR THE ISLE OF SKYE
▲Eilean Donan Castle

This postcard-perfect castle, watching over a sea loch from its island perch, is scenically (and conveniently) situated on the road between the Isle of Skye and Loch Ness. While the photo op is worth ▲▲, the interior—with cozy rooms—is worth only a peek and closer to ▲. Eilean Donan (EH-lan DOHN-an) might be Scotland's most photogenic countryside castle. Strategically situated at the confluence of three sea lochs, this was, for 500 years, the stronghold of the Macken- zies—a powerful clan that was, like the MacLeods at Dunvegan, a serious rival to the mighty MacDon- alds (see sidebar). Though it looks ancient, the cur- rent castle is actually less

than a century old. The original castle on this site (dating from 800 years ago) was destroyed in battle in 1719, then rebuilt between 1912 and 1932 by the Macrae family as their residence. (The Mac- raes became bodyguards to the Mackenzies in the 14th century and later took over from their bosses as holders of the castle.)

Cost and Hours: £10, daily 10:00-18:00, last entry one hour before closing, July-Aug from 9:00, closed mid-Dec-Jan; audiogu- ide-£3, good guidebook-£6, no backpacks, café, +44 1599 555 202, www.eileandonancastle.com.

Getting There: It's not actually on the Isle of Skye, but it's quite close, in the mainland town of Dornie. Follow the A-87 about 15 minutes east of Skye Bridge, through Kyle of Lochalsh and toward Loch Ness and Inverness. The castle is on the right side of the road, just after a long bridge (pay parking). Buses that run between Portree and Inverness stop at Dornie, a short walk from the castle (#917, 4/day, 1.5 hours from Portree).

Visiting the Castle: Buy tickets at the visitors center, then walk across the bridge and into the castle complex. "Eilean" means "island"—and this strategic location was both easily defensible (be- cause of the constantly shifting tides) and sustainable (because of a natural freshwater supply).

Enter just to the left of the main gate, where you'll begin with some audiovisual introductory exhibits. Then you'll continue deeper into the castle complex, climbing stairs into the bulky main keep, and work your way through the historic rooms. While the castle is a footnote on a Scottish scale, the exhibits work hard to make its story engaging. Docents posted throughout can tell you more.

First you'll see the claustrophobic, vaulted Billeting Room (where soldiers had their barracks), then head upstairs to the in- viting Banqueting Room, with grand portraits of the honorable John Macrae-Gilstrap and his wife (who spearheaded the modern rebuilding of the castle). This room comes to life when you get a docent to explain the paintings and artifacts here. After the reno- vation, this was a sort of living room.

Another flight of stairs takes you to the circa-1930 bedrooms, which feel more cozy and accessible than those in many other castles—and do a great job of evoking the lifestyles of the aristocrats who built the current version of Eilean Donan as their personal castle playset.

Downstairs is a cute kitchen exhibit, with mannequins preparing a meal and a very well-stocked larder. Finally, you'll pass the gears for operating the portcullis and some WWI memorials on your way to the exit.

To extend your visit, stairs lead down to a path around the base of the castle, where you can observe kelp swaying in the currents. Watch for the WWI memorial, flanked by two cannons; it lists MacRaes from around the world who were lost in that conflict.

Heading back over the bridge to the mainland, notice the trail on the left, following the coastline to the village of Dornie—offering more great views back on the castle.

INVERNESS & LOCH NESS

Inverness • Culloden Battlefield • Clava Cairns • Cawdor Castle • Loch Ness • Urquhart Castle

Inverness, the Highlands' de facto capital, is an almost-unavoidable stop on the Scottish tourist circuit. It's a pleasant town and an ideal springboard for some of the country's most famous sights. Hear the music of the Highlands in Inverness and the echo of muskets at Culloden, where government troops drove Bonnie Prince Charlie into exile and conquered his Jacobite supporters. Ponder the mysteries of Scotland's murky prehistoric past at Clava Cairns, and enjoy a peek at Highland aristocratic life at Cawdor Castle. Just to the southwest of Inverness, explore the locks and lochs of the Caledonian Canal while playing hide-and-seek with the Loch Ness monster.

PLANNING YOUR TIME

Though it has little in the way of sights, Inverness does have a workaday charm and is a handy spot to spend a night or two between other Highland destinations. With two nights, you can find a full day's worth of sightseeing nearby.

With a car, the day trips around Inverness are easy. Without a car, you can get to Inverness by train (better from Edinburgh, Stirling, Glasgow, or Pitlochry) or by bus (better from Skye, Oban, or Glencoe), then side-trip to Culloden, Loch Ness, and other nearby sights by public bus or with a package tour.

Note that Loch Ness is between Inverness and Oban, Glencoe, and the Isle of Skye. If you're heading to or from one of those places, it makes sense to see Loch Ness en route, rather than as a side-trip from Inverness. (And, frankly, for most visitors it's not worth more than an on-the-way glance anyway.)

Inverness

Inverness is situated on the River Ness at the base of a castle (now used as a courthouse, but with a public viewpoint). Inverness'

charm is its normalcy—it's a nice, midsize Scottish city that gives you a palatable taste of the "urban" Highlands and a contrast to cutesy tourist towns. It has a disheveled, ruddy-cheeked grittiness and is well located for enjoying the surrounding countryside sights. Check out the bustling, pedestrianized downtown, or meander the picnic-friendly riverside paths and islands— best at sunset, when the light hits the castle and couples hold hands while strolling along the water and over its footbridges. Perhaps best of all, Inverness is an ideal place to find some traditional Scottish folk music—the perfect place to unwind at the end of a busy day of sightseeing.

Orientation to Inverness

Inverness, with about 70,000 people, is one of the fastest-growing cities in Scotland. Yet it still feels almost like a small town. Marked

by its castle, Inverness clusters along the River Ness. The TI is on High Street, an appealing pedestrian shopping zone a few blocks away from the river; nearby are the train and bus stations. Most of my recommended B&Bs huddle atop a gentle hill behind the castle (a 10-minute uphill walk from the city center).

TOURIST INFORMATION

The TI is on High Street in the center of town. At the TI, you can pick up the self-guided *City Centre Trail* walking-tour leaflet and check out racks upon racks of brochures about nearby attractions (daily 9:00-17:00, possibly longer in peak season, 36 High Street, +44 1463 252 401, www.visitscotland.com and www. visitinvernesslochness.com).

ARRIVAL IN INVERNESS

By Train: At the small, modern train station, you'll find lockers near the tracks. Exit straight ahead, between the waiting room and ticket office, to emerge into a parking lot where taxis wait (about £8 to recommended accommodations). It's possible to walk from the station, but keep in mind that my B&Bs in "The Crown" neighborhood require lots of stairs: Walk out to the busy street (Academy Street), cross it, and turn left. Carry on straight where this narrows and becomes Inglis Street, in the pedestrian zone. At the end of Inglis, you'll run into the Market Brae steps, which take you up to Ardconnel Street in The Crown.

By Bus: The bus station is a block over from the train station. Exit straight ahead—in the direction the buses are pointed—and walk one block to Academy Street, then turn left and follow the instructions above.

By Car: Drivers should ask their accommodations about parking. For those dipping into town and wanting to park centrally, a variety of affordable options are close to the city center: the Old Town **Rose Street** garage (just off the busy A-82 on Rose Street); the **Cathedral** parking lot (south of the cathedral on the west bank of the River Ness); and—up in "The Crown" B&B neighborhood—the **Rainings Stairs** lot (at the top of the stairs down into town). It's generally not too difficult to find **street parking** (pay-and-display, typically around £1/hour, free overnight, check signs carefully to avoid permit-only spaces).

HELPFUL HINTS

Charity Shops: Like many Scottish cities, Inverness is home to several pop-up charity shops. Occupying vacant rental spaces, these are staffed by volunteers who are happy to talk about their philanthropy. You can pick up a memorable knickknack, adjust your wardrobe for the weather, and learn about local causes.

Festivals and Events: The summer is busy with special events; book far ahead during these times: Etape Loch Ness bike race (early June), Highland Games (late July), Belladrum Tartan Heart Festival (music, early Aug), Black Isle farm show (early Aug), and Loch Ness Marathon (late Sept).

In summer (June-Sept), the TI can let you know whether a *ceilidh* (traditional dance and music) is scheduled at City Hall.

For a real Highland treat, catch a **shinty match** (a combination of field hockey, hurling, and American football—but without pads). Inverness Shinty Club plays at Bught Park, along Ness Walk. The TI or your B&B can tell you if there are any matches on, or check www.invernessshinty.com.

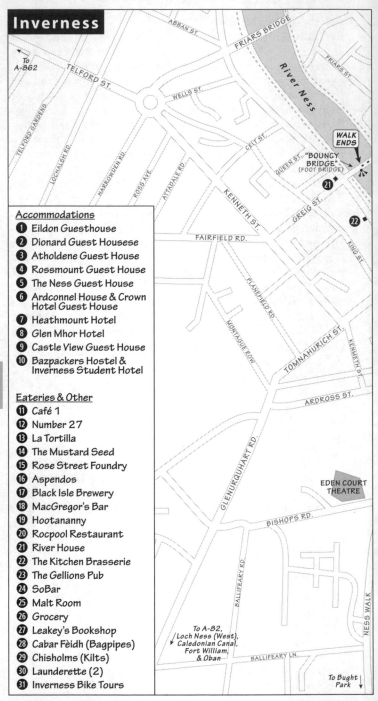

Inverness

To A-862

ABBAN ST.

FRIARS BRIDGE

River Ness

FRIARS ST.

TELFORD ST.

WELLS ST.

TELFORD GARDENS

LOCHALSH RD.

HARROWDEN RD.

ROSS AVE.

AYLDALE RD.

CELT ST.

QUEEN ST.

WALK ENDS

"BOUNCY BRIDGE" (FOOT BRIDGE)

KENNETH ST.

GREIG ST.

KING ST.

FAIRFIELD RD.

PLANEFIELD RD.

MONTAGUE ROW

TOMNAHURICH ST.

KENNETH ST.

ARDROSS ST.

GLENURQUHART RD.

EDEN COURT THEATRE

BISHOPS RD.

BALLIFEARY RD.

NESS WALK

To A-82, Loch Ness (West), Caledonian Canal, Fort William, & Oban

BALLIFEARY LN.

To Bught Park

Accommodations
1. Eildon Guesthouse
2. Dionard Guest Housese
3. Atholdene Guest House
4. Rossmount Guest House
5. The Ness Guest House
6. Ardconnel House & Crown Hotel Guest House
7. Heathmount Hotel
8. Glen Mhor Hotel
9. Castle View Guest House
10. Bazpackers Hostel & Inverness Student Hotel

Eateries & Other
11. Café 1
12. Number 27
13. La Tortilla
14. The Mustard Seed
15. Rose Street Foundry
16. Aspendos
17. Black Isle Brewery
18. MacGregor's Bar
19. Hootananny
20. Rocpool Restaurant
21. River House
22. The Kitchen Brasserie
23. The Gellions Pub
24. SoBar
25. Malt Room
26. Grocery
27. Leakey's Bookshop
28. Cabar Fèidh (Bagpipes)
29. Chisholms (Kilts)
30. Launderette (2)
31. Inverness Bike Tours

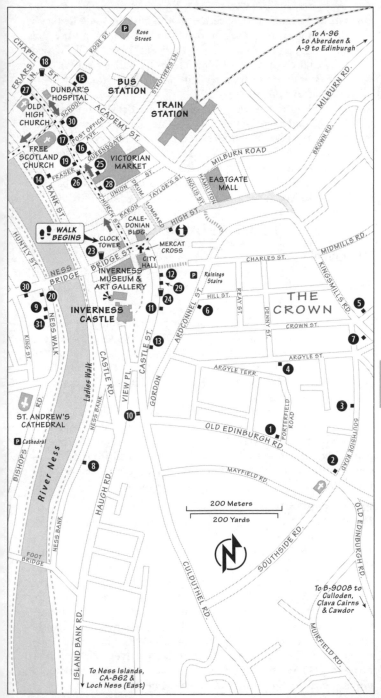

Bookstore: Located in a converted church built in 1649, **Leakey's Bookshop** is the place to browse through teetering towers of old books and vintage maps (Mon-Sat 10:00-17:30, closed Sun, Church Street, +44 1463 239 947, Charles Leakey).

Baggage Storage: The train station has lockers (Mon-Sat 6:40-20:30, Sun from 10:40).

Laundry: Head to the west end of the Ness Bridge to find **New City Launderette** (self-service or same-day full-service, Mon-Sat 8:00-20:00, Sun 10:00-16:00, last load one hour before closing, 17 Young Street, +44 1463 242 507). **Thirty Degrees Laundry** on Church Street is another option (full-service only, Mon-Fri 9:00-15:00, closed Sat-Sun, a few blocks beyond Victorian Market at 84 Church Street, +44 1463 710 380).

Tours in Inverness

IN TOWN

Skip the City Sightseeing hop-on, hop-off bus tour (this format doesn't work well in Inverness).

Walking Tours

Two different companies offer walking tours through Inverness. I enjoy **Walk Inverness,** run by Cath Findlay and her associates. They offer 2-hour walking tours departing from the TI most days through the summer at 11:00 (or daily in peak season). You'll learn about the history of Inverness, its castle, Victorian Market, and Old High Church, with a few *Outlander* landmarks thrown in for good measure (£12.50, www.walkinverness.com). They also organize private tours—see website for details. Another company—called **Walking Tours in Inverness**—runs 1.5-hour tours that depart each morning (£12, daily at 11:30 from in front of TI, in summer they do a second walk at 17:30, www.walkingtoursin.com/inverness).

Inverness Bike Tours

Hardworking Alison leads small groups on two-hour bike tours. Her six-mile route is nearly all on traffic-free paths along canals and lochs outside of the city and comes with light guiding along the way. You'll pedal through Ness Island, stop at the Botanical Gardens, ride along the Caledonian Canal with its system of locks (you may even catch a boat passing through the locks), and cycle through a nature preserve (£23, generally no kids under 14, 10-person max; daily in season at 10:00 and 14:45; best to book a spot in advance online, goes even in light rain, meet at the Prime Restaurant, near the west end of Ness Bridge at 4 Ness Walk, call or text +44 7443 866 619, www.invernessbiketours.co.uk). Arrive 15 minutes early to size up your bike and helmet.

EXCURSIONS FROM INVERNESS

Inverness is a popular home base for day trips. A variety of tour companies offer excursions: Details and tickets are available on each company's website, or through the TI. While the big sellers are the many Loch Ness tours, I far prefer an all-day trip to the Isle of Skye, which provides a good-enough look at Loch Ness and Urquhart Castle along the way. Especially for the longer-distance tours (such as the Isle of Skye), things can book up early in high season. It's smart to reserve well in advance.

Loch Ness

The (in)famous loch is just a 20-minute drive from Inverness. Tours often include a short boat ride, a visit to Urquhart Castle, and a stop at the Loch Ness monster exhibits. The loch is not particularly scenic, the castle is just a shell, and the monster is basically a promotional gimmick—but if you're determined to tick this off your list, a tour is an efficient way to do it. One well-established outfit is **Jacobite Tours,** with options from a one-hour basic boat ride to a seven-hour extravaganza (+44 1463 233 999, www.jacobite.co.uk). Many of the companies listed below also offer Loch Ness trips.

Isle of Skye

Several companies do good day tours to the Isle of Skye. They typically depart Inverness between 8:00 and 8:30 and travel 110 miles (a 2.5-hour drive) to Portree, in the heart of Skye. With about six hours of driving, and one hour for lunch in Portree, that leaves two or three hours for a handful of quick and scenic photo stops. The tours travel along Loch Ness (so you can see Urquhart Castle and pretend to look for a sea monster) and stop for a view of Eilean Donan Castle. The longer versions (12 hours-plus) loop around the stunning Trotternish Peninsula—worth adding on, if the weather's decent and you have the stamina.

Wow Scotland's ambitious 12-hour "Ultimate" big-bus itinerary includes short but smart and adequate stops all along the way—including the Trotternish Peninsula and a chance to hike at the Fairy Pools (£94, nearly daily June-Aug, fewer departures April-May and Sept, none Oct-March, +44 1808 511 773, www. wowscotlandtours.com). I'd pay the extra £20 for front row (or £5 for the second row).

Highland Experience Tours offers a similar tour—but without the Fairy Pools hike—in a smaller, 24-seat bus (£53, nearly 12 hours, daily April-Oct, fewer off-season, 10 hours, +44 131 285 3314, www.highlandexperience.com).

Happy Tours Scotland organizes daily minibus tours on a nine-hour joy ride (getting all the way to Quiraing) with top-notch guides (£85, 8 people per minibus, +44 7828 154 683, www.happytours.biz, Cameron).

By Train Plus Tour: To avoid a long bus ride or to skip the sights along the way to Skye, ride the train from Inverness to Kyle of Lochalsh, where the locally based **Skye Tours** will pick you up and take you around (+44 1471 822 716, www.skye-tours.co.uk). The train leaves Inverness before 9:00 and arrives around 11:30; the return train is around 17:15.

Other Destinations

Many of the above companies also offer a wide variety of other options from Inverness. Popular choices include Culloden and Clava Cairns, Cairngorms National Park, Royal Deeside and the Speyside Whisky Trail, longer trips to the far north of the Highlands and John O'Groats, *Outlander*-themed tours, and more. One tempting option for an extremely ambitious, but rewarding, day trip is to the Orkney Islands (which demand 15-plus hours, lots of bus time, and a ferry both ways). Peruse websites for your options, or ask at the TI.

Inverness Walk

Although humble Inverness is best as a jumping-off point for exploring the countryside, spare an hour or two for the town's fun history and quirky charm with this short self-guided walk (walk route shown on map earlier in this chapter).

• *Start right in the heart of town, along Bridge Street, in front of the clock tower.*

Clock Tower: This structure, looming 130 feet above you, is all that remains of a tollbooth building erected in 1791. This is the highest spire in town, and for generations was a collection point for local taxes. Here, four streets—Church, Castle, Bridge, and High—come together, integrating God, defense, and trade—everything necessary for a fine city.

About 800 years ago, a castle was built on the bluff overhead and the town of Inverness coalesced right about here. For centuries, this backwater town's economy was based on cottage industries. Artisans who made things also sold them. In 1854, the train arrived, injecting energy and money from Edinburgh and Glasgow, and the Victorian boom hit. With the Industrial Age came wholesalers, distributors, mass production, and affluence. Much of the city was built during this era, in Neo-Gothic style—over-the-top and fanciful, like the City Hall (from 1882, kitty-corner to the clock tower). With the Victorian Age also came tourism.

Notice the **Gaelic language** on directional and street signs all around you. While virtually no-one speaks Gaelic as a first language (and only about 60,000 Scottish people speak it fluently), this old Celtic language symbolizes the strength of Scottish Highland culture.

• *Take a few steps up (away from the river) High Street.*

High Street: At the next building, look up to see the **Bible quotes** chiseled into the facade (upper floor). A civic leader, tired of his council members being drunkards, edited these Bible verses for maximum impact, especially the bottom two.

Now do an about-face. Hiding just up the hill (behind the eyesore concrete home of the Inverness Museum and Art Gallery) is **Inverness Castle,** which is in the midst of an ambitious renovation project to convert it into a cultural center/community gathering point. It's worth hiking up to the castle at some point during your visit to enjoy some of the best views of Inverness and its river. The castle has served as a courthouse in modern times, but it doesn't see a lot of action. In the last few decades, there have been only two murders to prosecute. As locals like to say, "no guns, no problems." While hunters can own a rifle, gun ownership in Scotland is tightly regulated.

The next building up the street, called **The Caledonian,** faces McDonald's at the base of High Street. (Caledonia was the ancient Roman name for Scotland.) It was built in 1847, complete with Corinthian columns and a Greek-style pediment, as the leading bank in town, back when banks were designed to hold the money of the rich and powerful...and intimidate working blokes. Just a few steps up from here, notice how nicely pedestrianized High Street welcomes people and seagulls...but not cars.

• *Now cross the street to stand in front of the **City Hall** (which is known here as the "**Town House**"). Standing immediately in front of it is the well-worn...*

Mercat Cross: This cross designated the market in centuries past. This is where the townspeople gathered to hear important proclamations, share news, watch hangings, gossip, and so on. The scant remains of a prehistoric stone at the base of the cross are what's left of Inverness' "Stone of Destiny." According to tradition, whenever someone moved away from Inverness, they'd take a tiny bit of home with them in the form of a chip of this stone—so it's been chipped and pecked almost to oblivion.

• *Next we'll head up Church Street, which begins between the clock tower and The Caledonian.*

Church Street: The street art you'll trip over at the start of

Church Street is called *Earth-quake*—a reminder of the quake that hit Inverness in 1816. As the slabs explain, the town's motto is "Open-heartedness, Insight, and Perseverance."

Stroll down Church Street. Look up above the modern storefronts to see centuries-old facades, more interesting than the town's regrettable post-WWII architecture. **Union Street** (the second corner on the right)—stately, symmetrical, and Neoclassical—was the fanciest street in the Highlands when it was built in the 19th century. Its buildings had indoor toilets. That was big news.

Midway down the next block of Church Street (on the right), an alley marked by a white canopy leads to the **Victorian Market.** Venturing down the alley, you'll pass **The Malt Room** (a small and friendly whisky bar eager to teach you to appreciate Scotland's national tipple; see "Nightlife in Inverness") and **The Old Market Inn** (a dive bar worth a peek). Stepping into the Victorian Market, you'll find a gallery of shops under an iron-

and-glass domed roof dating from 1876. The first section seems abandoned, but delve deeper to find some more active areas, where local shops mix with tacky "tartan tat" souvenir stands. (If you can't get into the market through here, loop around to enter from Union Street.)

Go back out of the market the way you came in and continue down Church Street. At the next corner, you come to **Hootananny,** famous locally for its live music (on the left; pop in to see what's on tonight). Just past that is **Abertarff House,** the oldest house in Inverness. It was the talk of the town in 1593 for its "turnpike" (spiral staircase) connecting the floors.

Continue about a block farther along Church Street. The lane on the left leads to the **"Bouncy Bridge"** (where we'll finish this walk). Opposite that lane (on the right) is **Dunbar's Hospital,** with four-foot-thick walls (now a pancake shop). In 1668, Alexander Dunbar was a wealthy landowner who built this as a poor folks' home. Try reading the auld script in his coat of arms above the door.

A few steps farther up Church Street, walk through the iron

gate on the left and into the **churchyard** (we're focusing on the shorter church on the right—ignore the bigger one on the left). Looking at the WWI and WWII memorials on the church's wall, it's clear which war hit Scotland harder. While no one famous is buried here, many tombstones go back to the 1700s.

• *Dodging rabbits, head for the bluff overlooking the river and turn around to see...*

Old High Church: There are a lot of churches in Inverness (46 Protestant, 2 Catholic, 2 Gaelic-language, and one offering a Mass in Polish), but these days, most are used for other purposes. This one, dating from the 11th century, is the most historic (but is generally closed). It was built on what was likely the site of a pagan holy ground. Early Christians called upon St. Michael to

take the fire out of pagan spirits, so it only made sense that the first Christians would build their church here and dedicate the spot as St. Michael's Mount.

In the sixth century, the Irish evangelist monk St. Columba brought Christianity to northern England, the Scottish islands (at Iona), and the Scottish Highlands (in Inverness). He stood here amongst the pagans and preached to King Brude and the Picts.

Study the bell tower from the 1600s. The small door to nowhere (one floor up) indicates that back before the castle offered protection, this tower was the place of last refuge for townsfolk under attack. They'd gather inside and pull up the ladder. Every night at 20:00, the bell in the tower rings 100 times. It has rung like this since 1730 to remind townsfolk that it's dangerous to be out after dinner.

This church became a prison for Jacobites after the Battle of Culloden; many of the prisoners were executed in the churchyard. (Look for marks where bullets hit the tower wall).

• *From here, you can circle back to the lane leading to the "Bouncy Bridge" and then hike out onto the pedestrian bridge. Or you can just survey the countryside from this bluff.*

The River Ness: Emptying out of Loch Ness and flowing seven miles to the sea (a mile from here), this is one

INVERNESS & LOCH NESS

of the shortest rivers in the country. While it's shallow (you can almost walk across it), there are plenty of fish in it. A 64-pound salmon was once pulled out of the river right here. In the 19th century, Inverness was smaller, with open fields across the river. Then, with the Victorian boom, the suspension footbridge (a.k.a. "Bouncy Bridge") was built in 1881 to connect new construction across the river with the town.

• *Your tour is over. Inverness is yours to explore.*

Sights in Inverness

Inverness Museum and Art Gallery

This free, likable town museum is worth poking around on a rainy day to get a taste of Inverness and the Highlands. The ground-floor exhibits on geology and archaeology peel back the layers of Highland history: Bronze and Iron ages, Picts (including some carved stones), Scots, Vikings, and Normans, plus wildlife. The upstairs covers the Jacobites to the present day, including traditional Highland music (fiddles and bagpipes), clothing, swords, muskets, and more. The Art Gallery hosts temporary exhibits.

Cost and Hours: Free; April-Oct Tue-Sat 10:00-17:00, shorter hours off-season, closed Sun-Mon year-round; cheap café, in the ugly modern building on the way up to the castle, +44 1349 781 730, more info under the visitor attractions tab at www.highlifehighland.com.

Inverness Castle

The scenic castle that caps the hill above the River Ness will likely be closed for your visit; a lengthy and ambitious renovation should wrap up in 2025. Once open, the newly reconfigured complex hopes to become a sort of community gathering spot, with eateries and public spaces designed to appreciate the grand views. You may also be able to climb the tower for a commanding vista.

The wooden fortress that first stood on this spot was replaced by a stone structure in the 15th century. In 1715, that castle was named Fort George to assert English control over the area. In 1745, it was destroyed by Bonnie Prince Charlie's Jacobite army and remained a ruin until the 1830s, when the present castle was built. Now town leaders are discussing plans to build a new museum here, linking the two castle towers with a large exhibit space, but no timetable has been set.

The statue outside (from 1899) depicts Flora MacDonald, who helped Bonnie Prince Charlie escape from the English (see page 105).

River Walks

As with most European cities, where there's a river, there's a walk. Inverness, with both the River Ness and the Caledonian Canal, does not disappoint. Consider an early-morning stroll along the Ness Bank to capture the castle at sunrise, or a post-dinner jaunt to Bught Park for a local shinty match. The path is lit at night. The forested islands in the middle of the River Ness—about a 10-minute walk south of the center—are a popular escape from the otherwise busy city.

Here's a good plan for your Inverness riverside constitutional: From the Ness Bridge, head along the riverbank under the castle (along the path called "Ladies Walk"). As you work your way up the river, you'll see the architecturally bold Eden Court Theatre (across the river), pass a white pedestrian bridge, see a WWI memorial, and peek into the gardens of several fine old Victorian sandstone riverfront homes. Nearing the tree-covered islands, watch for fly-fishers in hip waders on the pebbly banks. Reaching the first, skinny little island, take the bridge with the wavy, wrought-iron railing and head down the path along the middle of the island. Notice that this is part of the Great Glen Way, a footpath that stretches from here all the way to Fort William (79 miles). Enjoy this little nature break, with gurgling rapids—and, possibly, a few midges. Reaching the bigger bridge, cross it and enjoy strolling through tall forests. Continue upriver. After two more green-railinged bridges, traverse yet another island, and find one last white-iron bridge that takes you across to the opposite bank. You'll pop out at the corner of Bught Park, the site of shinty practices and games—are any going on today?

From here, you can simply head back into town on this bank. If you'd like to explore more, near Bught Park you'll find minigolf, a skate park, the Highland Archive building, the free Botanic Gardens (daily 10:00-17:00, until 16:00 Nov-March), and the huge Active Inverness leisure center, loaded with amusements including a swimming pool with adventure slides, a climbing wall, a sauna and steam area, and a gym (www.invernessleisure.co.uk).

Continuing west from these leisure areas, you'll soon hit the Caledonian Canal; to the south, this parallels the River Ness, and to the north it empties into Beauly Firth, then Moray Firth and the North Sea. From the Tomnahurich Bridge, paths on either bank allow you to walk along the Great Glen Way until you're ready to turn around. It takes about an hour to circle around from the center of Inverness all the way to Clachnaharry, where the river meets Beauly Firth.

Shopping in Inverness

This city has more "tartan tat" shops per square mile than perhaps any place in Scotland. So, if you're looking for the same knock-off souvenirs you can get anywhere, at least Inverness makes for easy comparison shopping. The city also has outlets of some higher-end (but still tourist-oriented) Scotland-wide chains. For something with a bit more serious quality, seek out the places noted here.

Cabar Fèidh is *the* place for those who are seriously into bagpipes. American expat Brian sells CDs and sheet music, and repairs and maintains the precious instruments of local musicians (Mon-Tue and Thu-Sat 10:00-16:00, closed Sun and Wed, upstairs at 28 Church Street, +44 1463 223 030).

Chisholms is a quality outfitter for finding traditional, properly manufactured kilts and other Highland dress (Mon-Sat 10:00-16:00, closed Sun, 47 Castle Street, +44 1463 234 599, www.kilts.co.uk).

Nightlife in Inverness

Scottish Folk Music

While you can find traditional folk-music sessions in pubs and hotel bars anywhere in town, these places are well established as *the* music pubs. There's rarely a cover charge, unless a bigger-name band is playing.

MacGregor's Bar is run by Bruce MacGregor, a founding member of the Scottish group Blazin' Fiddles, and his wife Jo. Their passion for local music (with several music evenings each week) is matched by good food, good local beers on tap, and a fun local crowd. From spring through fall, they also offer a twice-weekly whisky tasting (£39, Mon-Thu at 19:00) along with traditional Scottish music and stories (a few blocks past the pedestrian bridge at 113 Academy Street, +44 1463 719 629, www.macgregorsbars.com).

Hootananny is an energetic place that specializes in traditional folk music, but occasionally mixes in rock, blues, or cover bands as well. There's usually music nightly, often starting about 21:30 (traditional music sessions Sun-Thu, trad bands on weekends; also a daytime session on Sat afternoon at 14:30; 67 Church Street, +44 1463 233 651, www.hootanannyinverness.co.uk).

The Gellions has live folk and Scottish music nightly (from 21:30 or sometimes earlier). Very local and a bit rough, it has local ales on tap and brags it's the oldest bar in town (14 Bridge Street, +44 1463 233 648, www.gellions.co.uk).

Rose Street Foundry, described later under "Eating in Inverness," is another central spot with frequent live music—though they are less focused on traditional music.

Billiards and Darts

SoBar is a sprawling pub with dart boards, pool tables, a museum's worth of sports memorabilia, and the biggest TV screens in town (popular on big game nights). It's a fine place to hang out and meet locals if you'd rather not have live music (just across from the castle at 55 Castle Street, +44 1463 572 542).

Whisky Tastings

For a whisky education, or just a fine cocktail, drop in to the intimate **Malt Room,** with more than 300 different whiskies ranging from £4 to £195. The whisky-plus-chocolate flight, for £27, makes for a fun nightcap (daily 12:00-late, Sun from 15:00, just off Church Street in the alley leading to the Victorian Market, 34 Church Street, +44 1463 221 888, Matt).

MacGregor's Bar (listed earlier) also offers whisky tastings and beer flights.

Sleeping in Inverness

Accommodations in Inverness can book up very early—by March, the entire busy summer season (May-Sept, especially July-Aug) can already be spoken for. This is a place where, to get your choice of rooms, the early bird gets the worm.

In addition to the more personally run places listed here, Inverness has a number of big chain hotels. These tend to charge a lot when it's busy but are worth a look if the B&Bs are full or if it's outside the main tourist season. Options include the **Inverness Palace Hotel & Spa** (a Best Western fancy splurge right on the river with a pool and gym), **Premier Inn** (River Ness location), and **Mercure.**

B&BS IN "THE CROWN," JUST ABOVE THE TOWN CENTER

Inverness' best B&B neighborhood is the area called "The Crown," which sits on a ridge just over the town center. Most of these places are within about a 10-minute walk (often involving some stairs) from the town center. This area has a real "Goldilocks" appeal: It feels calm, welcoming, and residential, but you also have quick access to the very heart of town. Parking can be tricky: Some street parking requires a permit, others make you feed the meter, and some places have private parking (ask when you book).

$$ Eildon Guesthouse offers five tranquil rooms with spacious baths. The cute-as-a-button 1890s brick home is centrally located yet exudes countryside warmth and serenity from the moment you open the gate (family rooms, 2-night minimum in summer, no kids under 10, in-room fridges, parking, 29 Old Edinburgh Road, +44 1463 231 969, www.eildonguesthouse.co.uk, eildonguesthouse@yahoo.co.uk, Jacqueline).

$$ Dionard Guest House, wrapped in a fine hedged-in garden, has cheerful common spaces, seven lovely rooms, some fun stag art, and lively host Gail (family suite, in-room fridges, laundry service for a reasonable price, parking, 39 Old Edinburgh Road, +44 1463 233 557, www.dionardguesthouse.co.uk, enquiries@dionardguesthouse.co.uk).

$$ Atholdene Guest House, run by amiable Gillian and Andrew, welcomes many return visitors—maybe they come back for the homemade scones? Its nine rooms are comfortable; ones in the front are bigger but come with a bit of street noise. Classical music in the morning makes for a civilized breakfast (2-night minimum in summer, guests must be 18 or older, parking, 20 Southside Road, +44 1463 233 565, www.atholdene.com, info@atholdene.com).

$$ Rossmount Guest House feels like home, with its curl-up-on-the-couch lounge space, unfussy rooms (five in all), hardwood-meets-modern style, and friendly hosts Ruth and Robert, plus Milo the dog (family room, 2-night minimum in summer, Argyle Street, +44 1463 229 749, www.rossmount.co.uk, mail@rossmount.co.uk).

$$ The Ness Guest House, well-run by Susan and Richard, is small but friendly, cozy, and tidy, offering good value in its four rooms (private parking, 48 Union Road, tel. +44 1463 559 174, www.thenessguesthouse.com, rooms@thenessguesthouse.com).

On Ardconnel Street: These two options sit side-by-side very close to the top of the Market Brae steps into the town center. While convenient, they're a bit more basic than my other listings, and may have rooms when others are full.

$$ Ardconnel House is a classic, traditional place offering a large guest lounge, along with six spacious, if dated, rooms (family room, two-night minimum preferred in summer, no children under 5, 21 Ardconnel Street, +44 1463 418 242, www.ardconnel-inverness.co.uk, ardconnel@gmail.com, Elaine).

$ Crown Hotel Guest House isn't quite as homey as some, but its seven rooms (five en suite, two with separate but private bathrooms) are pleasant and a solid value (family room, 19 Ardconnel Street, +44 1463 231 135, www.crownhotel-inverness.co.uk, crownhotelguesthouse@gmail.com, Munawar and Asia).

Hotel: $$$$ Heathmount Hotel's understated facade hides a chic retreat for comfort-seeking travelers. Its eight elegant rooms—tucked in the heart of the B&B neighborhood—come with unique decoration, parking, and fancy extras (family room, no elevator, restaurant, parking, Kingsmill Road, +44 1463 235 877, www.heathmounthotel.com, info@heathounthotel.com).

ON THE RIVER

$$$$ Glen Mhor Hotel, with 122 rooms, sprawls across several buildings right along the river. The location can't be beat, even if the staff and rooms lack a personal touch (family rooms, restaurant and microbrewery/distillery on-site, Ness Bank, +44 1463 234 308, www.glen-mhor.com, enquiries@glen-mhor.com).

$$ Castle View Guest House sits right along the River Ness at the Ness Bridge—and, true to its name, it owns smashing views of the castle. Its five big and comfy rooms (some with views) are colorfully furnished, and the delightful place is lovingly run by Eleanor (family rooms, street parking or affordable lot nearby, 2A Ness Walk, +44 1463 241 443, www.castleviewguesthouseinverness.com, enquiries@castleviewguesthouseinverness.com).

HOSTELS

For funky and cheap dorm beds near the center and the recommended Castle Street restaurants, consider these friendly side-by-side hostels, geared toward younger travelers. They're about a 12-minute walk from the train station.

¢ **Bazpackers Hostel,** a stone's throw from the castle, has a quieter, more private feel for a hostel with dorm beds arranged in pods (private rooms with shared bath available, reception open 11:00-23:00, pay laundry service, 4 Culduthel Road, +44 1463 717 663, www.bazpackershostel.co.uk, info@bazpackershostel.co.uk). They also rent a small apartment nearby (sleeps up to 4).

¢ **Inverness Student Hotel** has brightly colored rooms and a laid-back lounge with a bay window overlooking the River Ness. The knowledgeable, friendly staff welcomes any traveler over 18. Dorms are a bit grungy, but each bunk has its own playful name (breakfast extra, free tea and coffee, pay laundry service, kitchen, 8 Culduthel Road, +44 1463 236 556, www.invernessstudenthotel.com, inverness@scotlandstophostels.com).

Eating in Inverness

In high season, Inverness' top restaurants (including many of those recommended below) fill up quickly—reservations are wise.

BY THE CASTLE

These eateries line Castle Street, facing the back of the castle.

$$$ **Café 1** serves up high-quality modern Scottish and international cuisine with trendy, chic bistro flair. Fresh meat from their farm adds to an appealing menu (lunch and early-bird dinner specials until 18:15; open Mon-Fri 12:00-14:30 & 17:00-21:30, Sat from 12:30 and 17:30, closed Sun; 75 Castle Street, +44 1463 226 200, www.cafe1.net).

$$ **Number 27** has a straightforward, crowd-pleasing menu that offers something for everyone—burgers, pastas, and more. The food is surprisingly elegant for this price range (daily 12:00-21:00, generous portions, local ales on tap, 27 Castle Street, +44 1463 241 999).

$$ **La Tortilla** has Spanish tapas, including spicy king prawns (the house specialty) and two-person paellas, plus a vegan menu. It's an appealing, colorfully tiled, and vivacious dining option that feels like Spain. With the tapas format, three family-style dishes make about one meal (daily 12:00-22:00, 99 Castle Street, +44 1463 709 809).

IN THE TOWN CENTER

$$$$ **The Mustard Seed** serves Scottish food with a modern twist in an old church with a river view. It's a lively place with nice outdoor tables over the river when sunny. Reserve well ahead for this popular spot (two-course lunch deals, early-bird specials before 18:30, open daily 12:00-15:00 & 17:30-22:00, on the corner of Bank and Fraser Streets, 16 Fraser Street, +44 1463 220 220, www.mustardseedrestaurant.co.uk).

$$ **Rose Street Foundry** is a modern-feeling, brassy space filling a former foundry building. Owned by Cairngorm Brewery, it has 20 beers on tap and serves Scottish pub grub. The food is often an afterthought to the live music—check to see what's playing before committing to a meal here, to make sure you'll enjoy it (Mon-Sat 12:00-23:00, Sun until 21:00, 96 Academy Street, +44 1463 630 263).

$$$$ **Aspendos** serves up freshly prepared, delicious, pricey Turkish dishes in a spacious, dressy, and exuberantly decorated dining room (daily 12:00-22:00, 26 Queensgate, +44 1463 711 950).

$$ **Black Isle Brewery,** a taphouse right in the center of town, produces organic beers and ciders just across the River Ness. Screens over the bar list 26 different choices—both their own and guest brews—and they also serve good wood-fired pizzas. If the main space is jammed—as it often is—follow signs upstairs to the "Secret Garden," a hidden roof deck with lots of fun and cozy alcoves (daily 12:00-24:00, 68 Church Street, +44 1463 229 920).

Nightlife Spots with Great Food: Two places listed earlier, under "Nightlife in Inverness," also have great food. $$ **MacGregor's Bar** does excellent traditional and updated Scottish dishes, often accompanied by live music and with ample outdoor seating. **$$ Hootananny** is a spacious pub with a hardwood-and-candlelight vibe and a fun menu of Scottish pub grub (no food served Sat-Sun).

Picnic: There's a **Co-op** market with plenty of cheap picnic grub at 59 Church Street (daily until 22:00).

ACROSS THE RIVER

$$$$ Rocpool Restaurant is a hit with locals, good for a splurge, and perhaps the best place in town. Owner/chef Steven Devlin serves creative modern European food to a smart clientele in a sleek, contemporary dining room. Reservations are essential (early-bird weekday special until 18:30; open Tue-Sat 12:00-14:30 & 17:30-22:00, closed Sun-Mon; across Ness Bridge at 1 Ness Walk, +44 1463 717 274, www.rocpoolrestaurant.com).

$$$$ River House, a classy, sophisticated, but unstuffy place, is the brainchild of Cornishman Alfie—who prides himself on melding the seafood know-how of both Cornwall and Scotland with Venetian-style *cicchetti* small plates. Reserve ahead (Tue-Sat 15:00-21:30, closed Sun-Mon, 1 Greig Street, +44 1463 222 033, www.riverhouseinverness.co.uk).

$$$$ The Kitchen Brasserie is a modern building with a wavy roof and big windows overlooking the river, serving a menu of elevated seafood and land food (early-bird special until 18:00; open daily 11:00-14:30 & 17:00-21:00; 15 Huntly Street, +44 1463 259 119, www.kitchenrestaurant.co.uk).

Inverness Connections

From Inverness by Train to: Pitlochry (nearly hourly, 1.5 hours), **Stirling** (7/day direct, 3 hours, more with transfer in Perth), **Kyle of Lochalsh** near Isle of Skye (4/day, 2.5 hours), **Edinburgh** (nearly hourly, 3.5 hours, some with change in Perth), **Glasgow** (4/day direct, 3 hours, more with change in Perth), **Thurso** (for ferries to Orkney; 4/day, 4 hours). The Caledonian Sleeper provides overnight service to **London** (www.sleeper.scot). Train info: +44 345 748 4950, NationalRail.co.uk.

By Bus: Inverness has a handy direct bus to **Portree** on the Isle of Skye (bus #917, 3-4/day, 3 hours), but for other destinations in western Scotland, you'll first head for **Fort William** (bus #919, 6/day, 2 hours, fewer on Sun). For connections onward to **Oban** (figure 4 hours total) or **Glencoe** (3 hours total), see "Fort William Connections" on page 74. Inverness is also connected by direct bus to **Edinburgh** (#M90, 8/day, 4 hours; stops en route at Pitlochry, 1.5 hours) and **Glasgow** (#M10, 5/day, 3 hours). Bus info: Citylink. co.uk.

Tickets are sold in advance online, by phone at +44 871 266 3333, or in person at the Inverness bus station (daily 8:30-17:00, 2 blocks from train station on Margaret Street, +44 1463 233 371).

By Plane: Inverness Airport is about 10 miles east of town (code: INV, www.hial.co.uk). Stagecoach Highlands bus #11 connects to the city center every half-hour (www.stagecoachbus.com); taxis also make the 20-minute trip.

ROUTE TIPS FOR DRIVERS

Inverness to Edinburgh (160 miles, 3.25 hours minimum): Leaving Inverness, follow signs to the A-9 (south, toward Perth). If you haven't seen Culloden Battlefield yet, it's an easy detour: Just as you leave Inverness, head four miles east off the A-9 on the B-9006. Back on the A-9, it's a wonderfully speedy, scenic drive (A-9, M-90, A-90) all the way to Edinburgh. If you have time, consider stopping en route in Pitlochry (just off the A-9; see the Eastern Scotland chapter).

Inverness to Portree, Isle of Skye (110 miles, 2.5 hours): The drive from Inverness to Skye is pretty but much less so than the valley of Glencoe or the Isle of Skye itself. You'll drive along boring Loch Ness, and then follow signs to Portree and Skye on A-87 along Loch Cluanie (a loch tamed by a dam built to generate hydroelectric power). This valley was once a "drovers' route" for the cattle drive from the islands to the market—home of the original Scottish cowboys.

Inverness to Fort William (65 miles, 1.5 hours): This city, southwest of Inverness via the A-82, is a good gateway to Oban and Glencoe. See page 75.

Near Inverness

Inverness puts you in the heart of the Highlands, within easy striking distance of several famous and worthwhile sights: Commune with the Scottish soul at historic Culloden Battlefield, where British history reached a turning point. Wonder at three mysterious Neolithic cairns, which remind visitors that Scotland's story goes back thousands of years. And enjoy a homey country castle at Cawdor. Loch Ness—with its elusive monster—is another popular and easy, if overrated, day trip.

In addition to the sights in this section, note that sights including the Speyside Whisky Trail, the Working Sheepdogs demonstration, and the Highland Folk Museum are also within side-tripping distance of Inverness (see the Eastern Scotland chapter).

CULLODEN BATTLEFIELD

Jacobite troops under Bonnie Prince Charlie were defeated at Culloden by supporters of the Hanover dynasty (King George II's family) in 1746. Sort of the "Scottish Alamo," this last major land battle fought on British soil spelled the end of Jacobite resistance and the beginning of the clan chiefs' fall from power. Wandering the desolate, solemn battlefield at Culloden (kuh-LAW-dehn), you sense that something terrible occurred here. Locals still bring white roses and speak of "The Forty-Five" (as Bonnie Prince Charlie's entire campaign is called) as if it just happened. Engaging even if you're not interested in military history, the battlefield at Culloden and

its high-tech visitors center together are worth ▲▲▲.

Orientation to Culloden

Cost and Hours: £14, free battlefield map, £5 guidebook; daily 9:00-16:00, likely open later during busy times—check online or call to confirm; café, +44 1463 796 090, http://www.nts.org/uk/culloden.

Tours: Free, 40-minute **battlefield tours** depart at the top of each hour; these are worth planning your visit around (see the exhibit on your own before or after the tour). Near the ticket desk, you'll also see a posted schedule for thoughtful, engaging, in-depth **presentations** about various topics that take place in the big room at the end of the exhibits. **Audioguides** for both the exhibit and the battlefield are available on request, but are mainly intended for non-English speakers.

Getting There: It's a 15-minute **drive** east of Inverness. Follow signs to *Aberdeen*, then *Culloden Moor*—the B-9006 takes you right there (well-signed on the right-hand side). Parking is £2 (cash or card). Public **buses** leave from Inverness' Queensgate Street and drop you off in front of the entrance (£5 round-trip, bus #2, roughly hourly, 40 minutes, ask at TI for route/schedule updates). A **taxi** costs around £15 one-way.

Length of This Tour: Allow 2 hours.

Background

The Battle of Culloden (April 16, 1746) marks the steep decline of the Scottish Highland clans and the start of years of cruel repression of Highland culture by the British. It was the culmination of a year's worth of battles, and at the center of it all was the charismatic, enigmatic Bonnie Prince Charlie (1720-1788).

Though usually depicted as a battle of the Scottish versus the English, in truth Culloden was a civil war between two opposing dynasties: Stuart (Charlie) and Hanover (George). However, as the history has faded into lore, the battle has come to be remembered as a Scottish-versus-English standoff—or, in the parlance of the Scots, the Highlanders versus the Strangers.

Charles Edward Stuart, from his first breath, was raised with a single purpose—to restore his family to the British throne. His grandfather was King James II (VII of Scotland), deposed in 1688 by the English Parliament for his tyranny and pro-Catholic bias. The Stuarts remained in exile in France and Italy, until 1745, when young Charlie crossed the Channel from France to retake the throne in the name of his father. He landed on the west coast of Scotland and rallied support for the Jacobite cause. Though Charles was not Scottish-born, he was the rightful heir directly down the line from Mary, Queen of Scots—and why so many Scots joined the rebellion out of resentment at being ruled by a "foreign" king (King George II, who was born in Germany, couldn't even speak English).

Bagpipes droned, and "Bonnie" (handsome) Charlie led an army of 2,000 tartan-wearing, Gaelic-speaking Highlanders across Scotland, seizing Edinburgh. They picked up other supporters of the Stuarts from the Lowlands and from England. Now 6,000 strong, they marched south toward London—quickly advancing as far as Derby, just 125 miles from the capital—and King George II made plans to flee the country. But anticipated support for the Jacobites failed to materialize in the numbers they were hoping for (both in England and from France). The Jacobites had so far been victorious in their battles against the Hanoverian government forces, but the odds now turned against them. Charles retreated to the Scottish Highlands, where many of his men knew the terrain and might gain an advantage when outnumbered. The English government troops followed closely on his heels.

Against the advice of his best military strategist, Charles' army faced the Hanoverian forces at Culloden Moor on flat, barren terrain that was unsuited to the Highlanders' guerrilla tactics. The Jacobites—many of them brandishing only broadswords, targes (wooden shields covered in leather and studs), and dirks (long daggers)—were mowed down by King George's cannons and horsemen. In less than

an hour, the government forces routed the Jacobite army, but that was just the start. They spent the next weeks methodically hunting down ringleaders and sympathizers (and many others in the Highlands who had nothing to do with the battle), ruthlessly killing, imprisoning, and banishing thousands.

Charles fled with a £30,000 price on his head (an equivalent of millions of today's pounds). He escaped to the Isle of Skye, hidden by a woman named Flora MacDonald (her grave is on the Isle of Skye, and her statue is outside Inverness Castle). Flora dressed Charles in women's clothes and passed him off as her maid. Later, Flora was arrested and thrown in the Tower of London before being released and treated like a celebrity.

Charles escaped to France. He spent the rest of his life wandering Europe trying to drum up support to retake the throne. He drifted through short-lived romantic affairs and alcohol, and died in obscurity, without an heir, in Rome.

The Battle of Culloden was the end of 60 years of Jacobite rebellions, the last major battle fought on British soil, and the final stand of the Highlanders. From then on, clan chiefs were deposed; kilts and tartans were outlawed; and farmers were cleared off their ancestral land, replaced by more-profitable sheep. Scottish culture would never fully recover from the events of the campaign called "The Forty Five."

❍ Self-Guided Tour

This tour takes you through two sections: the exhibit and the actual battlefield.

The Exhibit

Just past the ticket desk, note the **family tree:** Bonnie Prince Charlie ("Charles Edward Stuart") and George II were distant cousins. Then the exhibit's shadowy-figure **touchscreens** connect you with historical figures who give you details from both the Hanoverian and Jacobite perspectives. A **map** shows the other power struggles happening in and around Europe, putting this fight for political control of Britain in a wider context. This battle was no small regional skirmish, but rather a key part of a larger struggle between Britain and its neighbors, primarily France, for control over trade and colonial power. In the display case are **medals** from the early 1700s, made by both sides as propaganda.

(Vertical text in right margin:) **INVERNESS & LOCH NESS**

From here, your path through this building is cleverly designed to echo the course of the Jacobite army. Your short march (with lots of historic artifacts) gets under way as Charlie sails from France to Scotland, then finagles the support of Highland clan chiefs. As he heads south with his army to take London, you, too, are walking south. Along the way, maps show the movement of troops, and wall panels cover the buildup to the attack, as seen from both sides. Note the clever division of information: To the left and in red is the story of the "government" (a.k.a. Hanoverians/Whigs/English, led by the Duke of Cumberland); to the right, in blue, is the Jacobites' perspective (Prince Charlie and his Highlander/French supporters).

But you, like Charlie, don't make it to London—in the dark room where the route reverses, you can hear Jacobite commanders arguing over whether to retreat back to Scotland. Pessimistic about their chances of receiving more French support, they decide to U-turn, and so do you. Heading back up north, you'll get some insight into some of the strategizing that went on behind the scenes.

By the time you reach the end of the hall, it's the night before the battle. Round another bend into a dark passage, and listen to the voices of the anxious troops. While the English slept soundly in their tents (recovering from celebrating the Duke's 25th birthday), the scrappy and exhausted Jacobite Highlanders struggled through the night to reach the battlefield (abandoning their plan of a surprise night attack at Nairn and instead retreating back toward Inverness, before ultimately deciding to fight right here).

At last the two sides meet. As you wait outside the theater for the next showing, study the chart depicting how the forces were arranged on the battle-field. Once inside the theater, you'll soon be surrounded by the views and sounds of a wind-swept moor. An impressive four-minute **360° movie** projects the re-enacted battle with you right in the center of the action. The movie drives home just how out-matched the Jacobites were.

The last room has **period weapons,** including ammunition and artifacts found on the battlefield, as well as **historical depictions** of the battle. You'll also find a section describing the detective work required to piece together the story from historical evidence. The huge **virtual map** illustrates the combat you've just experienced while giving you a bird's-eye view of the field through which you're about to roam.

While you can head straight out to the battlefield from here, don't miss (on the way back to the ticket desk) the **aftermath corri-**

dor ("End of the Rising"), which covers the nearly genocidal years following the battle and the cultural wake of this event to this day.

The Battlefield
Leaving the visitors center, survey the battlefield. Red flags show the front line of the government army (8,000 troops). This is where most of the hand-to-hand fighting took place. The blue flags in the distance are where the Jacobite army (5,500 troops) lined up.

As you explore the battlefield, notice how uneven and boggy the ground is in parts, and imagine trying to run across this hummocky terrain with all your gear, toward almost-certain death.

The old stone **memorial cairn,** erected in 1881, commemorates the roughly 1,500 Jacobites buried in this field. It's known as the Graves of the Clans. As you wander the battlefield, following the audioguide, you'll pass by other **mass graves,** marked by small headstones, and ponder how entire clans fought, died, and were buried here. *Outlander* fans seek out the Fraser clan head-

stone (with the big cairn at your back, it's at 2 o'clock—often adorned with fresh flowers).

Near the visitor center, the restored stone-and-turf **Leanach Cottage** predates Culloden and may have been used as a field hospital during the battle. A small exhibit inside explains plans to preserve Culloden for future generations.

Heading back to the parking lot, consider climbing up the stairs to the **rooftop deck,** which provides a higher vantage point from which to consider this monumental event.

On your way out, walking alongside the building, notice the wall of **protruding bricks.** Each represents a soldier who died. The handful of Hanoverian casualties are on the left (about 50); the rest of the long wall's raised bricks represent the multitude of dead Jacobites.

CLAVA CAIRNS
Scotland is littered with reminders of prehistoric peoples—especially in Orkney and along the coast of the Moray Firth—but the Clava Cairns, worth ▲ for a quick visit, are among the best-preserved, most inter-

esting, and easiest to reach. You'll find them nestled in the countryside just beyond Culloden Battlefield.

Cost and Hours: Free, always open; just after passing Culloden Battlefield on the B-9006 coming from Inverness, signs on the right point to *Clava Cairns*. Follow this twisty road a couple miles, over the "weak bridge" and to the free parking lot by the stones. Skip the cairns if you don't have a car.

Visiting the Cairns: These "Balnauran of Clava" are Neolithic burial chambers dating from 3,000 to 4,000 years ago. Although they appear to be just some giant piles of rocks in a sparsely forested clearing, a closer look will help you appreciate the prehistoric logic behind them. (The site is explained by a few information plaques.) There are three structures: a central "ring cairn" with an open space in the center but no access to it, flanked by two "passage cairns," which were once buried under turf-covered mounds. The entrance shaft in each passage cairn lines up with the setting sun at the winter solstice. Each cairn is surrounded by a stone circle, and the entire ensemble is framed by evocative trees—injecting this site with even more mystery.

Enjoy the site's many enigmas: Were the stone circles part of a celestial calendar system? Or did they symbolize guardians? Why were the clamshell-sized hollows carved into the stones facing the chambers? Was the soul of the deceased transported into the next life by the ray of sunlight on that brief moment that it filled the inner chamber? How many *Outlander* fans have taken selfies in front of the split standing stone (which inspired a similar stone in the novel)? No one knows.

CAWDOR CASTLE

Atmospheric, intimate, and worth ▲, this castle is still the residence of the Dowager (read: widow) Countess of Cawdor, a local aristocratic branch of the Campbell family. While many associate the castle with Shakespeare's *Macbeth* (because "Cawdor" is mentioned more than a dozen times in the play), there is no actual connection with Shakespeare. *Macbeth* is set 300 years before the castle was even built. The castle is worth a visit simply

because it's historic and beautiful in its own right—and because the woman who owns it flies a Buddhist flag from its tower. She is from Eastern Europe and was the Earl's second wife.

Cost and Hours: Castle and gardens-£13.50, includes audioguide; gardens only-£8; May-Sept daily 10:00-17:30, closed Oct-April; +44 1667 404 401, www.cawdorcastle.com. The good £5.50 guidebook provides more detail on the family and the rooms. Storage is available for larger bags, which cannot be brought into the castle.

Getting There: It's on the B-9090, just off the A-96, about 15 miles east of Inverness (6 miles beyond Culloden and Clava Cairns). Public transportation to the castle is scant, but check at the TI for current options.

Visiting the Castle: You'll follow a one-way circuit around the castle with each room well-described with posted explanations written by the countess' late husband, the sixth Earl of Cawdor. His witty notes bring the castle to life and make you wish you'd known the old chap. Cawdor feels very lived-in because it is. While the Dowager Countess moves out during the tourist season, for the rest of the year this is her home. You can imagine her stretching out in front of the fireplace with a good book. Notice her geraniums in every room.

The drawing room (for "withdrawing" after dinner) is lined with a family tree of portraits looking down. In the Tapestry Bedroom you'll see the actual marriage bed of Sir Hugh Campbell from 1662 and 17th-century tapestries warming the walls. In the Yellow Room, a flat-screen TV hides inside an 18th-century cabinet (ask a docent to show you). In the Tartan Passage, lined with modern paintings, find today's dowager—Lady Angelika—in a beautiful 1970 pastel portrait, staring at her late husband's predecessors. Notice how their eyes follow you creepily down the hall—but hers do not.

A spiral stone staircase near the end of the tour leads down to the castle's proud symbol: a holly tree dating from 1372. According to the beloved legend, a donkey leaned against this tree to mark the spot where the castle was to be built...and it was, around the tree.

The **gardens,** included with the castle ticket, are worth exploring, with some 18th-century linden trees and several surprising species (including sequoia and redwood). The hedge maze,

INVERNESS & LOCH NESS

crowned by a minotaur and surrounded by a laburnum arbor (dripping with yellow blossoms in spring), is not open to the public.

The nine-hole **golf course** on the castle grounds provides a quick and affordable way to have a Scottish golfing experience. The par-32 course is bigger than pitch-and-putt and fun even for non-golfers (£20/person with clubs). If it's open, you're welcome to try the putting green for £5.

Nearby: The close but remote-feeling **village of Cawdor**—with a few houses, a village shop, and a tavern—is also worth a look if you've got time to kill.

Loch Ness

Don't let silly gimmicks distract you from this area's true grandeur: Loch Ness is 23 miles long, less than a mile wide, and 754 feet deep. It's essentially the vast chasm of a fault line, filled with water...lots and lots of water (its volume exceeds all the freshwater bodies of England and Wales combined).

The people of Inverness and environs adore the giant loch at their doorstep. They spend a lifetime's worth of weekends exploring its contours, and especially enjoy its untrampled eastern shore (along the B-852). If you've got ample time to spend, do some homework and really dig into Loch Ness beyond Nessie (for starters, check out www.lochnessliving.com).

But the local tourist industry—despite insisting that there's "so much more to Loch Ness"—seems cynically fixated on the legend of the Loch Ness monster. It seems like every visitor to this part of Scotland gets funneled into the extremely tacky lochside stretch of the A-82 at the small town of Drumnadrochit, which seems designed to extract as much of your money as possible. But if you want to say you've seen Loch Ness, this is the easiest place to do it.

Here's my recommended Loch Ness strategy: If you're driving past anyway, it can be worth a stop to soak in the hokeyness, snap a photo pretending you're "looking for Nessie," and maybe tour the well-presented Loch Ness Centre & Exhibition or visit the ruins of Urquhart Castle. I wouldn't go to special effort to side-trip to Loch Ness—there are far better places near Inverness to spend your limited time and money—but if you consider it a "must"...suit yourself.

Getting There: The Loch Ness sights are a 20-minute drive southwest of Inverness. To drive the full length of Loch Ness takes about 45 minutes. Fort William-bound bus #919 makes stops at Urquhart Castle and Drumnadrochit (8/day, 40 minutes).

Sights on Loch Ness

In July 1933, a couple swore they saw a giant sea monster shimmy across the road in front of their car by Loch Ness. Within days, ancient legends about giant monsters in the lake (dating as far back as the sixth century) were revived—and suddenly everyone was spotting "Nessie" poke its head above the waters of Loch Ness. Further sightings and photographic "evidence" have

bolstered the claim that there's something mysterious living in this unthinkably deep and murky lake. (Most sightings take place in the deepest part of the loch, near Urquhart Castle.) Most witnesses describe a water-bound dinosaur resembling the real, but extinct, plesiosaur. Others cling to the slightly more plausible theory of a gigantic eel. And skeptics figure the sightings can be explained by a combination of reflections, boat wakes, and mass hysteria. The most famous photo of the beast (dubbed the "Surgeon's Photo") was later discredited—the "monster's" head was actually attached to a toy submarine. But that hasn't stopped various cryptozoologists from seeking photographic, sonar, and other proof.

And that suits the thriving local tourist industry just fine. The Nessie commercialization is so tacky that there are two different monster exhibits within 100 yards of each other, both in the town of Drumnadrochit. Of the two competing sites, Nessieland is pretty cheesy while the Loch Ness Centre and Exhibition (described next) is surprisingly thoughtful. Each has a tour-bus parking lot and more square footage devoted to their kitschy shops than to the exhibits. While Nessieland is a tourist trap, the Loch Ness Centre may appease that small part of you that knows the *real* reason you wanted to see Loch Ness.

▲Loch Ness Centre & Exhibition

This attraction is better and more methodical than you might expect, and is worth visiting if you want to understand the geological and historical environment that bred the monster story. Housed in a big old manor house across the street from the loch, it's spearheaded by Adrian Shine, a naturalist fond of saying "I like mud,"

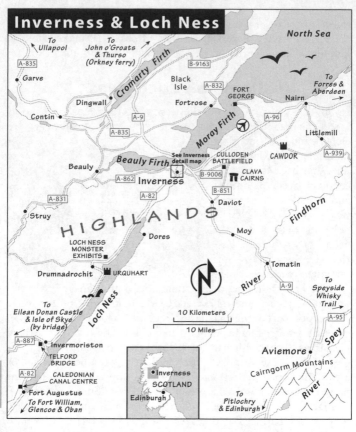

Inverness & Loch Ness

who has spent many years researching lake ecology and scientific phenomena.

Cost and Hours: £9, RS%—ask; daily Easter-Oct 10:00-17:45, Nov-Easter 10:00-15:45, last entry 45 minutes before closing; in the big stone mansion right on the main road to Inverness, +44 1456 450 573, www.lochness.com.

Visiting the Museum: The exhibit has two parts: First you go through a series of rooms with videos and special effects, taking about 30 minutes all together. Then you enter a small exhibit on the history of the Great Glen and Loch Ness...followed by a gigantic gift shop.

The videos detail the various searches that have been conducted; refreshingly, they retain an air of healthy skepticism instead of breathless monster-chasing. You'll also see some artifacts related to the search, such as a hippo-foot ashtray used to fake monster footprints and the *Viperfish*—a harpoon-equipped submarine used in a 1969 Nessie expedition. And you'll learn how, in 1952, record-seeker John Cobb died going 200 mph in his speedboat on the loch.

▲Urquhart Castle

The ruins at Urquhart (UR-kurt), just up the loch from the Nessie exhibits, are gloriously situated with a view of virtually the entire lake but create a traffic jam of tourism on busy days.

Cost and Hours: £13 (or £12 if you prebook online), guidebook-£5; daily April-Sept 9:30-18:00, Oct until 17:00, shorter hours off-season; last entry 45 minutes before closing, café, +44 1456 450 551, www.historicenvironment.scot.

Crowd-Beating Tips: The castle can be jammed, especially in July and August, when it's wise to prebook online to guarantee an entry time. The parking lot can also fill up—reserve a parking spot along with your ticket.

Tours: You can download a free audioguide; there are occasional free informational talks down amid the ruins (ask for schedule at entrance).

Visiting the Castle: The visitors center has a tiny exhibit with interesting castle artifacts and an eight-minute film taking you on a sweep through a thousand years of tumultuous history—from St. Columba's visit to the castle's final destruction in 1689. The castle itself, while dramatically situated and fun to climb through, is an empty shell. After its owners (who supported the crown) blew it up to keep the Jacobites from taking it, the largest medieval castle in Scotland (and the most important in the Highlands) wasn't considered worth rebuilding or defending, and was abandoned. Well-placed, descriptive signs help you piece together this once-mighty fortress. As you walk toward the ruins, take a close look at the trebuchet (a working replica of one of the most destructive weapons of English King Edward I), and ponder how this giant catapult helped Edward grab almost every castle in the country away from the native Scots.

Loch Ness Cruises

Cruises on Loch Ness are as popular as they are pointless. The lake is far from Scotland's prettiest—and the time-consuming boat trips show you little more than what you'll see from the road. As it seems that Loch Ness cruises are a mandatory part of every "Highlands Highlights" day tour, there are several options, leaving from the top, bottom, and middle of the loch. The basic one-hour loop

The Caledonian Canal

Two hundred million years ago, two tectonic plates collided, creating the landmass we know as Scotland and leaving a crevice of thin lakes slashing diagonally across the country. This Great Glen Fault, from Inverness to Oban, is easily visible on any map.

Scottish engineer Thomas Telford connected the lakes 200 years ago with a series of canals so ships could avoid the long trip around the north of the country. The Caledonian Canal runs 62 miles from Scotland's east to west coasts; 22 miles of it is man-made. Telford's great feat of engineering took 19 years to complete, opening in 1822 at a cost of one million pounds. But bad timing made the canal a disaster commercially. Napoleon's defeat in 1815 meant that ships could sail the open seas more freely. And by the time the canal opened, commercial ships were too big for its 15-foot depth. Just a couple of decades after the Caledonian Canal opened, trains made the canal almost useless...except  for Romantic Age tourism. From the time of Queen Victoria (who cruised the canal in 1873), the canal has been a popular tourist attraction. To this day the canal is a hit with vacationers, recreational boaters, and lock-keepers who compete for the best-kept lock.

The scenic drive from Inverness along the canal is entertaining, with Drumnadrochit (Nessie centers), Urquhart Castle, Fort Augustus (five locks), and Fort William (under Ben Nevis, with the eight-lock "Neptune's Staircase"). As you cross Scotland, you'll follow Telford's work—22 miles of canals and locks between three lochs, raising ships from sea level to 51 feet (Ness), 93 feet (Lochy), and 106 feet (Oich).

While Neptune's Staircase, a series of eight locks near Fort William, has been cleverly named to sound intriguing (see page 76), the best lock stop is midway, at Fort Augustus, where the canal hits the south end of Loch Ness. In Fort Augustus, the **Caledonian Canal Centre,** overlooking the canal just off the main road, gives a good rundown on Telford's work (see "Fort Augustus" at the end of this chapter). Stroll past several shops and eateries to the top for a fine view.

Seven miles north, in the town of **Invermoriston,** is another Telford structure: a stone bridge, dating from 1805, that spans the Morriston Falls as part of the original road. Look for a small parking lot just before the junction at A-82 and A-887, on your right as you drive from Fort Augustus. Cross the A-82 and walk three minutes back the way you came. The bridge, which took eight years to build and is still in use, is on your right.

costs around £18 and includes views of Urquhart Castle and lots of legends and romantic history (Jacobite is the dominant outfit of the many cruise companies, www.jacobite.co.uk). I'd rather spend my time and money at Fort Augustus or Urquhart Castle.

▲Fort Augustus

Perhaps the most idyllic stop along the Caledonian Canal is the little lochside town of Fort Augustus. It was founded in the 1700s—before there was a canal here—as part of a series of garrisons and military roads built by the English to quell the Highland clansmen, even as the Jacobites kept trying to take the throne in London. Before then, there were no developed roads in the Highlands—and without roads, it's hard to keep indigenous people down.

From 1725 to 1733, the English built 250 miles of hard roads and 40 bridges to open up the region; Fort Augustus was a central Highlands garrison at the southern tip of Loch Ness, designed to awe clansmen. It was named for William Augustus, Duke of Cumberland—notorious for his role in destroying the clan way of life in the Highlands. (When there's no media and no photographs to get in the way, ethnic cleansing has little effect on one's reputation.)

Fort Augustus makes for a delightful stop if you're driving through the area. Parking is easy. There are plenty of B&Bs, charming eateries, and an inviting park along the town's five locks. You can still see the capstans, surviving from the days when the locks were cranked open by hand.

The fine little **Caledonian Canal Centre** tells the story of the canal's construction (free, daily, +44 1320 725 581). Also, consider the pleasant little canalside stroll out to the head of the loch.

Eating in Fort Augustus: You can eat reasonably at a string of $ eateries lining the same side of the canal. Consider **The Lock Inn,** cozy and pub-like with great canalside tables, ideal if it's sunny; **The Bothy,** another pub with decent food; and the **Canalside Chip Shop** offering fish-and-chips to go (no seating, but plenty of nice spots on the canal). A small grocery store is at the gas station, next to the TI, which is a few steps from the canal just after crossing the River Oich (also housing the post office, a WC, and an ATM).

EASTERN SCOTLAND

Pitlochry • Between Inverness & Pitlochry • Loch Tay •
Speyside Whisky Trail • Balmoral Castle & Royal Deeside
• On the Aberdeenshire Coast

Between Edinburgh and Inverness, the eastern expanse of Scotland bulges out into the North Sea. The main geological landmark is Cairngorms National Park, with gently rugged Highland scenery and great hiking terrain. And surrounding the Cairngorms on all sides are worthwhile stopovers. This region is easily accessible—you'll likely pass through at some point—and has a lot to offer.

Those in a hurry should focus on the sights lined up along the busy A-9 corridor, which traces the western boundary of the Cairngorms between the Lowlands (Edinburgh, Glasgow, Stirling, etc.) and Inverness. Welcoming Pitlochry has a green-hills-and-sandstone charm and a pair of great distilleries linked by a nice hike, making it a fine overnight stop. Nearby, you'll find a fascinating trip back into prehistory (at the Scottish Crannog Centre on Loch Tay), a fun sheepdog show, and an open-air folk museum.

The eastern and northern edges of the Cairngorms, farther off the beaten path, offer a closer look at rural Scotland and some worth-the-effort treasures: Whisky connoisseurs flock to Speyside (also doable as a day trip from Inverness); royalists visit Balmoral Castle; hikers enjoy exploring the mountains and moors around Ballater; and ruined-castle fans favor Dunnottar. These stops are handy for those heading between St. Andrews and Inverness, but they're also ideal for anyone wanting to linger over a slightly longer, far more scenic drive between the Lowlands and Inverness—ideally with an overnight or two along the way (best in Ballater).

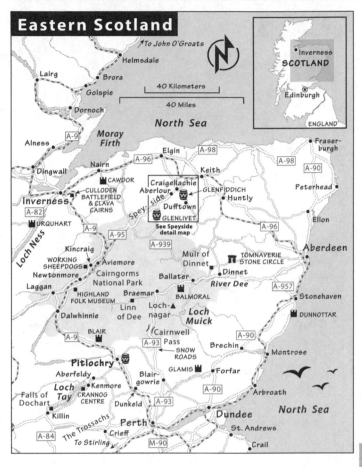

Pitlochry

This likable tourist town, famous for its whisky and its hillwalking (both beloved by Scots), makes an enjoyable overnight stop while exploring attractions along the busy A-9 highway. Just outside the craggy Highlands, Pitlochry is set amid pastoral rolling hills that offer plenty of forest hikes and riverside strolls. It seems that tourism is the town's only industry—with perhaps Scotland's

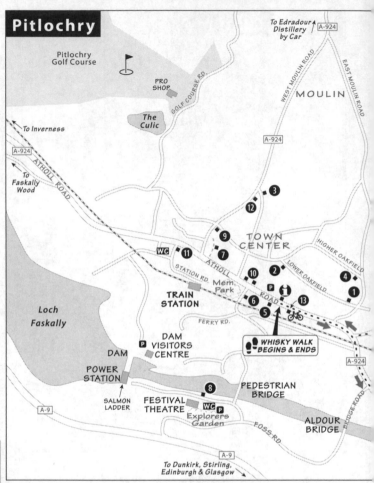

Pitlochry

Pitlochry Golf Course

PRO SHOP

To Edradour Distillery by Car A-924

WEST MOULIN ROAD

EAST MOULIN ROAD

MOULIN

GOLF COURSE RD.

The Culic

To Inverness

A-924

A-924

ATHOLL ROAD

To Faskally Wood

3

12

9

TOWN CENTER

HIGHER OAKFIELD

WC

11

7

ATHOLL

STATION RD.

Mem. Park

10

2

LOWER OAKFIELD

4

1

TRAIN STATION

ROAD

P

6

1

13

5

FERRY RD.

Loch Faskally

DAM VISITORS CENTRE

P

DAM

POWER STATION

SALMON LADDER

A-9

FESTIVAL THEATRE

8

WC

P

Explorers Garden

WHISKY WALK BEGINS & ENDS

A-924

PEDESTRIAN BRIDGE

BRIDGE ROAD

FOSS RD.

ALDOUR BRIDGE

A-9

To Dunkirk, Stirling, Edinburgh & Glasgow

highest concentration of woolens shops and outdoor outfitters. (The name "Pitlochry" must come from an old Pictish word for "tourist trap.") But Pitlochry also has the feel of a real community. People here are friendly and bursting with town pride: They love to chat about everything from the high-quality local theater to the salmon ladder at the hydroelectric dam. It's also a restful place, where—after the last tour bus pulls out—you can feel your pulse slow as you listen to gurgling streams.

Orientation to Pitlochry

Plucky little Pitlochry (pop. 4,000) lines up along its tidy, tourist-minded main street, Atholl Road, which runs parallel to the River Tummel. The train station is on Station Road, off the main street.

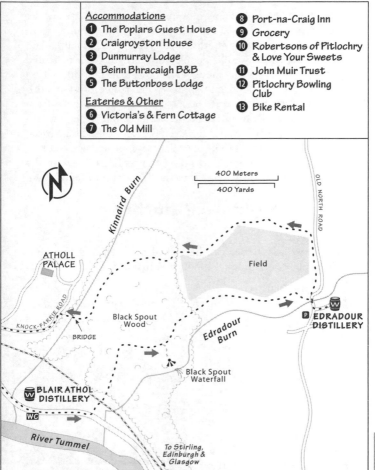

Accommodations
1 The Poplars Guest House
2 Craigroyston House
3 Dunmurray Lodge
4 Beinn Bhracaigh B&B
5 The Buttonboss Lodge

Eateries & Other
6 Victoria's & Fern Cottage
7 The Old Mill

8 Port-na-Craig Inn
9 Grocery
10 Robertsons of Pitlochry & Love Your Sweets
11 John Muir Trust
12 Pitlochry Bowling Club
13 Bike Rental

Its two distilleries are a walk—or short drive—out of town (see my self-guided whisky walk). Navigate by following the black directional signs to Pitlochry's handful of sights.

TOURIST INFORMATION

The helpful TI, at one end of town, sells maps for local hill walks and scenic drives. Their good *Pitlochry Path Network* brochure is handy (Mon-Sat 9:30-17:00, Sun 10:00-16:00, shorter hours and closed Sun Nov-March; 22 Atholl Road, +44 1796 472 215, www. visitscotland.com, also see www.pitlochry.org).

HELPFUL HINTS

Special Events: In summer, a pipe band marches through town every Monday evening. From May through August, the salmon ladder at the dam comes to life (described later, under "Sights in Pitlochry"). Pitlochry's Highland Games are in early September (www.pitlochryhighlandgames.co.uk). And in October, over 80,000 people come to see the Enchanted Forest light-and-water show. Set to music, it illuminates Faskally Wood, just outside town (www.enchantedforest.org.uk).

Bike Rental: Across the street and a block from the TI (away from town), **Escape Route Bikes** rents e-bikes for £45 per day (includes helmet and lock, Tue-Sat 9:00-17:00, closed Sun-Mon, 3 Atholl Road, +44 1796 473 859, www.escape-route.co.uk).

Parking: Drivers who aren't spending the night can park in the large pay-and-display lot next to the TI, in the center of town.

Sights in Pitlochry

DISTILLERIES

Pitlochry's two distilleries can be linked by a relaxing two-hour hike (described later, under "Pitlochry Whisky Walk.")

▲▲Edradour Distillery

This cute distillery (pronounced ED-rah-dower)—the smallest historic distillery in Scotland (est. 1825)—takes pride in making its

whisky with a minimum of machinery, and maintains a proud emphasis on tradition. Small white-and-red buildings are nestled in a delightfully green Scottish hillside. ("Edradour"—also the name of the stream that gurgles through the complex—means "land between two rivers.") With its idyllic setting and gregarious spirit, it's one of the most enjoyable distillery tours in Scotland. Unlike the bigger distilleries, they allow you to take photos of the equipment. If you like the whisky, see if their shop is open and buy some here to support the Pitlochry economy—this is one of the few independently owned distilleries left in Scotland.

Cost and Hours: £12 for a one-hour tour when offered—check ahead before heading out; tours usually depart 3/hour, April-Oct Mon-Sat 10:00-17:00; off-season Mon-Fri 10:00-16:00, closed Sat; closed Sun year-round, last tour departs one hour before closing, +44 1796 472 095, www.edradour.com.

Getting There: Most come to the distillery by car—follow signs from the main (A-924) road, 2.5 miles into the countryside—

but you can also get there on a peaceful hiking trail that you'll have all to yourself (follow my "Pitlochry Whisky Walk," later).

Visiting the Distillery: You'll watch a 10-minute orientation film, then enjoy a sit-down education while tasting two different drams. Then the guided tour proceeds through the facility: from the malt barn (where the barley is germinated and dried) to the still (where giant copper stills turn distiller's beer into whisky) to the warehouse (where 6,000 casks age in the darkness). Take a deep whiff of the rich aroma—you're smelling the so-called "angels' share," the tiny percentage of each cask that's lost to evaporation.

Blair Athol Distillery

This big, ivy-covered facility is conveniently located (about a half-mile from the town center) and more corporate-feeling, offering 45-minute tours with a taste of three whiskies. I'd tour this only if you're a whisky completist, or if you lack the wheels or hiking stamina to reach Edradour.

Cost and Hours: £16, May-Sept daily 10:00-17:00, tours depart roughly hourly, last tour departs one hour before closing; fewer tours and shorter hours off-season; +44 1796 482 003, www.malts.com—search for "Blair Athol."

Pitlochry Whisky Walk

A fun way to visit the distilleries is to hill-walk from downtown Pitlochry. The entire loop trip takes 2-3 hours, depending on how long you linger in the distilleries (at least an hour of walking each way). You'll see lush fern forests and a pretty decent waterfall. The walk is largely uphill on the way to the Edradour Distillery; wear good shoes, bring a rain jacket just in case, and be happy that you'll stroll easily downhill *after* you've had your whisky samples.

At the TI, pick up the *Pitlochry Path Network* brochure and follow along with its map. You'll be taking the **Edradour Walk** (marked on directional signs with yellow hiker icons; on the map it's a series of yellow dots). Leave the TI and head left along the busy A-924. The walk can be done in either direction, but I'll describe it counterclockwise.

Within 10 minutes, you'll walk under the railroad tracks and then come to **Blair Athol Distillery** on your left. If you're a whisky buff, stop in here. Otherwise, hold out for the much more atmospheric Edradour. You'll pass a few B&Bs and suburban homes, then a sign marked *Black Spout* on a lamppost. Just after this, you'll cross a bridge, then take the next left, walking under another stone rail overpass and away from the road. Following this path, you'll come to a clearing, and as the road gets steeper, you'll see signs directing you 50 yards off the main path to see the "Black Spout"—a wonderful waterfall well worth the few extra steps on your right.

At the top of the hill, you'll arrive in another clearing, where a narrow path hugs a huge field on your left. Low rolling hills surround you in all directions. It seems like there's not another person around for miles, with just the thistles to keep you company. From here it's an easy 20 minutes to the **Edradour Distillery.**

Leaving the distillery, to complete the loop, head right, following the paved road (Old North Road). In about 50 yards, a sign points left into the field. Take the small footpath that runs along the left side of the road. (If you see the driveway with stone lions on both sides, you've gone a few steps too far.) You'll walk parallel to the route you took getting to the distillery, hugging the far side of the same huge field. The trail then swoops back downhill through the forest, until you cross the footbridge and make a left. You'll soon reach Knockfarrie Road—take this downhill; you'll pass a B&B and hear traffic noises as you emerge from the forest. The trail leads back to the highway, with the TI a few blocks ahead on the right.

TOWN CENTER
Strolling the High Street

Pitlochry's main street is a pleasant place to wander and window-shop. As you stroll, consider this: The town exists thanks to the arrival of the train, which conveniently brought Romantic Age tourists from the big cities in the south to this lovely bit of Scotland. Queen Victoria herself visited three times in the 1860s, putting Pitlochry on the tourist map. The postcard-perfect Victorian sandstone architecture on the main street makes it clear that this was a delightful escape for city folks back in the 19th century.

Here are some things to look for, listed in order of how you'll reach them from the TI. Just past the recommended Victoria's restaurant, the **memorial park** with the Celtic cross honors men from the local parish whose lives were lost fighting in World War I—a reminder of Scotland's disproportionate sacrifices in that conflict. Throughout Scotland, even many tiny villages have similar monuments.

Ferry Road, next to the

park, branches off under the rail bridge and leads to a footbridge that takes you to the other side of the river—home to Pitlochry's spunky Festival Theatre, as well as a power station with a salmon ladder (a fun excuse for a lazy walk—described later).

Pop into **Robertsons of Pitlochry** whisky shop, stocked with over 400 whiskies and other Scottish spirits. The collection is fun to peruse, and if you don't make it to one of Pitlochry's distilleries, ask Ewan for a wee dram here. You can book tastings of five drams in their bar (£15, open Mon-Sat 10:00-18:00, Sun 11:00-17:00, +44 1796 472 011, www.robertsonsofpitlochry.co.uk).

A few doors down, the **Love Your Sweets** shop, with a purple awning, stocks a staggering variety of uniquely Scottish candies in bulk. Step in to buy a mixed bag of some unusual flavors of hard candies, such as clove, rhubarb, or Irn-Bru. At the next little park on the right, a surging stream angles away from the main road and to the recommended Old Mill restaurant.

On the corner with Station Road is the headquarters of the **John Muir Trust.** John Muir (1838-1914) was born in Scotland, moved to the US when he was 10, and later helped establish the world's first national park system in his adopted country. Inside is a free tiny exhibit called Wild Space, with a feel-good nature video and a small art gallery. They also sell books, maps, and other conservation-themed souvenirs (Mon-Sat 10:00-17:00, Sun 11:00-16:30, shorter hours off-season, +44 1796 470 080, www. johnmuirtrust.org).

Lawn Bowls

The **Pitlochry Bowling Club** lets outsiders rent shoes and balls and try their hand at the game (£3, May-Sept generally daily 14:00-16:00 & 18:30-22:00, 24 West Moulin Road, +44 1796 473 459).

Pitlochry Golf Course

A 10-minute walk from the town center, the pleasant Pitlochry Golf Course and driving range offers a delightful way to spend an afternoon in Pitlochry, with views of the Tummel Valley (£50-60, short course available, open dawn until dusk, Golf Course Road, +44 1796 472 792, www.pitlochrygolf.co.uk).

ACROSS THE RIVER

These sights lie along the largely undeveloped riverbank opposite Pitlochry's town center. While neither are knockouts, they're a fine excuse for a pretty stroll or drive. Walkers can reach this area easily in about 15 minutes: Head down Ferry Road (near the memorial park), cross the footbridge, and turn right.

Pitlochry Dam Visitors Centre and Salmon Ladder

Pitlochry's dam on the River Tummel provides a nice place to go for a stroll, and comes with a salmon ladder—a series of chambers that allow salmon to "step" their way upstream next to the dam (salmon generally run May-Aug).

The well-designed and family-friendly visitors center celebrates hydroelectric power in the Highlands. Its fine nine-minute video, "Power from the Glens," explains the epic vision of generating clean power from—and for—the Highlands. You can also walk all the way across the top of the dam, pausing to read informational plaques and to peer through windows into the hydroelectric plant (free, Tue-Sun 10:00-16:30, closed Mon; Nov-March closed Mon-Tue; https://pitlochrydam.com). Their cafeteria is delightful, with a nice river view. As you walk along the top of the dam, be sure to look back at the sleek, modern visitors center protruding from the trees.

Pitlochry Festival Theatre

This theater company rotates its productions, putting on a different play every few nights. Most are classics, with a few musicals and new shows mixed in (£16-35; plays generally run May-Oct Mon-Sat). The theater hosts concerts on Sunday evenings—usually tribute acts—and a variety of other performances in winter (purchase tickets online or at the theater on Port-na-Craig Road—box office open daily 10:00-20:00, +44 1796 484 626, www.pitlochryfestivaltheatre.com).

Nearby: Just above the theater's parking lot, the six-acre **Explorers Garden** features plants and wildflowers from around the world (£4, daily 10:00-17:00, closed Nov-March, last entry 45 minutes before closing, +44 1796 484 626, www.explorersgarden.com).

Sleeping in Pitlochry

All of these have free parking.

$$ The Poplars Guest House, perched regally on a meticulously landscaped hill high above the main road, has been stylishly renovated by charming Jason and Nathalie. The huge home has a spacious lounge with views, and six rooms that combine modern comforts with a respect for tradition. Start the day off right with their whisky porridge (family room, closed in winter, at the end of Lower Oakfield at #27, +44 1796 472 129, www.poplars-pitlochry.com, info@poplars-pitlochry.com).

$$ Craigroyston House, my sentimental favorite in Pitlochry, is a quaint, updated Victorian country house with eight large and luxe bedrooms. Their terraced yard is a great place to sip some wine or play croquet. Vaughan and Susan, originally from Orkney, are welcoming and generous (family rooms, no kids under 7, right above the TI parking lot at 2 Lower Oakfield, +44 1796 472 053, www.craigroyston.co.uk, reservations@craigroyston.co.uk). Drivers can reach it on Lower Oakfield Road; walkers can hike up from the huge parking lot next to the TI on Atholl Road (find the small gate at the back of the lot).

$$ Dunmurray Lodge is a calming place to call home, with four springtime-colored rooms, and friendly hosts (family room, apartment, no kids under 5; breakfast includes gluten-free, vegetarian, and other options; 5-minute walk from town at 72 Bonnethill Road, +44 7783 462 625, www.dunmurray.co.uk, info@dunmurray.co.uk, Lorraine and Mike).

$$ Beinn Bhracaigh (pronounced "benny vrackie," meaning "speckled mountain") is a guesthouse with a hotel feel. The 13 rooms are modern and tasteful (each named after a different salmon river), and they have a sitting room where you can serve yourself at the well-stocked honesty bar. It sits high above the main road—still within a (longish, steep) walk, but easier by car. Most rooms come with fine views across the town center, the River Tummel, and valley beyond (minimum two-night stay in peak season and on weekends, room-only rates available, no kids under 8, no elevator, 14 Higher Oakfield, +44 1796 470 355, www.beinnbhracaigh.com, info@beinnbhracaigh.com, James and Kirsty).

$ The Buttonboss Lodge has a less idyllic setting, right along the busy main road across from the TI (expect some traffic noise). But it's affordable and convenient for train travelers. The eight rooms, managed by Cristian, are straightforward and a bit old-fashioned (family suite with kitchenette and private entry, 25 Atholl Road, +44 1796 472 065, +44 7902 074 309, www. buttonbosslodge.co.uk, info@buttonbosslodge.co.uk).

Eating in Pitlochry

Pitlochry may be small and touristy, but its restaurants offer quality local flavor. Several options line the main drag, including a couple of bakeries selling picnic supplies.

$$ Victoria's restaurant and coffee shop, a local favorite, feels like a dressed-up diner, serving up an eclectic menu of comfort food and gourmet dishes—including a hearty baked goat cheese salad (daily 10:00-21:00, patio seating, at corner of memorial park, 45 Atholl Road, +44 1796 472 670).

$$$ Fern Cottage, just behind Victoria's, has a darker, cozy lodge ambience and a Mediterranean spin on their gourmet menu (patio tables, daily 12:00-16:00 & 17:00-21:00, Ferry Road, +44 1796 473 840).

$$$ The Old Mill, tucked a block behind the main drag

in an actual old mill, has good Scottish food, plus some pastas and salads. Sit in their popular, high-energy pub, calmer restaurant in back, or at picnic tables outside (food served daily 12:00-15:00 & 17:00-21:00, +44 1796 474 020).

$$$ Port-na-Craig Inn, on the river just downhill from the theater, is a fancier option catering to theatergoers. For a calmer experience, go at 20:00, after the show has started. In good weather, their outdoor patio makes a nice riverside hangout (soup-and-sandwich lunch specials, reservations smart, daily 11:00-21:00, +44 1796 472 777, www.portnacraig.com).

Supermarket: A well-stocked **Co-op** grocery has everything for a healthy picnic (daily 6:00-22:00, West Moulin Road, +44 1796 474 088).

Pitlochry Connections

The train station is open Monday to Saturday 8:00-18:30 and Sunday 10:30-18:00.

From Pitlochry by Train to: Inverness (nearly hourly, 1.5 hours), **Stirling** (5/day direct, 1 hour, more with transfer in Perth), **Edinburgh** (6/day direct, 2 hours, more with transfer), **Glasgow** (almost hourly, 4/day direct, 2 hours, some transfer in Perth). Train info: +44 8457 484 950, www.nationalrail.co.uk.

By Bus to: Glasgow (5/day on #M10, 2 hours), **Edinburgh** (8/day on #M90, 2.5 hours).

Between Inverness and Pitlochry

The A-9 highway, connecting Inverness, Stirling, and Edinburgh, may be Scotland's most touristy road—and it's scenic, too. Heading south soon after leaving Inverness, the highway begins to skirt around the curved west edge of Cairngorms National Park, which it follows almost all the way to Pitlochry. These bald, heather-covered hills are what many people picture when they imagine Highland scenery.

As you follow the A-9, it seems every exit is stacked with brown "tourist attraction" signs. For the most part, the options along here are more convenient than good; they tend to pale in comparison to alternatives elsewhere in the country. But if your trip to Scotland isn't taking you beyond this Highland corridor, some of these may be worth a stop. I've listed them in the order you'll reach them traveling south from Inverness; the "Near Pitlochry" section, next, explores attractions just south of Pitlochry. For more remote sojourns, see later in this chapter. Note that most of these—especially the sheepdog show—are also reachable as a day trip from Inverness.

▲▲Working Sheepdogs

Each afternoon, Neil Ross—a salt-of-the-earth farmer who was born and raised right on this property—presents a 45-minute demonstration of his well-trained  sheepdogs. As Neil describes his work, he'll explain why shepherds have used a crook for thousands of years, why sheep and cows are actually "man's best friends," and why farmers get frustrated when "fancy people with numbers after their names" try to tell them how to manage their land. Then the dogs get to work: With shouts and whistles, each dog follows individual commands, demonstrating an impressive mastery over the sheep. (Watching in awe, you can't help but think: Sheepdogs are smart...and sheep are idiots.) Neil may also demonstrate shearing a sheep—using old-fashioned, rusty metal shears, which supposedly are better for the sheep than modern electric ones. (Volunteers are welcome to try a few snips.) After the presentation, you'll meet (and pet) the border collie stars of the show, and may have the chance to feed some lambs. If they happen to have a litter of border collie puppies, even those who think they dislike dogs may find it hard to resist smuggling one home. The entire show is outdoors, so come prepared for all types of weather. They may be adding more wool-working activities, such as spinning wool into yarn—ask when you call to confirm.

Cost and Hours: £12.50; typically the demo occurs May-Oct Sun-Fri at 16:00—however, it may not happen every day, so it's important to call ahead to confirm the schedule and driving directions; closed to the public at other times, no demonstrations Sat or Nov-April, no WC except the bushes, +44 1540 651 402, https://workingsheepdogs.uk.

Getting There: Finding the farm can be tricky—don't count on your GPS to get you there correctly—but this should work: Heading south on A-9 from Inverness, exit at Kincraig, then follow B-9152 for several miles as it parallels A-9 south. After going through Kincraig, watch on the right for the *Highland Wildlife Park* signs. Head up this access road (going under the highway) and watch on the right for the *Welcome to Working Sheepdogs—Leault*

EASTERN SCOTLAND

Farm signs. Taking this road, you'll rumble over red cattle grates, then immediately take the (unmarked) left fork and drive another mile or so through the hills to the farm. Look for the big pen with sheep. If you're traveling north on A-9, exit for Kingussie and Kincraig, get on B-9152 northbound, and watch for the *Highland Wildlife Park* signs on the left, then follow the above directions. Note that access can change, so it's smart to reconfirm these directions when you call.

▲Highland Folk Museum

Scotland doesn't have a top-notch open-air folk museum—but this is close enough. Just off the highway on the outskirts of Newtonmore, the museum features re-creations of traditional buildings from the surrounding area from the 1700s through the 1930s. The buildings are a bit spread out, and it's quiet outside of frequent "activity days" (check the schedule online).

Cost and Hours: Free but donations strongly encouraged, daily April-Aug 10:00-17:00, Sept-Oct 10:30-16:00, closed Nov-March, helpful £5 guidebook, +44 1349 781 650, www.highlifehighland.com/highlandfolkmuseum.

Getting There: Exit the A-9 in Newtonmore, then follow brown signs for about five minutes through the village to the museum (free parking).

Visiting the Museum: The highlight of the museum is a circa-1700, thatched-roof Highland township called **Baile Gean,** a gathering of four primitive stone homes and three barns, each furnished as it would have been in the Jacobite era (it's a 15-minute walk from the entry—go to the right through a pine forest and up a small hill). Although built for the museum, the township was closely based on an actual settlement a few miles away that was populated until the 1830s. Costumed docents can explain traditional Highland lifestyles, and you'll likely see—and smell—a peat fire filling one of the homes with its rich smoke. (Because peat doesn't spit or spark, it was much safer to burn than wood—which was too valuable to feed fires anyway, as most tools were made of wood.) This area provided an ideal backdrop for some of the rural-life scenes in the TV production of *Outlander.*

With more time, visit the other structures in the rest of the open-air museum, such as the tweed shop; the schoolhouse, where you'll learn about early-20th-century classrooms; or the Lochanhully House (look for the house with red eaves, past the playground), which depicts a 1950s Scottish home. At the far end of the complex, you may see some hairy coos.

▲Blair Castle

If you like Scottish history, aristocratic furnishings, and antlers, you'll like Blair Castle. It's a convenient stop for those zipping past

on the A-9. In Gaelic, a "blàr" or "blair" is a flat bit of land surrounded by hills. And sure enough, this stately, white palace rises up from a broad clearing. A stout fortress during the Jacobite wars, it was later renovated and expanded as a mansion in the Scottish Baronial style.

The former residence of the Dukes of Atholl (a.k.a. Clan Murray) is now owned and run as a business by a trust. Filled with art, historic artifacts, and Clan Murray mementoes, it offers a fine look at 19th-century upper-crust life. Follow the self-guided, one-way route up the creaky "picture staircase" and try to spot the portrait of the cross-eyed forebear. Other highlights include the truly palatial main drawing room, where you can imagine the elite soirées that once took place, and the wood-paneled ballroom at the end, draped in tartan and bristling with antlers. In contrast, the WWI room recalls how the house was used as a hospital during that conflict.

If time allows, explore the grounds—especially the walled Hercules Garden, where rugged plantings surround a lily-padded pond, overlooked by a statue of Hercules (accessed via the trail near the parking lot).

Cost and Hours: £16, April-Oct daily 9:30-17:30, closed Nov-March, last entry one hour before closing, good cafeteria, +44 1796 481 207, https://blair-castle.co.uk.

Getting There: From the town of Blair Atholl (just off of the A-9), drive down the long, tree-lined driveway to the free parking lot. From Pitlochry, you can take the more scenic B-8019/B-8079 instead of the A-9. Bus #87 runs from Pitlochry (5/day in summer, fewer off-season, 15 minutes, www.elizabethyulecoaches.co.uk).

Nearby: The **Atholl Country Life Museum** is a humble, volunteer-run museum literally across the street from the entrance to the Blair Castle grounds. A local teacher created these exhibits, filling an old school to show the other side of the social and economic coin. Chatting with the volunteers makes a visit extra fun (£5, Mon-Sat 10:00-16:00, Sun 13:00-16:00, closed Nov-March, www.facebook.com/athollcountrylifemuseum).

EASTERN SCOTLAND

Near Pitlochry

ON LOCH TAY

A 30-minute drive southwest of Pitlochry, Loch Tay is worth visiting mostly for its excellent Scottish Crannog Centre—the best place in Scotland to learn about early Iron Age life. You can also drive along Loch Tay (and past the thundering Falls of Dochart) to connect Pitlochry and the A-9 corridor with the Trossachs and Loch Lomond.

▲▲Scottish Crannog Centre

Across Scotland, archaeologists know that little round islands on the lochs are evidence of crannogs—circular houses on stilts, dating to 500 years before the Christian era. During the Iron Age, Scots built on the water because people traveled by boat, and because waterways were easily defended against rampaging animals (or people). Scientists have found evidence of 18 such crannogs on Loch Tay alone. Families of up to 20 people, along with their livestock, lived in just one crannog.

A facsimile crannog built using mostly traditional methods was the centerpiece of a visit here—until a 2021 fire destroyed it.

While the crannog is reconstructed, your stop here includes a museum with a collection of Iron Age artifacts and a living history area with hands-on demonstrations of ancient crafts and technologies— turning a lathe, grinding flour, spinning yarn, and even starting a fire using nothing but wood and string. A modest exhibit just off the gift shop explains the history of crannogs, excavation efforts, and the building of the new one.

Cost and Hours: £5, daily 10:00-16:30, closed Dec-Jan, well marked just outside Kenmore on the south bank of Loch Tay, +44 1887 830 583, http://www.crannog.co.uk.

Kenmore

Located where Loch Tay empties into the River Tay, Kenmore is a sleepy, one-street, black-and-white village with a big hotel, a church, and a post office/general store. There's not much to do here, other than visit the nearby Scottish Crannog Centre, enjoy the Loch Tay scenery, and consider hiking through the woods to the Taymouth Castle (though the castle is usually closed to visitors). With its classic old hotel, Kenmore can be a handy home base for this area.

Sleeping and Eating in Kenmore: Dominating the village center, the **$$ Kenmore Hotel** feels like a classic Scottish country hotel—it claims to be the oldest inn in Scotland (dating from 1572). The 33 rooms are old-fashioned but cozy,

and welcoming lounges, terraces, and other public spaces sprawl through the building. Look for the Robert Burns poem above the fireplace in one of the bars (elevator, The Square, Kenmore, +44 1887 830 205, www.kenmorehotel.com, reception@kenmorehotel.com). The **$$$** pub, dining room, and various outdoor dining areas all share the same menu.

Falls of Dochart

At the far end of Loch Tay from Kenmore, in the village of Killin, the road passes on a stone bridge over a churning waterfall

where the peat-brown waters of the River Dochart tumble dramatically into the loch. The romantic bridge is busy with passing motorists enjoying a photo op; eateries and gift shops surround the scene. You can clamber down onto the flat stones for a closer look. From the bridge, notice the stone archway marking the burial ground of the Clan Macnab.

SOUTHEAST OF PITLOCHRY
▲Dunkeld

This appealing wee town, just off the A-9, is worth a stretch-your-legs break. While the town center is pleasant—with flower boxes, cleverly named shops, folk music, and a growing foodie scene—its claim to fame is its partially ruined cathedral on the banks of the River Tay.

Pay-and-display parking is at both ends of town (the north end has a WC). The TI and cathedral are just down High Street from the main drag, Atholl Street.

The **Cathedral of St. Columba** was actually Scotland's leading church for a brief time in the ninth century, when that important saint's relics were being stored here during Viking raids. Later it blossomed into a large cathedral complex in a secluded riverside setting. But it was devastated by the one-two punch of Reformation iconoclasts (who tore down most of the building) and Jacobites (who fought the Battle of Dunkeld near here). Duck inside to see the stony interior and its one-room museum (pick up the

free info sheet or consider borrowing the good audioguide for a small donation). Outside, as you circle the entire complex, you'll discover that the current church is merely the choir of the original structure—a huge, ruined nave (currently undergoing restoration) stretches behind it.

The **$ Scottish Deli** is nice for a drop in, with soups, sandwiches, and salads (a few tables inside, corner of High Street and Atholl Street, +44 1350 728 028).

Speyside and Royal Deeside: Whisky Country and Castles

While the A-9 corridor is studded with touristy amusements, the region north and east of the Cairngorms (while hardly undiscovered) feels more rugged and lets you dig deeper into the countryside. In this area, I've focused on two river valleys with very different claims to fame. Speyside, curling along the top of the Cairngorms, is famous for its many distilleries. Royal Deeside, cutting through the middle of the Cairngorms, is the home of the late Queen Elizabeth II's country retreat at Balmoral and the neighboring village of Ballater. Overnighting in Ballater is an ideal way to linger in this region and sleep immersed in Cairngorms splendor, a land rich with hiking opportunities—from easy to challenging.

Speyside Whisky Trail

Of the hundred or so distilleries in Scotland, half lie near the valley of the River Spey—a small area called Speyside. The abundant waters of the river, along with generous peat deposits, have attracted distillers here for centuries. While I prefer some of the smaller, more intimate distillery tours elsewhere in Scotland (including Oban Distillery in Oban, Talisker on the Isle of Skye, and Edradour near Pitlochry), Speyside is convenient to Inverness—about a

1.5-hour drive—and practically a pilgrimage for aficionados. The distilleries here feel bigger and more corporate, but they also include some famous names (including the world's two best-selling brands of single malts, Glenfiddich and Glenlivet). And for whisky lovers, it's simply enjoyable to spend time in a region steeped in such reverence for your favorite drink.

PLANNING YOUR TIME

A quick car tour of Speyside takes about a half-day, and it's a scenic way to connect Inverness to Royal Deeside (it also works as a side trip from Inverness). Whisky aficionados will have their own list of distilleries they want to hit. But, for the typical traveler, here is an easy plan for the day:

Enjoy the scenic drive to Aberlour, tour the Speyside Cooperage, tour the Glenfiddich distillery, and finally have a short stop in Dufftown. All are within about five miles of each other. With an early start, you could easily do these stops and then drive down to Balmoral Castle to tour it and sleep nearby in Ballater. Or, if you have more time and a special interest, you could add on a visit to Glenlivet and/or Cardhu.

Orientation to Speyside

The A-95, which parallels the River Spey, is the region's artery (to reach it, take the A-9 south from Inverness and turn off toward Grantown-on-Spey). Brown *Malt Whisky Trail* signs help connect the dots. While several distilleries lie along the main road, even more are a short side trip away. Three humdrum villages form the nucleus of Speyside: Aberlour (the biggest), Craigellachie (a wide spot in the road), and Dufftown (with a clock tower and a good dose of stony charm).

Because public transit connections aren't ideal, Speyside works best for drivers—though if you're determined, you could take the train from Inverness to Elgin and catch the "whisky bus" from there (Stagecoach bus #36, stops in Craigellachie and Aberlour on the way to Dufftown, about hourly, none Sun).

Each distillery is a working facility with a tasting room, shop, and lounge/bar. If you're making the long trip here, most visitors enjoy taking a tour, which typically costs around £20, lasts an hour and a half, and includes some background information on the distillery's history, a walk through the production facilities, and a tasting of three or four whiskies. Most offer additional, in-depth experiences for aficionados, which includes higher-quality whiskies and can cost much more. Tours fill up—weeks in advance at busy times—so if you have your heart set on a particular place, book online well ahead.

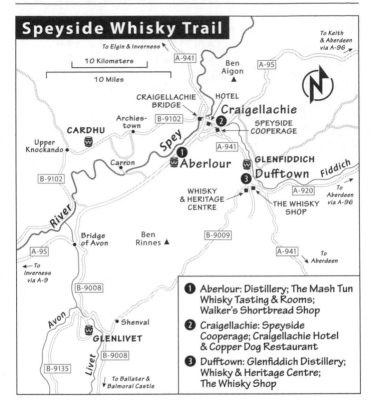

Speyside Whisky Trail

① Aberlour: Distillery; The Mash Tun Whisky Tasting & Rooms; Walker's Shortbread Shop

② Craigellachie: Speyside Cooperage; Craigellachie Hotel & Copper Dog Restaurant

③ Dufftown: Glenfiddich Distillery; Whisky & Heritage Centre; The Whisky Shop

It's interesting to see the reverence each distillery has for its founders—you'll see cast-bronze statues of them, as if they're saints, and their personal belongings are displayed as if holy relics.

While each distillery has a bar, most don't serve food. Keep an eye out for roadside restaurants between the stops; I've noted a few good options, too.

A word of caution: In Scotland, DUI standards are very low (0.05 percent) and strictly enforced. Go easy on the tastings, or bring a designated driver. Distilleries are often happy to give drivers their dram "to go" so they can enjoy it safely later.

Which Distillery to Tour? The two big distilleries of Speyside—Glenfiddich and Glenlivet—each offer good-quality tours and tastings. **Glenlivet** is more of an "innovator," with a fancier campus, glitzier facilities, and an upscale, corporate vibe. But I prefer **Glenfiddich,** which feels more historic and is closer to other sights. I've also mentioned **Cardhu,** which feels more "countryside" and is the most casual of the bunch; as they supply Johnnie Walker, they'd be a good choice for fans.

Sights in Speyside

ALONG THE MALT WHISKY TRAIL

I've listed these roughly west to east, as you'll reach them approaching Speyside on the A-95 from the Inverness area (or the A-9).

Aberlour

Officially named "Charlestown of Aberlour" for its founder, this attractive sandstone town lines up along the A-95. It's famous both for its namesake whisky distillery (www.aberlour.com) and as the home of Walkers Shortbread, which you'll see sold in red-tartan boxes all over Scotland. (You can stop off at the factory store—you'll see the giant complex at the east end of town—or just drop into the Joseph Walkers shop on the cute main street.)

Eating in Aberlour: Just off the main road toward the river, **$$ The Mash Tun** is an atmospheric whisky bar that serves good lunches and dinners, and rents rooms upstairs (+44 1340 881 771, www.mashtun-aberlour.com).

Craigellachie

The blink-and-you'll-miss-it village of Craigellachie (craig-ELL-a-kee) is home to the landmark **$$$ Craigellachie Hotel.** This classic, grand old hotel, a handy home base for whisky pilgrims, is famous for its whisky bar—stocking more than 800 bottles (opens daily at 17:00, the receptionist may let you in for a peek at other times, 26 rooms, +44 1340 881 204, www.craigellachiehotel.co.uk). Downstairs, the hotel's **$$ Copper Dog** restaurant is handy for lunch.

Just past the hotel on the A-941, keep an eye out on the left for the picturesque, multi-turreted **Craigellachie Bridge,** built by the great Scottish industrial architect Thomas Telford.

Note that the A-95 takes a sharp turn to the right in Craigellachie (just before the hotel), leading to the cooperage described next, and beyond that, to the Glenfiddich Distillery and Dufftown; the main road (past the hotel and the bridge) becomes A-941.

▲Speyside Cooperage

Perhaps the single biggest factor in defining whisky's unique flavor is the barrel it's aged in. At this busy workshop on the outskirts of Craigellachie, you can watch master coopers build or refurbish casks for distilleries throughout Scotland. The 14 coopers who work here—who must first complete a four-year apprenticeship to get the gig—are some of the

EASTERN SCOTLAND

last of a dying breed; while just about everything used to be transported in barrels, today it's just booze. The place can be visited only on a guided tour, which often sell out; call a day or two ahead to confirm the schedule and sign up. They also have a café with basic food and nice outdoor seating, which can also be reserved ahead.

Cost and Hours: £5, tours depart hourly, Mon-Fri 9:00-16:00, last tour at 15:00, closed Sat-Sun, Dufftown Road, Craigellachie, +44 1340 871 108, www.speysidecooperage.co.uk.

Visiting the Cooperage: First you'll view an engaging 15-minute film, then you'll follow your guide up to an observation deck peering down over the factory floor. Oak timber is shaped into staves, which are gathered into metal hoops, then steamed to make them more pliable. Finally the inside is charred with a gas flame, creating a carbonized coating that helps give whisky its golden hue and flavor. Because the vast majority of casks used in Scotland are hand-me-downs from the US (where bourbon laws only allow one use per barrel), you're more likely to see reassembly of old casks (with new ends) rather than from-scratch creation of new ones. But the process is equally fascinating. Apart from observing the barrel-making, it's also interesting to see the intensity of the workers—who are paid by the piece.

▲Glenfiddich Distillery

Before you enter Dufftown, keep an eye out on the left for the home of Scotland's top-selling single malt whisky—with a name that means "Valley of the Deer" (Note: The -ch at the end is pronounced like "loch," not like "itch"). This sprawling yet charming factory offers excellent tours and tastings, which are a good all-around choice for curious visitors. After a 15-minute promotional video, your guide will walk you through the impressive plant, which includes a busy bottling hall. Your tour finishes with an extensive tasting session. While it's smart to prebook, they tend to hold back a few slots for walk-ins as well.

Cost and Hours: Standard £20 visit includes 1.5-hour tour and 4 tastings (departs every 45 minutes), more expensive options available, Wed-Sun 9:30-16:30 (last tour), closed Mon-Tue, +44 1340 822 373, www.glenfiddich.com.

Dufftown

This charming, sleepy town has a characteristic crossroads street plan radiating from its clock-tower-topped main square. A few steps up Conval Street from the tower, the humble, one-room **Whisky and Heritage Centre** doubles as the TI.

You'll see a small selection of historical displays and tools from the whisky trade. Most importantly, you'll have a chance to chat with the fun retirees who run the place (free, intermittently closed as it's staffed by volunteers—but generally daily 10:00-16:00 in summer, +44 1340 821 591). **The Whisky Shop,** directly behind the tower, is a serious place selling 650 types of whisky (daily 10:30-17:00, closed Sun in winter, 1 Fife Street, +44 1340 821 097, www.whiskyshopdufftown.com). Dufftown has only very basic eateries (best avoided).

DISTILLERIES FARTHER FROM THE HIGHWAY

These two options require a 10- to 15-minute drive from the main Whisky Trail artery on A-95, but may be worth it for those interested. While each of these is well-signposted, it's easiest to simply plug them into your GPS.

Glenlivet Distillery

Sitting five miles south of the A-95 (turn off at Bridge of Avon), or 13 miles southwest of Dufftown, Glenlivet is the most posh and polished—and one of the biggest and most fa- mous—of the area's many distilleries. The sprawling visitors center feels rich and glitzy: a cozy fireplace drawing room displaying lore from founder George Smith (including the pis- tols he was given to defend

his fledgling business); a wall of cinematically lit bottles filled with amber liquid; a well-stocked and luxuriously displayed shop; and the Drawing Room bar, which invites visitors to relax and sip a dram or a cocktail in surroundings that are both lavish and cozy.

Glenlivet brags that their tour isn't just about their own whis- ky, but about Speyside production generally, and makes a point to highlight workers who participate every step of the way—from barley farmers to the people who manage the cask-aging process. Glenlivet also prides itself on innovation; for example, the bar dis- penses "cocktail capsules" that dissolve in your mouth with explo- sive flavors. This place is very popular, which means its tours tend to sell out well in advance; book as far ahead as possible on their website. Even if they're already booked up, the rest of the facility is enjoyable enough that fans may still enjoy stopping by just for a browse and dram in the bar.

Cost and Hours: "The Original" 1.5-hour distillery tour and three-whisky tasting costs £20; you can also book a more in-depth tasting (with no tour) for £40, or an "archives" tasting—including a visit to the extensive warehouse—for £100; review options and book on website; daily 10:00-17:00, Oct-April closed Sun-Mon; +44 1340 821 720, www.theglenlivet.com/en. Note: This is just a short detour for those connecting Speyside to Ballater on the scenic route through the mountains (B-9008/A-939).

Cardhu Distillery

This smaller, countryside spot has two claims to fame: First, it was founded by two women (Helen Cumming, who made whisky illegally before it was legit; and her daughter-in-law, Elizabeth, who carried on the tradition). And second, it's the "Speyside home of Johnnie Walker," sending 70 percent of its mature spirit to that big, famous producer. Because Cardhu is a short drive—on twisty, scenic roads—from the main Whisky Trail highway, it feels a bit calmer and more personal. Just above the parking lot, a short walk leads past hairy coos to a statue of Elizabeth Cumming and the Striding Man from the Johnnie Walker logo.

Cost and Hours: £19 includes 1.5-hour tour and three whiskies, plus a cocktail, daily 10:00-17:00, shorter hours in winter, in the village of Cardow, +44 1479 874 635, www.malts.com/en.

Balmoral Castle and Royal Deeside

Royal Deeside—the forested valley of the River Dee—is two sights in one: the Scottish home of the British royal family, wrapped in some of the most gorgeous scenery of Cairngorms National Park. The central spine of this area—a 30-minute stretch between the towns of Ballater and Braemar, with Balmoral Castle right in the middle—feels far from the congestion of the A-9 highway on the other side of the park, yet still fully accessible. It's a splendid place for a walk or a hike.

Driving through the Cairngorms, you'll see pockets of Scots pine (Scotland's national tree). While no longer widespread, these once blanketed the Scottish countryside. In fact, 2,000 years ago, the Romans must have been impressed. They called this land "Caledonia Silva," meaning "wooded land." Driving on, closer to Balmoral, you'll enter a high, treeless moorland with lots of broom plants (what we'd call Scotch broom) and wild thistles (Scotland's national flower).

As you drive, cresting hills to meet vast views, you can imagine royals out on the hunt. (In fact, you'll spot wee huts used by hunters to hide out while they await the stag of their dreams.) The only game you'll likely see is hairy coos and lots of roadkill—mostly rabbit. (Hare today...)

For those who enjoy exploring ruins and coastal scenery, it's worth a speedy detour to Dunnottar Castle on your way south from Ballater and Balmoral.

Getting There: The Royal Deeside works best for **drivers.** Getting here requires a twisty, picturesque mountain drive, either from points south (Edinburgh, Glasgow, Stirling via the summer-only "Snow Roads") or from the north (Inverness and Speyside)—for details, see "Route Tips for Drivers," near the end of this chapter. If you are determined, carless, and patient, **Stagecoach North Scotland bus #201** departs about hourly from Aberdeen and makes frequent stops on its approximately two-hour journey to Ballater; about half of the buses carry on 15 minutes to Balmoral Castle (Crathie stop), then 15 minutes farther to Braemar.

Sights in Royal Deeside

▲▲Balmoral Castle

This 50,000-acre private estate, located within Cairngorms National Park, was Queen Elizabeth II's home for several months of

the year, and where she passed away in September 2022. Outside of royal visits, the grounds and the castle's ballroom are open to visitors. While royalists will enjoy this glimpse into the place where royals unwind, be aware that it's a mainly outdoor visit of the grounds, gardens, and palace exterior; only one room (the ballroom) is open to the public, and that room is rather modest. But for those who enjoy royal sights as well as beautiful nature, it's worth ▲▲.

Cost and Hours: £15, includes audioguide, April-July daily 10:00-17:00, closed Aug-March, arrive at least an hour before closing, café on site, +44 1339 742 534, www.balmoralcastle.com.

Getting There: Balmoral is in the country near the village of Crathie, between the towns of Ballater and Braemar (about 15 minutes' drive from each one). The parking lot is right along the B-976 road that follows the River Dee (£5; parking lot also has a handy post office/shop/visitor information center with WCs downstairs).

Luxury Land Rover Expedition Tours: The royals famously move about their sprawling estate in beefy Land Rovers. If you'd like to follow their example, you can invest in a (very pricey) ranger-led Land Rover "safari" through the grounds; book well in advance

(£300/carload—up to 5, 3 hours, 2/day during the open season, www.balmoralcastle.com).

Background: Queen Victoria and Prince Albert purchased the Balmoral estate in 1848. The thickly forested hills all around reminded Albert of his Thuringian homeland, but Victoria adored it as well—calling it her "Highland paradise." Balmoral Castle was built in the Scottish Baronial style—a romantic, faux-antique look resembling turreted Scottish Renaissance castles from the 16th century—helping to further popularize that look. Victoria felt a particularly strong connection to Scotland—spending a total of eight years of her life here, particularly while she was mourning after Albert's untimely death—and the Scots loved her for it. Ever since, each British monarch has enjoyed retreating to this sprawling property, designed for hunting (red deer) and fishing (salmon). Queen Elizabeth II spent each August through October here, and it was here that she passed away in 2022 at age 96, the realm's longest-reigning monarch. Today Balmoral has a huge staff (including ranger-like fishing and hunting assistants called "ghillies"), 80 miles of roads, a herd of Highland cattle, and a flock of Highland ponies—stout little miniature horses useful for hauling deer carcasses over the hills.

Visiting the Castle: Touring the grounds and ballroom takes about an hour and a half, with audioguide narration, and requires a good bit of level walking.

From the parking lot, walk across the River Dee to reach the ticket booth. You'll receive your audioguide and map, which will lead you on the 10-minute walk to the heart of the palace grounds. When you reach the round deer larder building, you can either follow the audioguide for the full tour around the **grounds** (produce garden, conservatory, garden cottage—all with great palace views—then around the left side of the palace, past the sunken garden, to the ballroom). Or, if the weather's bad, you can cut to the chase and head straight for the **palace.**

As you walk through the produce and flower gardens, ponder the unenviable challenge of trying to time all of the flowers to bloom and the produce to ripen at the same time, coinciding with the royal family's arrival the first week of August (especially difficult given Scotland's notoriously uncooperative climate).

Finally you'll reach the single room in the palace open to the public: the **ballroom.** Its humbleness is a reminder that Balmoral is a private vacation home rather than a state residence designed for pomp and circumstance. And yet, it has a certain understated, rustic charm, with historic paintings and photographs of fond royal vacation memories, and many stag heads mounted on the walls. When the monarch visits, they pull up the carpets (which are here only to protect the hardwoods from the soiled soles of us commoners) and kick off the season with a "Ghillies Ball," in honor of the rugged Scots outdoorsmen who "help" the royals hunt and fish. The ballroom is filled with an exhibition about the palace, which changes each year. You'll likely see some clothing worn by the royals, and there's often a display the miniature automobiles that future kings and queens have enjoyed driving around (such as the miniature 1966 Austin Martin—James Bond-style—and an "American Style Imperial 1" from 1955).

You'll exit out back and head to the sprawling **$ café** (with lots of outdoor tables, and indoor seating under wood rafters). Beyond that you'll reach the **mews,** or stables, with a gigantic gift shop and a couple of small exhibits in the garages—often including a vintage royal Land Rover, as if to remind us that Queen Elizabeth was trained as an auto mechanic during World War II, before she took the throne.

You can walk back to the parking lot the way you came. Or—for a more scenic return—follow the river back.

Nearby: Two more royal landmarks hide out a short walk from the parking lot.

First, just up the hill and across the road (head up the driveway with the read telephone box) is **Crathie Kirk,** the small stony parish church where the royal family worships when they are at Balmoral (interior is often closed).

If you're interested in the story of **John Brown**—the ghillie who became Queen Victoria's trusted companion for decades after Prince Albert's death (as depicted in the film *Mrs. Brown*)—you can find his grave in the kirkyard that surrounds the ruins of St. Manir's Church (which was replaced by the Cathie Kirk in 1804). To find it, head along the small lane (on the Balmoral side of the highway) that curves down just past the post office/shop at the end of the parking lot. John Brown's grave is in the second of the two graveyards. It's roughly in the middle—look for the tall, gray headstone, with a pointed top, that's taller than most others, immediately next to the similarly shaped headstone of his relatives. The inscription reads: "In affectionate and grateful remembrance...the devoted and faithful personal attendant and beloved friend of Queen Victoria." It's said that the queen came here to mourn frequently. In order to do so in privacy, she asked the upper windows of the neighboring house to be frosted...and they still are today.

▲▲Ballater

Ballater (BAH-lah-tur) is the place where you'll feel as much royal-ist sentiment as anywhere in Scotland. For the people of Ballater (many of whom work, either directly or indirectly, with Bal-moral Castle), the Windsors are, simply, their neighbors. Royal connections aside, Ballater is a pleasant, unpretentious, ex-tremely tidy little town. Just big enough to have all the essential tourist services—but neatly nes-tled in the wooded hills of the

Cairngorms, and a bit more "away from it all" than Pitlochry—Ballater is an ideal home base for those wanting to spend a night in this part of Scotland.

It was local springs—which bubbled up supposedly healing waters—that first put Ballater on the map. But the town is what it is today thanks to Queen Victoria and Prince Albert, who bought the nearby Balmoral Castle in 1848, then built a train station in Ballater to access it. Today, the town's best attraction may be its residents, who revel in telling tales of royal encounters. King Charles III, who maintains a private residence at Birkhall (not open to the public), has a particular affection for this part of the Cairngorms. He supports Ballater charities and has been known to show up unannounced at town events...and locals love him for it. ("King Charles is a really nice guy," one of them told me. "Not at all like the chap you see on TV.")

Sights in Ballater

The town's only real sight—the old **train station** built by Queen Victoria to more easily commute to her new summer home at Bal-moral Castle—has been rebuilt after a fire in 2015. Inside is a space shared by the TI and the town library (daily 10:00-17:00). In the back is a fine photographic exhibit telling the story of Victoria and Albert's presence here, and an actual royal train car, permanently parked at the platform. (The line stopped running in 1966.) You can peek in the windows to see the plush sofa, writing desk, and upholstered walls and ceiling.

The other part of the train station is occupied by the **Rothesay Rooms Restaurant,** sponsored by Then-Prince Charles as a charity project after the town suffered devastating floods. They use Queen Victoria's royal waiting room as a private dining hall. This high-end place, which recently relocated here, may not yet be open for your visit; if it is, and if you'd like a splurge, consider a meal here (www.rothesay-rooms.co.uk).

The town is also fun for a wander. Facing the station are two stately sandstone buildings honoring the couple that put this little village on the map: the **Prince Albert Hall** and the **Victoria Hall.** To the left, tucked at the end of the street, find the sweet little **Dee Valley Confectioners,** which produces fudge, chocolate, and all manner of very traditional Scottish candies: clove and rhubarb rock, soor plooms, granny sours, and brandy balls. The shop originally opened in Aberdeen in 1965, but has "only" been here since 1980.

Head out to the **main street** (Bridge Street) and do some window shopping. It's like a British Mayberry. The one block that runs from the train station to the church has virtually everything you could need: cafés, bookstore, clothing, deli, hardware store, optician. Notice that several shops in town boast the coveted seals announcing "By Appointment of his Majesty the King"—meaning that they're authorized to sell their wares directly to the gang at Balmoral.

Follow Bridge Street one block to the left—past the Balmoral Bar, with its turrets that echo its namesake castle—to the unusually fine **parish church** surrounded by an inviting green, with benches, flower gardens, and royal flourishes... like everything in Ballater.

Sleeping in Ballater

The town has several fine B&Bs; given the royal proximity and generally touristy nature of Ballater, prices are high...but so is quality. Many places have "drying rooms" where hikers and hunters can hang up their sopping-wet gear.

$$$ The Auld Kirk—in, you guessed it, an old church (from 1843) right along the main drag into town—has seven rooms, which mingle traditional woodwork and modern flourishes (nicely renovated bathrooms) above a popular café that serves afternoon tea, with sprawling outdoor seating. Forthright Helen runs a very tight ship (family rooms, 31 Braemar Road, +44 1339 755 762, www.theauldkirk.com, info@theauldkirk.com).

$$ No. 45, well and warmly run by Alison, has eight rooms in a classic stone hotel building (from 1880) along the main road into town. The lounges and public spaces feel big and inviting, with Cairngorms charm, and their great breakfast is served in a glassed-in conservatory surrounded by the lovely garden (family rooms, 45

Braemar Road, +44 1339 755 420, +44 7377 342 901, www.no45. co.uk, mail@no45.co.uk).

$$ Gordon Guest House is smack-dab in the center of town. Filling the former home of a bank manager, it sits upstairs over storefronts facing the historic train station and main street. Steve and Beth offer a warm welcome, lots of helpful advice, and a great breakfast in their four rooms. Steve parks his classic Morris cars in the side yard—a great conversation starter (family room, Station Square, +44 7379 164 086, www.thegordonguesthouse.com, info@ thegordonguesthouse.com).

Eating in Ballater

This little town has a nice variety of eateries. For a quick bite, consider one of the cafés along the main drag, Bridge Street (good options include old-school **$ The Bothy** and the more modern **$ Orka**). There's also a handy, long-hours **Co-op grocery store** facing the parish church, and nice tables on the green.

$$$$ Clachan Grill is the town's "destination restaurant" for a high-quality meal. In their smart, classy dining room or out on their inviting patio, they serve modern Scottish cuisine; the menu brags about the provenance of each ingredient. It's worth reserving ahead (Wed-Mon 17:00-21:00, closed Tue, look down a side lane near the bridge at 5 Bridge Square, +44 1339 755 999).

$$ Lochnagar Indian Brasserie, specializing in *balti* but offering a wide variety of Indian dishes, is far better than a small-town curry house deserves to be (on the corner at the back of the church green).

Other places in town solid for a meal include the **$$ Alexandra Hotel** (at the bridge end of town) and **$$ The Balmoral Bar** (right in the center).

BRAEMAR

Deeper in the mountains of the Cairngorms, the town of Braemar (bray-MAR) is famous for hosting Scotland's most famous Highland Games—called the **Braemar Gathering**—which begin the first Sunday in September (www.braemargathering.org). The royals are usually in attendance.

At other times of year, Braemar is also worth a quick wander if you're passing through. Turn off the main road (onto Old Military Road) and cross the bridge over a jagged gorge to discover Braemar's cute, if slightly Disney-esque, town center. The road—lined with over-the-top pubs and Highland swag—leads to the **Braemar Highland Games Centre.** You'll see the various playing fields, surrounded by a giant green grandstand; looking across the field, find the small but lavishly decorated royal box. The Highland Games Pavilion and Exhibition Hall is shared by a **$** café and a small museum about the history of the Braemar Gathering (free, £5 donation suggested, daily 10:00-16:00, www.highlandgamescentre. org). You'll see exhibits on each type of activity—bagpiping, footraces, Highland dancing, and the famous "heavy events"—as well as full Highland regalia from various areas. It's all well described, and may be of interest if you can't see an actual Highland Games.

Braemar Castle, on the edge of town toward Balmoral and Ballater, generally isn't worth a visit.

Note that the **Linn of Dee** hiking area, described in the next section, is near Braemar.

▲▲WALKS AND HIKES IN THE ROYAL DEESIDE

The main reason many people visit this area is for the royal connection. But once here, they realize why the royals love it so much: It's a beautiful landscape, ideal for communing with nature. In case the weather cooperates, I've suggested a few easy-to-appreciate hiking areas below. These options—all within a 15- to 20-minute drive of either Ballater or Braemar—are for people seeking an easy and scenic taste of the Cairngorms. In many cases, the drive is nearly as nice as the hike. Each of these has parking, but you may have to pay (usually around £3; some machines accept credit cards, others only cash). The TIs and shops sell maps, and locals love to give advice. Remember: Weather can change in a hurry. Bring along gear for all weather, plus food, water, and, of course, midge spray. As elsewhere in Scotland, Walkhighlands (www.walkhighlands.co.uk) is a great resource for hiking tips.

Near Ballater

The town of Ballater itself can be an enjoyable place to stroll. The TI loves to tell about the **Seven Bridges Hike** that rambles up and down the River Dee around Ballater, plus a short detour up to Knock Castle (mostly level, figure about six miles and three hours—or do just part of the walk). Or, drive a few minutes out of town for one of the options below.

Muir of Dinnet National Nature Reserve

A 10-minute drive east of Ballater takes you to this nature reserve, with some easy and pleasant (if not quite spectacular) nature walks. And it comes with a fun little roadside stopover: Leave town on the A-93 (Ballater Road). After four miles, you'll approach the turnoff on the left for B-9119 to the nature reserve. But just before turning off, watch on the right side of the road for an old **AA call box.** Pull over here and open the door to the call box to discover a fun and whimsical mini-museum of AA roadside assistance (Britain's equivalent of the AAA). Back in the day, AA members had a little emblem affixed to their automobile. And if an AA employee saw that emblem drive by, they were required to stop and salute.

Turning off on B-9119, it's just another mile or so to the **Muir of Dinnet** parking lot. For an easy, rewarding hike, take the **Burn O'Vat trail** (a less than one-mile loop, only a short uphill stretch): Follow the burn (brook) up to the waterfall, where you can (carefully) carry on over some big rocks and through a big hole in the cliff to reach the "vat"—a nearly enclosed space tucked back away from the trail. Then backtrack to the bridge, cross it, climb up to the ridge, and circle back to your car; along the way, a viewing platform overlooks a nearby loch.

For a more ambitious walk at Muir of Dinnet, you can try the **Parkin's Moss Trail,** a two-mile, 1.5-hour loop that follows a boardwalk over a bog—offering a close-up look at this distinct ecosystem.

Tomnaverie Stone Circle

A visit to this stone circle, capping a hill overlooking Cairngorms scenery, combines well with the Muir of Dinnet. (It's not much of a "hike," but the views are grand). You'll find it on the B-9094, a scenic back road about a 15-minute drive northeast of Ballater (from Muir of Dinnet, continue on the B-9119, and then turn right onto the B-9094). Driving past, keep a close eye out for the official parking lot. From here, you can walk up the gravel path to see an evocative stone circle on the summit of a wee hill. Notice that the main stone is "recumbent" (lying on its side, almost like an altar)—which is typical for stone circles only in this northeastern part of Scotland. It lines up with Lochnagar peak on the horizon, surrounded by heather, rolling hills, and cute villages. On the adjacent hill, you may notice a modern structure. This is venting for an underground nuclear bunker.

Above Ballater: Loch Muick and Lochnagar

This is the granddaddy of area hikes, and the place that really has you feeling above it all. Lochnagar, at 3,789 feet, is the peak that you can see (sometimes) on the horizon from Ballater; Loch Muick is the two-mile-long loch that sits at its base. While officially part of the sprawling Balmoral Estate, this area is just a 15- to 20-minute drive above Ballater's town center. (Note that the parking lot can fill up; on busy days, try to arrive early.)

The drive can be worthwhile for the scenery alone: At the east end of town, go over the bridge, turn right on the B-976, and head into the settlement called Bridge of Muick. Here the main road bends right, but you'll carry on straight, following *Glen Muick* signs. From here, the road follows the River Muick, narrows to single-track, and heads up, up, up for seven miles. The last half is through classic, remote Cairngorms moorland, a wild landscape with scrubby heather fringing bald mountains. You'll arrive at a parking lot near the settlement called Spittal of Glenmuick. (As you're on Balmoral Estate property, the parking is pricey.)

From the parking lot, you have a few hiking choices. The simplest option is the **Lochend hike** (about 3 miles and 1.5 hours), which loops along the edge of Loch Muick and past the small hunting settlement called Allt-na-guibhsaich (with the trailhead to Lochnagar).

For a longer walk, the **Loch Muick Circuit**—all the way around the loch—is about eight miles (figure 3.5 hours). En route, you'll pass the remote stone hunting lodge called Glas-Allt-Shiel. After Prince Albert's death, Queen Victoria wanted to escape into nature but couldn't bear staying at Allt-na-guibhsaich...so this became her Loch Muick home.

And for an even more ambitious hike, you could do the demanding **summit of Lochnagar,** which requires 12 miles and about seven hours (with a gain of about 3,000 feet)—with commanding views over Loch Muick and this scenic stretch of the Cairngorms.

Near Balmoral

Because the area around Balmoral Castle is a private estate, there's less hiking here than you might hope. One good option is the **Balmoral Cairns Walk,** a six-mile, three-hour, moderately strenuous hike that connects various cairns (stone-stacked monuments)—each one dedicated to important events in the lives of Queen Victoria, Prince Albert, or their children. As this is not well marked, it's important to get clear instructions before heading out (check Walkhighlands.com for tips and map).

Linn of Dee (near Braemar)

While farther from Ballater, this thickly forested, riverside natural area offers a nice excuse to also check out the town of Braemar (which you'll pass through to get here). From the big roundabout just below the Braemar Highland Games Centre, follow brown signs to *Linn of Dee* and follow the country road about six miles (15 minutes) to the nature reserve. The road takes you over a beautiful stretch of the River Dee as it runs through a wide valley. The landscape grows rocky and you cross a stone bridge over a narrow and very scenic gorge where the Dee squeezes between jagged cliffs. Just beyond is the pay parking lot at the Mar Lodge Estate. From here, two handy walks are well-signposted: Yellow signs outline an easy, half-mile loop down to the riverside for a view of the gorge and bridge, then back up again; blue signs send you on a longer, 1.75-mile loop that follows the river farther, and detours up along a smaller stream. For a quick, satisfying visit, you could start out on the shorter trail and then follow the longer one along the river, as long as time and stamina permit, before heading back to your car. This is a popular area to look for wildlife, from birds to red squirrels (which don't sound all that exciting...until you spot one).

ROUTE TIPS FOR DRIVERS

If connecting south to **Stirling, Edinburgh, or Glasgow,** you'll take the super-scenic "Snow Roads"—the highest public road in Great Britain (A-93 via Perth; the Braemar-Blairgowrie stretch is particularly striking). You'll notice roadside ski centers with lifts designed to get Scots high into the mountains for winter sports. Red-and-white striped poles along the side of the road help measure snowfall. The highest point, at 2,199 feet, is Cairnwell Pass; a nearby old road, with a treacherous hairpin turn, is called the "Devil's Elbow"—thankfully, the main road has been straightened out.

If connecting north to **Inverness,** it makes sense to go by way of the Speyside whisky country—take A-939 north from Ballater (following signs to Tomintoul), then turn off on B-9008 to Duff-town. The Glenlivet distillery is just a short detour from this route.

Either of these routes takes you over high-altitude moor scenery, with views of distant, sleepy valleys, castles, and manor houses—vintage Cairngorms.

If you're traveling along Scotland's east coast—between Aberdeen and Dundee (or St. Andrews) on A-90—you'll go right past Dunnottar Castle (described next) near the town of Stonehaven. From here, it's a one-hour drive to Ballater.

Aberdeenshire Coast

▲Dunnottar Castle

The mostly ruined and empty castle of Dunnottar (duh-NAW-tur) owns a privileged position: clinging to the top of a bulbous bluff, flanked by pebbly beaches and surrounded nearly 360 degrees by the North Sea. It's scenic and strategic. From the parking lot, you'll walk five minutes to a fork: To the right, you'll come to a ridge with a panoramic view of the castle's fine setting; to the left, you'll hike steeply down (almost all the way to the beach), then steeply back up, to the castle itself. Inside, there's not much to see. The only important thing that happened here was the Battle for the Honours of Scot-

EASTERN SCOTLAND

land, when the Scottish crown jewels were briefly hidden away in the castle from Oliver Cromwell's army, which laid siege to Dunnottar (unsuccessfully) for three days. But don't worry too much about the history, or the scant posted descriptions—just explore the stately ruins while enjoying the panoramic views, sea spray, and cry of the gulls.

Cost and Hours: The photo-op view is free (and enough for many); entering the castle costs £9.50, daily 9:00-18:00, shorter hours Oct-March, +44 1569 762 173, www.dunnottarcastle.co.uk.

Getting There: It's just off the busy A-90 expressway, which runs parallel to the coast between Aberdeen and Dundee; exit for Stonehaven, and you'll find Dunnottar well signed just to the south.

Nearby: Dunnottar sits just beyond **Stonehaven,** a pleasant, workaday seafront town that's a handy place to stretch your legs or grab some lunch (big pay parking lot right in the town center, ringed by eateries and grocery stores).

NORTHERN SCOTLAND

Wester Ross & the North Coast • Orkney Islands

Scotland's far north is its rugged and desolate "Big Sky Country"—with towering mountains, vast and moody moors, achingly desolate glens, and a jagged coastline peppered with silver-sand beaches. Far less discovered than the big destinations to the south, this is where you can escape the crowds and touristy "tartan tat" of the Edinburgh-Stirling-Oban-Inverness rut, and get a picturesque corner of Scotland all to yourself.

The area is tied together by a heavily promoted driving route called the North Coast 500 (NC-500)—Scotland's answer to Iceland's Ring Road or America's Route 66. This 516-mile loop drive—beginning and ending in Inverness—ties together the destinations in this chapter, except Orkney (which is a ferry ride away). You can buy maps and guidebooks that outline and narrate the route in local bookstores, and the official website www.north-coast500.com. But whether or not you stick strictly to the official route, this stunning swath of Scotland is ideal for a meandering road trip. Even on a sunny summer weekend, you may not pass another car for miles. It's just you and the Munro baggers. There's no real "destination" in the north (other than Orkney)—it's all about the journey.

This chapter covers the area north of the Isle of Skye and Inverness: the scenic west coast (called Wester Ross) and the sandy north coast; plus the fascinating Orkney archipelago just offshore from Britain's northernmost point.

Fully exploring northern Scotland takes some serious time. The roads are narrow, twisty, and slow, and the pockets of civilization are few and far between. With two weeks or less in Scotland, this area doesn't make the cut (except maybe Orkney). But if you have time to linger, and you appreciate desolate scenery and an end-of-the-world feeling, the untrampled north is worth considering.

Even on a shorter visit, Orkney may be alluring for adventurous travelers seeking a contrast to the rest of Scotland. The islands' claims to fame—astonishing prehistoric sites, Old Norse (Norwegian) heritage, and recent history as a WWI and WWII naval base—combine to spur travelers' imaginations.

PLANNING YOUR TIME

For a scenic loop through this area, try this four-day plan, which hits most of the official North Coast 500 stops (except the 60-mile overland stretch between Inverness and Loch Carron). For some, this may be a borderline-unreasonable amount of driving, on twisty, challenging, often one-lane roads (especially on days 1 and 2). Connecting Skye or Glencoe to Ullapool takes a full day. If you don't have someone to split the time behind the wheel, or if you want to really slow down, consider adding another overnight to break up the trip.

Day 1 From the Isle of Skye, drive up the west coast (including the Applecross detour, if time permits), overnighting in Torridon or Ullapool.

Day 2 Continue the rest of the way up the west coast, then trace the north coast from west to east, catching the late-afternoon ferry to Orkney. Overnight in tidy Kirkwall (2 nights).

Day 3 Spend all day on Orkney.

Day 4 Take the ferry from Orkney back to the mainland; with enough time and interest, squeeze in a visit to John O'Groats before driving three hours back to Inverness (on the relatively speedy A-9).

Planning Tips: To reach Orkney most efficiently—without the slow-going west-coast scenery—consider zipping up on a flight (easy and frequent from Inverness, Edinburgh, or Aberdeen), or make good time on the A-9 highway from Inverness up to Thurso (figure 3 hours one-way) to catch the ferry.

Without a car I'd skip this area. (It's very slow to traverse this area by bus.) If you're flying to Orkney, consider renting a car for your time here.

Wester Ross & the North Coast

North of the Isle of Skye, Scotland's scenic Wester Ross coast (the western part of the region of Ross), is remote, sparsely populated, mountainous, and slashed with jagged "sea lochs." (That's "inlets" in American English, or "fjords" in Norwegian.) After seeing Wester Ross' towering peaks, you'll understand why George R.R. Martin named the primary setting of his *Game of Thrones* epic "Westeros."

The area is a big draw for travelers seeking stunning views without the crowds—though it's slowly becoming more well known as the most dramatic stretch of the North Coast 500. For casual visitors, the views in Glencoe and on the Isle of Skye are much more accessible and just as good as what you'll find farther north. But diehards enjoy getting away from it all in Wester Ross.

Scotland's 100-mile-long north coast, which stretches from Cape Wrath in the northwest corner to John O'Groats in the northeast, is gently scenic, but less dramatic than Wester Ross. Views in this region are dominated by an alternating array of moors and rugged coastline. This is a good place to make up the long miles of Wester Ross.

Scenic Drives in the North

This section outlines three drives that, when combined, take you along this region's west and north coasts. The first Wester Ross leg (from Eilean Donan Castle to Ullapool) is the most scenic, with a fine variety of landscapes—but not many towns—along the way. The next Wester Ross leg gets you to Scotland's northwest corner and the town of Durness. The final leg sweeps you across the north coast, to John O'Groats.

PLANNING YOUR DRIVE

Note that the route I've described here—if you take all of the optional scenic detours—covers about 325 miles of the full North Coast 500 loop (plus another 120 miles as you zip from John O'Groats back to Inverness).

Northern Scotland

40 Kilometers

40 Miles

Westray

Rousay

SCOTLAND

• Inverness

⊛ Edinburgh

ENGLAND

North Atlantic Ocean

See Orkney Islands detail map

Mainland

SKARA BRAE 🏰 Kirkwall

Stromness

Hoy

Scapa Flow

Orkney Islands

Pentland Firth

Cape Wrath

Smoo Cave

Dunnet Head

Scabster

Gills

John O'Groats

Durness

Thurso

MEY

Kyle of Durness →

Loch Eriboll

A-836

Halkirk

Wick

A-838

Tongue

A-99

Loch Glendhu

Scourie •

A-894

Kinbrace •

A-9

B-869

Kyleksu

ARDVRECK

A-836

The Minch

Lochinver •

Inchnadamph

Helmsdale •

Loch Assynt

A-835

Loch Shin

Knockan Crag

DUNROBIN

Brora

INVEREWE GARDENS

Strathcanaird

Lairg •

Golspie •

Ardmare •

Ullapool

North Sea

A-832

Loch Broom

Braemore

Dornoch •

Poolewe

Loch Maree

A-835

Alness •

A-9

Moray Firth

Elgin •

Gairloch •

W E S T E R   R O S S

Loch Torridon

Kinlochwe

Dingwall •

Nairn •

CAWDOR

Achnasheen

Torridon

A-890

Inverness

CULLODEN BATTLEFIELD

Speyside

Applecross •

APPLECROSS ROAD

A-82

CLAVA CAIRNS

A-95

Loch Carron

EILEAN DONAN

URQUHART

Loch Ness

A-9

A-939

Kyle •

Dornie

Ballater •

Isle of Skye

Kyleakin

A-87

Fort Augusta

Aviemore •

• Mallaig

CALEDONIAN CANAL

Laggan •

Newtonmore •

BALMORAL

A-830

NORTHERN SCOTLAND

   If you want just a taste of this rugged landscape—without going farther north—you can drive the Wester Ross coastline almost as far as Ullapool, then turn off on the A-835 for a quick one-hour drive to Inverness.

   In this region, roads are twisty and often only a single lane, so don't judge a drive by its mileage alone. Allow plenty of extra time.

EILEAN DONAN CASTLE TO ULLAPOOL

This long drive, worth ▲▲, connects the picture-perfect island castle of Eilean Donan to the humble fishing village of Ullapool, the logical halfway point up the coast. Figure about 130 miles and nearly a full day for this drive, plus another 20 slow-going miles if you take the Applecross detour (described below).

From the A-87, a few miles east of Kyle of Lochalsh (and the Skye Bridge), follow signs for the A-890 north toward *Lochcarron*. (Note that **Eilean Donan Castle** is just a couple of miles farther east from this turnoff; for details see page 116). From here on out, carefully track the brown *Wester Ross Coastal Trail* signs.

Follow the A-890 as it cuts across a hilly spine, then twists down and runs alongside **Loch Carron.** At the end of the loch, just after the village of Strathcarron, you'll reach a T-intersection. Turn left, following the A-896 and signs for *Lochcarron*. This is also where you pick up the official North Coast 500/NC-500 driving loop. From here, you'll follow the opposite bank of Loch Carron. (For the faster route to Ullapool—which skips much of the best scenery, take a right at the T-intersection, which brings you to the A-890, toward Inverness.)

Applecross Detour: Soon after you pull away from the loch-side, you'll cross over a high meadow and see a well-marked turnoff on the left for a super-scenic—but challenging—alternate route: the **Applecross Road,** over a pass called Bealach na Bà (Gaelic for "Pass of the Cattle"). Intimidating signs suggest a much more straightforward alternate route that keeps you on the A-896 straight up to Loch Torridon (if doing this, skip down to the  "Loch Torridon" section, later). But if you're relatively comfortable negotiating steep switchbacks, and have time to spare (adding about 20 miles to the total journey), this road is drivable. You'll twist up, up, up—hearing your engine struggle up gradients of up to 20 per-cent—and finally over, with rugged-moonscape views over peaks and lochs. From the summit (at 2,053 feet), the jagged mountains rising from the sea are the Cuillin Hills on the Isle of Skye. Finally, you'll corkscrew back down the other side, arriving at the humble seafront town of Applecross.

Once in **Applecross,** you could either return over the same pass to pick up the A-896 (slightly faster), or, for a meandering but very scenic route that sticks with the NC-500, carry on all the way around the northern headland of the peninsula. This provides you with further views of Raasay and Skye, through a deserted-feeling landscape on one-lane roads. Then, turning the corner at the top of the peninsula, you'll begin to drive above Loch Torridon, with some of the finest views on this drive.

Loch Torridon: Whether you take the Applecross detour or the direct route, you'll wind up at the stunning sea loch called **Loch Torridon**—hemmed in by thickly forested pine-covered hills, it resembles the Rockies. You'll pass through an idyllic fjord-side town, Shieldaig, then cross over a finger of land and plunge deeper into Upper Loch Torridon. Near the end of the loch,  keep an eye out for **The Torridon**—a luxurious lochfront grand hotel with gorgeous Victorian Age architecture, a café serving afternoon tea, and expensive rooms (www.thetorridon.com).

As you loop past the far end of the loch—with the option to turn off for the village of **Torridon** (which has a good youth hostel, www.hostellingscotland.org.uk)—the landscape has shifted dramatically, from pine-covered hills to a hauntingly desolate glen. You'll cut through this valley—bookended by towering peaks and popular with hikers—before reaching the town of Kinlochewe.

At Kinlochewe, take the A-832 west (following *Ullapool* signs from here on out), and soon you'll be tracing the bonnie, bonnie banks of **Loch Maree**—considered by many connoisseurs to be one of Scotland's finest lochs. You'll see campgrounds, nature areas, and scenic pullouts as you make good time on the speedy two-lane lochside road. (The best scenery is near the beginning, so don't put off that photo op.)

Nearing the end of Loch Maree, the road becomes single-track again as you twist up over another saddle of scrubby land. On the other side, you'll get glimpses of Gair Loch through the trees, before finally arriving at the little harbor of **Gairloch.** Just beyond the harbor, where the road straightens out as it follows the coast, keep an eye out (on the right) for the handy Gale Center. Run as a charity, it has WCs, a small café with treats baked by locals, a fine shop of books and crafts, and comfortable tables and couches for taking a break (www.galeactionforum.co.uk).

NORTHERN SCOTLAND

True to its name, Gair Loch ("Short Loch") doesn't last long, and soon you'll head up a hill (keep an eye out for the pullout on the left, offering fine views over the village). The next village is Polewe, on **Loch Ewe.** Just after the village, on the left, is the **Inverewe Gardens.** These beautiful gardens, run by the

National Trust for Scotland, were the pet project of Osgood Mackenzie, who in 1862 began transforming 50 acres of his lochside estate into a subtropical paradise. The warming Gulf Stream and—in some places—stout stone walls help make this oasis possible. If you have time and need to stretch your legs from all that shifting, spend an hour wandering its sprawling grounds. The walled garden, near the entrance, is a highlight, with each bed thoughtfully labeled (£13, closed Nov-March, www.nts.org.uk).

Continuing on the A-832 toward Ullapool, you'll stay above Loch Ewe, then briefly pass above the open ocean. Soon you'll find yourself following **Little Loch Broom** (with imposing mountains on your right). At the end of that loch, you'll carry on straight and work your way past a lush strip of farmland at the apex of the loch. Soon you'll meet the big A-835 highway; turn left and take this speedy road the rest of the way into Ullapool. (Or you can turn right to zip on the A-835 all the way to Inverness—just an hour away.) Whew!

Ullapool

A gorgeously set, hardworking town of about 1,500 people, Ullapool (ulla-PEWL) is what passes for a metropolis in Wester Ross. Its most prominent feature is its big, efficient ferry dock, connecting the mainland with Stornoway on the Isle of Lewis (Scotland's biggest, in the Outer Hebrides). Facing the dock is a strip of cute little houses, today housing restaurants, shops, B&Bs, and residences. Behind the waterfront,

the town is only a few blocks deep—you can get the lay of the land in a few minutes' stroll. Curving around the back side of the town—along a big, grassy campground—is an inviting rocky beach, facing across the loch in one direction and out toward the open sea in the other.

Orientation to Ullapool: Ullapool has several handy services for travelers. An excellent **bookshop** is a block up, straight ahead from the ferry dock. Many services line Argyle Street, which runs parallel to the harbor one block up the hill: the **TI** is to the right, while a Bank of Scotland **ATM** and the **post office** are to the left. On this same street, the town runs a fine little **museum** with well-done exhibits about local history (closed Sun and Nov-March, www.ullapoolmuseum.co.uk). This street, nicknamed "Art-gyle Street," also has a smattering of local art **galleries.**

Sleeping in Ullapool: Several guesthouses line the harborfront Shore Street, including **$ Waterside House** (3 rooms, minimum two-night stay in peak season, https://waterside.uk.net) and the town's official **¢ youth hostel** (closed Nov-March, www.hostellingscotland.org.uk).

Eating in Ullapool: The two most reliable places are the **$$ Ceilidh Place,** on West Argyle Street a block above the harbor (www.theceilidhplace.com); and **$$$ The Arch Inn,** facing the water a half-block from the ferry dock (www.thearchinn.co.uk). Both have a nice pubby vibe as well as sit-down dining rooms with a focus on locally caught seafood. Both also rent rooms and frequently host live music. For a quick meal, two **$ chippies** (around the corner from each other, facing the ferry dock) keep the breakwater promenade busy with al fresco budget diners and happy seagulls.

ULLAPOOL TO THE NORTH COAST

This shorter drive, worth ▲, connects one quaint seaside town (Ullapool) to another (Durness—on the north coast) through rolling hills sprinkled with wee lochs and the dramatic landscape. Expect this drive (about 70 miles) to take another couple scenic hours, depending on your sightseeing stops.

Leaving Ullapool, follow signs that read simply *North (A-835)*. You'll pass through the cute little beachside village of **Ardmair,** then pull away from the coast.

About 15 minutes after leaving Ullapool, just after you exit the village of Strathcanaird and head uphill, watch on the left for a pullout with a handy orientation panel describing the panorama of **towering peaks** that line the road. It looks like a mossy Monument Valley. Enjoy the scenery for about four more miles—surrounded by lochs and gigantic peaks—and watch for the **Knockan Crag** visitors center, above you on the right, with exhibits on local geology, flora, and fauna and suggestions for area hikes (unmanned and open daily 24 hours, WCs, www.nnr.scot).

Continuing north along the A-835, you'll soon pass out of the region of Ross and Cromarty and enter Sutherland. At the T-intersection, turn left for *Kylesku* and *Lochinver* (on the A-837). From here on out, you can start following the *North & West Highlands Tourist Route;* you'll also see your first sign for John O'Groats at the northeastern corner of Scotland (152 miles away).

You'll roll through moors, surrounded on all sides by hills. Just after the barely there village of Inchnadamph, keep an eye out on the left for the ruins of

Ardvrech Castle, which sits in crumbled majesty upon its own little island in Loch Assynt, connected to the world by a narrow sandy spit. Just after these ruins, you'll have another choice: For the fastest route to the north coast, turn right to follow A-894 (toward *Kylesku* and *Durness*). If you have some time to spare, you could stick with the NC-500 route and carry on straight to scenically follow Loch Assynt toward the sleepy fishing village of **Lochinver** (12 miles). After seeing the village, you could go back the way you came to the main road, or continue along the NC-500 route all the way around the little peninsula on the B-869, passing several appealing sandy beaches and villages.

Back on the main A-894, you'll pass through an almost lunar landscape, with peaks all around, finally emerging at the gorgeous, mountain-rimmed **Loch Glendhu,** which you'll cross on a stout modern bridge. From here, it's a serene landscape of rock, heather, and ferns, with occasional glimpses of the coast—such as at **Scourie,** with a particularly nice sandy beach. Finally (after the road becomes A-838—keep left at the fork, toward *Durness*), you'll head up, over, and through a vast and dramatic glen. At the end of the glen, you'll start to see sand below you on the left; this is **Kyle of Durness,** which goes on for miles. You'll see the turnoff for the ferry to Cape Wrath, then follow tidy stone walls the rest of the way into **Durness.**

THE NORTH COAST

This driving route—which sticks with the official NC-500 the whole way—takes you along the picturesque, remote north coast from west (Durness village) to east (the touristy town of John O'Groats). Allow at least 2.5 hours for this 90-mile drive (add more time for stops along the way).

Durness Town

This beachy village of cow meadows is delightfully perched on a bluff above sandy shores. This area has a different feel from Wester Ross—it's more manicured, with tidy farms hemmed in by neatly stacked stone walls. There's not much to see or do in the town, but there is a 24-hour gas station (gas up now—this is your last chance for a while...trust me) and a handy TI (by the big parking lot with an electric-car charging station, on the east end of town, +44 1971 509 005).

Head east out of the village on the A-838, watching for brown signs on your right to *Durness Village Hall.* Pull over here to stroll through the small **memorial garden for John Lennon,** who enjoyed his boyhood vacations in Durness.

Just after the village hall, on the left, pull over at **Smoo Cave** (free WCs in parking lot). Its goofy-sounding name comes from the Old Norse *smúga,* for "cave." (Many places along the north coast—which had a strong Viking influence—have Norse rather than Gaelic or Anglo-Saxon place names.) It's free to hike down the well-marked stairs to a protected cove, where an  underground river has carved a deep cave into the bluff. Walk inside the cave to get a free peek at the waterfall; for a longer visit, you can pay for a 20-minute boat trip and guided walk (unnecessary for most; sign up at the mouth of the cave).

Back on the road, soon after Smoo Cave, on the left, is the gorgeous **Ceannabeinne Beach** (Gaelic for "End of the Mountains"). Of the many Durness-area beaches, this is the locals' favorite.

Durness to Thurso

Heading east from the Durness area, you'll traverse many sparsely populated miles—long roads that cut in and out from the coast, with scrubby moorland and distant peaks on the other side. You'll emerge at the gigantic **Loch Eriboll,** which you'll circumnavigate—passing lamb farms and crumbling stone walls—to continue your way east. Leaving this fjord, you'll cut through some classic fjord scenery until you finally pop out at the scenic **Kyle of Tongue.** You'll cross over the big, modern bridge, then twist up through the village of Tongue and continue your way eastward (the A-838 becomes the A-836)—through more of the same scrubby moorland scenery. Make good time for the next 40 lonely miles. Notice how many place names along here use the term "strath"—a wide valley (as opposed to a narrower "glen"), such

as where jagged mountains open up to the sea.

Finally—after going through little settlements like Bettyhill and Melvich—the moors begin to give way to working farms as you approach Thurso. The main population center of northern Scotland (pop. 8,000), Thurso is a functional transit hub with a charming old core. As you face out to sea, the heavily industrialized point on the left is **Scrabster,** with the easiest ferry crossing to Orkney (for details, see "Getting to Orkney," later).

Several sights near Thurso are worth the extra couple miles.

Dunnet Head: About eight miles east of Thurso (following brown *John O'Groats* signs on the A-836) is the village of Dunnet. If you have time for some rugged scenery, turn off here to drive the four miles (each way) to the Dunnet Head peninsula.

While John O'Groats is often dubbed "Britain's northernmost point," Dunnet Head pokes up just a bit farther. And, while it lacks the too-cute signpost marking distances to faraway landmarks, views from here are better than from John O'Groats. Out at the tip of Dunnet Head, a lonely lighthouse enjoys panoramic views across the Pentland Firth to Orkney, while a higher vantage point is just up the hill. Keep an eye out for seabirds, including puffins.

Mary-Ann's Cottage: In the village of Dunnet, between the main road and Dunnet Head, this little stone house explains traditional crofting lifestyles. It appears just as it was when 92-year-old Mary-Ann Calder moved out in 1990 (closed Oct-May, very limited hours).

Castle of Mey: About four miles east of Mary-Ann's Cottage (on the main A-836) is the Castle of Mey. The Queen Mother grew up at Glamis Castle, but after her daughter became Queen Elizabeth II, she purchased and renovated this sprawling property as an escape from the bustle of royal life...and you couldn't get much farther from civilization than this. For nearly 50 years, the Queen Mum stayed here for

annual visits in August and October. Today it welcomes visitors to tour its homey interior and 30 acres of manicured gardens (closed Oct-April, www.castleofmey.org.uk).

From Mey, it's another six miles east to John O'Groats. About halfway there, in Gills Bay, is another ferry dock for cars heading to Orkney (see "Getting to Orkney," later).

John O'Groats

A total tourist trap that's somehow also genuinely stirring, John O'Groats marks the northeastern corner of the Isle of Britain—bookending the country with Land's End, 874 miles to the southwest in Cornwall. People enjoy traversing the length of Britain by motorcycle, by bicycle, or even by foot (it takes about eight weeks to trudge along the "E2E" trail—that's "End to End"). And upon arrival, whether they've walked for two months or just driven up for the day from Inverness, everyone wants to snap a "been there, done that" photo with the landmark signpost. Surrounding that is a huge parking lot, a souvenir stand masquerading as a TI, and lots of tacky "first and last" shops and restaurants. Orkney looms just off the coast.

Nearby: The real target of "End to End" pilgrims isn't the signpost, but the **Duncansby Head Lighthouse**—about two miles to the east, it's the actual northeasternmost point, with an even more end-of-the-world vibe. (By car, head away from the John O'Groats area on A-99, and watch for the Duncansby Head turnoff on the left, just past the Seaview Hotel.) If you have time for a hike, about a mile south of the lighthouse are the **Duncansby Stacks**—dramatic sea stacks rising up above a sandy beach.

RETURNING TO INVERNESS

Compared to the rest of this drive, the 120-mile route back to Inverness is speedy, straightforward, and anticlimactic: From John O'Groats, meander south along the A-99, through the town of Wick; in Latheron, you'll pick up the A-9, which zips south to Inverness. (If you're coming back on the Orkney ferry to Thurso, you can cut the corner by taking the A-9 overland from there.) Enjoy the gentle seaside scenery on your way down.

Dunrobin Castle: The picturesque traditional home of Clan Sutherland is a worthwhile stop. This huge, French-château-style castle—"the largest house in the Highlands," has 189 rooms, gardens, a museum, and a falconry show (closed Nov-March, 50 miles north of Inverness just outside Golspie, www.dunrobincastle.co.uk).

The Orkney Islands

The Orkney Islands, perched just an hour's ferry ride north of the mainland, are uniquely remote, historic, and—for the right traveler—well worth the effort.

Crossing the 10-mile Pentland Firth separating Orkney from northern Scotland, you leave the Highlands behind and enter a new world. With no real tradition for clans, tartans, or bagpipes, Orkney feels not "Highlander" or even "Scottish," but Orcadian (as locals are called). Though Orkney was inhabited by Picts from the sixth century BC, during most of its formative history—from 875 all the way until 1468—it was a prized trading hub of the Norwegian realm, giving it a feel more Scandinavian than Celtic. The Vikings (who sailed from Norway, just 170 miles away) left their mark, both literally (runes carved into prehistoric stone monuments) and culturally: Many place names are derived from Old Norse, and the Orkney flag looks like the Norwegian flag with a few yellow accents.

There are other historic connections. In later times, Canada's Hudson's Bay Company recruited many Orcadians to staff its outposts. And given its status as the Royal Navy headquarters during both World Wars, Orkney remains one of the most pro-British corners of Scotland. In the 2014 independence referendum, Orkney cast the loudest "no" vote in the entire country (67 percent against).

Orkney's landscape is also a world apart: Aside from some dramatic sea cliffs hiding along its perimeter, the main island is mostly flat and bald, with few trees, the small town of Kirkwall, and lots of tidy farms with gently mooing cows. While the blustery weather (which can change several times a day) keeps the vegetation on the scrubby side, for extra greenery each town has a sheltered community garden run by volunteers. Orkney's fine sandy beaches seem always empty—as if lying on them will give you hypothermia. Sparsely populated, the islands have no traffic lights and most roads are single lane with "passing places" politely spaced as necessary.

Today's economy is based mostly on North Sea oil, renewable energy, and fishing. The boats you'll see are creel boats with nets and cages to collect crabs, lobsters, scallops, and oysters. Unless a cruise ship drops by, tourism seems to be secondary.

For the sightseer, Orkney has two draws unmatched elsewhere in Scotland: It has some of the finest prehistoric sites in northern Europe, left behind by an advanced Stone Age civilization that flourished here. And the harbor called Scapa Flow has fascinating remnants of its important military role during the World Wars—from intentional shipwrecks designed to seal off the harbor, to muscular Churchill-built barriers to finish the job a generation later.

Orientation to Orkney

Orkney (as the entire archipelago is called) is made up of 70 islands, with a total population of 24,500. The main island—with the primary town (Kirkwall) and ferry ports connecting Orkney to northern Scotland (Stromness and St. Margaret's Hope)—is called, confusingly, Mainland. (It just goes to show you: One man's island is another man's mainland.)

PLANNING YOUR TIME

Orkney merits at least two nights and one full day. Some people (especially WWII aficionados) spend days exploring Orkney, but I've focused on the main sights to see in a short visit—all on the biggest island.

The only town of any substance, Kirkwall is your best home base. You can see its sights in a few hours (a town stroll, the fine Orkney Museum, and its striking cathedral). From there, to see the best of Orkney in a single day, plan on driving about 70 miles, looping out from Kirkwall in two directions: Spend the morning at the prehistoric sites (Maeshowe and nearby sites, Skara Brae), and the afternoon driving along the Churchill Barriers and visiting the Italian Chapel.

Cruise Crowds: Orkney is Scotland's busiest cruise port; on days when ships are in port, normally sleepy destinations can be jammed. Check the cruise schedule (www.orkneyharbours.com) and plan accordingly to avoid busy times at popular sights (such as Skara Brae and the Italian Chapel).

NORTHERN SCOTLAND

Orkney Islands

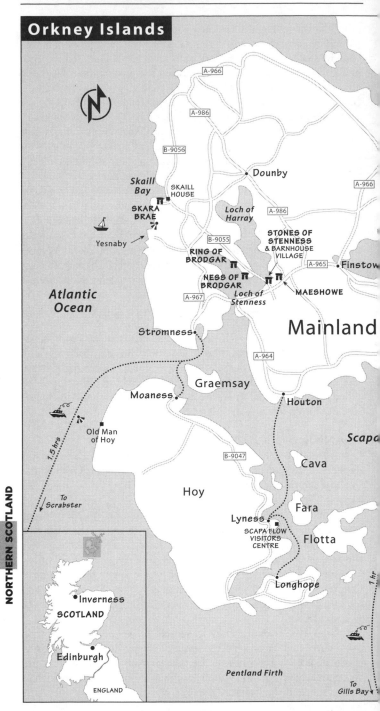

A-966

A-986

B-9056

Dounby

A-966

Skaill
Bay

SKAILL
HOUSE

Loch of
Harray

A-986

SKARA
BRAE

STONES OF
STENNESS
& BARNHOUSE
VILLAGE

Yesnaby

RING OF
BRODGAR

B-9055

A-965

Finstow

NESS OF
BRODGAR

A-967

Loch of
Stenness

MAESHOWE

Atlantic
Ocean

Mainland

Stromness

A-964

Graemsay

Moaness

Houton

Scapa

1.5 hrs

Old Man
of Hoy

Cava

To
Scrabster

B-9047

Hoy

Fara

Lyness

SCAPA FLOW
VISITORS
CENTRE

Flotta

1 hr

NORTHERN SCOTLAND

Longhope

Inverness

SCOTLAND

Edinburgh

Pentland Firth

To
Gills Bay

ENGLAND

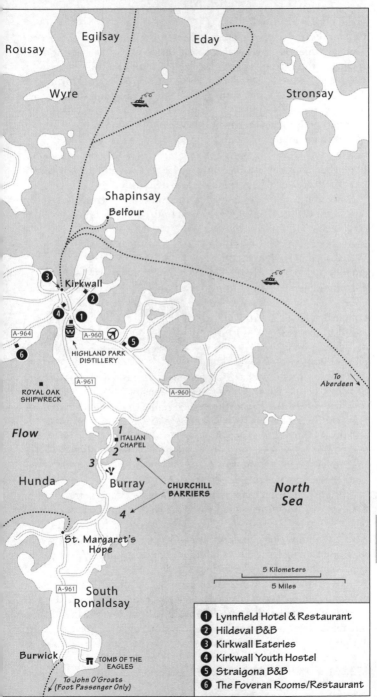

Rousay

Egilsay

Eday

Wyre

Stronsay

Shapinsay

Belfour

3 Kirkwall

2

4 1

A-964

W

A-960

5

6

HIGHLAND PARK
DISTILLERY

To
Aberdeen

A-961

A-960

ROYAL OAK
SHIPWRECK

Flow

1

ITALIAN
CHAPEL

2

3

Hunda

Burray

CHURCHILL
BARRIERS

North
Sea

4

St. Margaret's
Hope

5 Kilometers

5 Miles

A-961

South
Ronaldsay

Burwick

TOMB OF THE
EAGLES

To John O'Groats
(Foot Passenger Only)

1 Lynnfield Hotel & Restaurant
2 Hildeval B&B
3 Kirkwall Eateries
4 Kirkwall Youth Hostel
5 Straigona B&B
6 The Foveran Rooms/Restaurant

GETTING TO ORKNEY

By Car/Ferry: Two different car-ferry options depart from near Thurso, which is about a three-hour drive from Inverness (on the A-9); for the scenic longer route, you could loop all the way up Wester Ross, and then along the north coast from Durness to Thurso (see earlier in this chapter). The two companies land at opposite corners of Orkney, at Stromness and St. Margaret's Hope; from either, it's about a 30-minute drive to Kirkwall.

Plan on about £75 round-trip for a car on the Northlink ferry, or £80 round-trip on the Pentland ferry, plus £34 per passenger. For either company, reserve online at least a day in advance; check in at the ferry dock 30 minutes before departure.

For most, the best choice is the **Scrabster-Stromness** ferry, operated by NorthLink (3/day in each direction in summer, 2/day off-season, 1.5-hour crossing, www.northlinkferries.co.uk). While it's a slightly longer crossing, it's also a bigger boat, with more services (including a good sit-down cafeteria—and famously tasty fish-and-chips), and it glides past the Old Man of Hoy, giving you an easy glimpse at one of Orkney's top landmarks. This ferry is coordinated with bus #X99, connecting Scrabster to Inverness (www.stagecoachbus.com).

The **Gills Bay-St. Margaret's Hope** route is operated by Pentland Ferries; its main advantage is the proximity of Gills Bay to John O'Groats, making it easy to visit Britain's northeastern-most point on your way to or from the ferry—but Gills Bay is also that much farther from Inverness (3/day in each direction, one-hour crossing, www.pentlandferries.co.uk).

There's also a **passenger-only boat** directly from John O'Groats to Burwick, which connects conveniently to an onward bus to Kirkwall (3/day June-Aug, 2/day May and Sept, none Oct-April, 40-minute crossing, www.jogferry.co.uk). While this works for those leaving their car at John O'Groats for a quick Orkney day trip, it's more weather-dependent.

By Plane: Kirkwall's little airport has direct flights to Inverness, Edinburgh, Glasgow, and Aberdeen. Landing at the airport, you're four miles from Kirkwall; pick up a town map at the info desk. It's convenient to pick up a rental car at the airport. There are not many taxis, so without a car your best bet is the bus that runs every 30 minutes—just pay the driver (code: KOI, +44 1856 872 421, www.hial.co.uk/kirkwall-airport).

By Tour from Inverness: The John O'Groats foot ferry operates a very long all-day tour from Inverness that includes bus and ferry transfers, and a guided tour around the main sights (£79, none Oct-April, www.jogferry.co.uk).

GETTING AROUND ORKNEY

While this chapter is designed for travelers with a car (or a driver/guide—see next), **public buses** do connect sights on Mainland (operated by Stagecoach, www.stagecoachbus.com). From Mainland, **ferries** fan out to outlying islets (www.orkneyferries. co.uk); the main ports are Kirkwall (for points north) and Houton (for Hoy). If taking a car on a ferry, it's always smart to book ahead.

Local Guide: Husband-and-wife team Kinlay and Kirsty run **Orkney Uncovered.** Energetic and passionate about sharing their adopted home with visitors, they'll show you both prehistoric and wartime highlights (everything in this chapter—which Kinlay helped research). They're also happy to tailor an itinerary to your interests and offer a special price for Rick Steves readers (RS%—£425 for a full-day, 8-hour tour in a comfy van, more for 5 or more people, multiday tours and cruise excursions possible, +44 1856 878 822, www.orkneyuncovered.co.uk, enquiries@ orkneyuncovered.co.uk).

Kirkwall

Kirkwall (pop. 9,000) is tidy and functional. Like the rest of the island, most of its buildings are more practical than pretty. But it has an entertaining and interesting old center and is a smart home base from which to explore the island. Whether sleeping here or not, you'll likely pass through at some point (to gas up, change buses, use the airport, or stock up on groceries).

Orientation to Kirkwall

Historic Kirkwall's shop-lined, pedestrian-only main drag leads from the cathedral down to the harbor, changing names several times as it curls through town. It's a workaday strip, lined with a combination of humble local shops and places trying to be trendy. You'll pop out at the little harbor, where fishing boats bob and ferries fan out to the northern islets.

NORTHERN SCOTLAND

The handy **TI** is at the bus station (on West Castle Street, daily 9:00-17:00, closed Sun Oct-March, +44 1856 872 856, www.visitscotland.com, but see also the helpful www.orkney.com). They produce a handy weekly "What's On" bulletin with events and tourist news—ask where you might find live music at night. If you don't have a car, **Craigies Taxi** is reliable and responds quickly to a call (+44 1856 878 787).

Sights in Kirkwall

▲St. Magnus Cathedral

This grand edifice, whose pointy steeple is visible from just about anywhere in town, is one of Scotland's most enjoyable churches to visit (free, daily). The build-

ing dates from the 12th century, back when this was part of the Parish of Trondheim, Norway. Built from vibrant red sandstone by many of the same stonemasons who worked on Durham's showpiece cathedral, St. Magnus is harmonious Romanesque inside and out: stout columns and small, rounded windows and arches. Inside, it boasts a delightful array of engaging monuments, all well described by the self-guided tour brochure: a bell from the *Royal Oak* battleship, sunk in Scapa Flow in 1939 (explained later); a reclining monument of arctic explorer John Rae, who appears to be enjoying a very satisfying eternal nap; the likely bones of St. Magnus (a beloved local saint); and many other characteristic flourishes. But the highlight is the gravestones that line the walls of the nave, each one carved with reminders of mortality: skull and crossbones, coffin, hourglass, and the shovel used by the undertaker. Read some of the poignant epitaphs: "She lived regarded and dyed regreted."

Nearby: The **Bishop and Earl's Palaces** (across the street) are a pair of once-grand, now-empty ruined buildings—for most, they're not worth the admission fee.

▲▲Orkney Museum

Just across the street from the cathedral, this museum packs the old parsonage with well-described exhibits covering virtually every dimension of history and life on the island. A visit here (to see the Stone Age, Iron Age, and Viking artifacts) can

be good preparation before exploring the islands' archaeological sites. Poking around, you'll see a 1539 map showing how "Orcadia" was part of Scandinavia, an exhibit about the crazy annual brawl called The Ba', and lots of century-old photos of traditional life (free, Mon-Sat 10:30-12:30 & 13:30-17:00, closed Sun, fine book shop, +44 1856 873 535, www.orkney.gov.uk).

Mercat Cross

In front of the cathedral stands Kirkwall's mercat cross (market cross), which is the starting point for the annual event called The Ba'. Short for "ball," this is a no-holds-barred, citywide rugby match that takes place every Christmas and New Year's Day. Hundreds of Kirkwall's rough-and-tumble young lads team up based on neighborhood (the Uppies and the Doonies), and attempt to deliver the ball to the opposing team's goal by any means necessary. The only rule: There are no rules. While it's usually just one gigantic scrum pushing back and forth through the streets, other tactics are used (such as the recent controversy when one team simply tossed the ball in a car and drove it to the goal). Ask locals about their stories—or scars—from The Ba'.

▲Highland Park Distillery

Outside the town center is a sprawling stone facility that's been distilling whisky since 1789 (legally). They give 75-minute tours simi-

lar to other distilleries, but this is one of only six in all of Scotland that malts its own barley—you'll see the malting floor (where the barley is spread and stirred while germinating) and the peat-fired kilns. Guides love to explain how the distillery's well-regarded whiskies get their flavor from Orkney's unique composition of peat (composed mostly of heather on this treeless island) and its high humidity (which minimizes alcohol "lost to the angels" during maturation). While the distillery is "silent" for much of July and August, its tour is good even if the workers are gone (£30, Tue-Sat 10:00-17:00, closed Sun-Mon, last tour at 16:00, reservations required, includes three tasty shots; on the edge of town to the south, toward the Scapa Flow WWII sites; +44 1856 885 604, www.highlandparkwhisky.com).

Sleeping in Kirkwall

These accommodations are in or near Kirkwall. Orkney's B&Bs are not well marked; get specific instructions from your host before you arrive.

In Kirkwall: **$$$ Lynnfield Hotel** rents 10 rooms that are a bit old-fashioned in decor, but with modern hotel amenities (on Holm Road/A-961, +44 1856 872 505, www.lynnfield.co.uk). High up in town, consider **$$ Hildeval B&B,** in a modern home with five contemporary-style rooms (on East Road, +44 1856 878 840, www.hildeval-orkney.co.uk). And ¢ the **Kirkwall Youth Hostel** rents both dorm beds and private rooms (Old Scapa Road, 15-minute walk from center, +44 1856 872 243, www.hostellingscotland.org.uk).

In the Countryside: Just past the airport, **$$ Straigona B&B,** about a five-minute drive outside of Kirkwall, has three rooms in a cozy modern home, run by helpful Julie and Mike (two-night minimum stay in summer, +44 1856 861 328, www.straigona.co.uk). For more anonymity and grand views over Scapa Flow, the recommended restaurant **$$ The Foveran** has eight rooms, some with contemporary flourish and others more traditional (5 minutes from Kirkwall by car on the A-964, +44 1856 872 389, www.thefoveran.com).

Eating in Kirkwall

The first place is near the cathedral; the next two are on the harbor. The main pedestrian street connecting the harbor and cathedral is lined with other options. Hotels along the harbor are also a good bet for dinner.

$$ Judith Glue Shop is a souvenir-and-craft shop across from the cathedral, with a cutesy café in the back (25 Broad Street, +44 1856 874 225).

$ The Harbour Fry is the best place for fish-and-chips, with both eat-in and takeaway options (daily 12:00-21:00, half a block off the harbor at 3 Bridge Street, +44 1856 873 170).

$$ Helgi's Pub, facing the harbor, serves quality food and is popular for its fun menu and burgers. Upstairs is boring, the ground floor is more fun, and you're welcome to sit at the bar if the tables are full. Reservations are smart for dinner (daily 12:00-14:00 & 17:00-21:00, 14 Harbor Street, +44 1856 879 293, www.helgis.co.uk).

DESTINATION RESTAURANTS NEAR KIRKWALL

With talented chefs working hard to elevate Orcadian cuisine—using traditional local ingredients, but with international flourish, these are considered the best restaurants around.

$$$$ The Foveran, perched on a bluff with smashing views over Scapa Flow, has a cool, contemporary dining room with a wall of windows (dinner nightly May-Sept, weekends-only in winter, southwest of Kirkwall on the A-964, +44 1856 872 389, www.thefoveran.com).

$$$$ Lynnfield Hotel, near the Highland Park Distillery on the way out of town, has a more traditional feel (open daily for lunch and dinner, reservations smart in the evening, on Holm Road/A-961, +44 1856 872 505, www.lynnfield.co.uk).

Sights in Orkney

PREHISTORIC SITES

Orkney boasts an astonishing concentration of 5,000-year-old Neolithic monuments worth ▲▲▲—one of the best such collections in Great Britain (and that's saying something). And here on Orkney, there's also a unique Bronze and Iron Age overlay, during which Picts, and then Vikings, built their own monuments to complement the ones they inherited. The best of these sites are easily toured along a single stretch of road, as described below.

Background: Five thousand years ago—centuries before Stonehenge—Orkney had a bustling settlement with some 30,000 people (a population larger than today's). The climate, already milder than most of Scotland thanks to the Gulf Stream, was even warmer then, making this a desirable place to live. Orkney's prehistoric residents left behind structures from every walk of life: humble residential settlements (Skara Brae, Barnhouse Village), mysterious stone circles (Ring of Brodgar, Stenness Stones), more than 100 tombs (Maeshowe, Tomb of the Eagles), and what appears to be a sprawling ensemble of spiritual buildings (the Ness of Brodgar). And, this being the Stone Age, all of this was accomplished using tools made not of metal, but of stone and bone. Many more sites await excavation. (Any time you see a lump or a bump in a field, it's likely an ancient site—identified with the help of ground-penetrating radar—and protected by the government.) While you could spend days poring over all of Orkney's majestic prehistoric monuments, on a short visit focus on the following highlights. (Actual artifacts from these sites are on display only in the Orkney Museum in Kirkwall.)

Maeshowe

The finest chambered tomb north of the Alps, Maeshowe (mays-HOW) was built around 3500 BC. From the outside, it looks like

yet another big mound. But inside, the burial chamber is remarkably intact. The only way to go inside is on a fascinating 30-minute tour. You'll squeeze through the entrance tunnel and emerge into a space designed for ancestor worship, surrounded by three smaller cells. At the winter solstice, the setting sun shines through the entrance tunnel, illuminating the entrance to the main cell. How they managed to cut and transport gigantic slabs of sandstone, then assemble this dry-stone, corbeled pyramid—all in an age before metal tools—still puzzles present-day engineers. Adding to this place's mystique, in the 12th century, a band of Norsemen took shelter here for three days during a storm, and entertained themselves by carving runic messages into the walls— many of them still readable (£10.50—book online in advance to guarantee entry, daily 9:30-17:30, Oct-March 10:00-16:00, closes in bad weather, +44 1856 761 606, www.historicenvironment.scot).

Prehistoric Sites near Maeshowe

A narrow spit of land just a few hundred yards from Maeshowe is lined with several stunning, free-to-visit, always-"open" Neolithic sites (from Maeshowe, head south on the A-965 and immediately turn right onto the B-9056, following *Bay of Skaill* signs). Along this road, you'll reach the following sites, in this order (watch for the brown signs). Conveniently, these line up on the way to Skara Brae.

Stones of Stenness: Three-and-a-half standing stones survive from an original 12 that formed a 100-foot-diameter ring. Dating from around 3000 BC, these are some of the oldest standing stones in Britain (a millennium older than Stonehenge).

Barnhouse Village: From the Stones of Stenness, a footpath continues through the field to the Barnhouse Village. Likely built around the same time as the Stones of Stenness, this was probably a residential area for the priests and custodians of the ceremonial monuments all around. Discovered in 1984, much of what you see today has been reconstructed—making this the least favorite site of archaeological purists. Still, it provides an illuminating contrast to Skara Brae (described later): While those Skara Brae homes were built underground, the ones at Barnhouse were thatched stone huts not unlike ones you still see around Great Britain today. The entire gathering was enclosed by a defensive wall.

Back on the road, just before the **causeway** between two lochs—saltwater on the left and freshwater on the right—two pillars flank the road (one intact, the other stubby). These formed a gateway of sorts to the important Neolithic structures just beyond.

Ness of Brodgar: On the left, look for a busy excavation site in action. The Ness of Brodgar offers an exciting opportunity to observe an actual archaeo-

logical dig in progress (discovered only in 2003). The work site you see covers only one-tenth of the entire complex, which was likely an ensemble of important ceremonial buildings...think of it as the "Orkney Vatican." The biggest foundation, nicknamed "the Cathedral," appears to have been a focal point for pilgrimages. Don't be surprised if there's no action—due to limited funding, archaeologists are likely at work here only in July and August (at other times, it's carefully covered, with nothing to see). The archaeologists hope to raise enough funds to build a permanent visitors center. Free guided tours are sometimes available (check www.nessofbrodgar.co.uk for details).

The Ring of Brodgar: Farther along on the left, look for stones capping a ridge above the road. The Ring of Brodgar is more than three times larger than the Stones of Stenness (and about 500 years newer). Of the original 60 or so stones—creating a circle as wide as a football field—25 still stand. The ring, which sits amidst a marshy moor, was surrounded by a henge (moat) that was 30 feet wide and 20 feet deep. Walking around the ring, notice that some are carved with "graffiti"—names of visitors from the late 19th century to the early 20th century, as well as some faint Norse runes carved by a Viking named Bjorn around AD 1150 (park 300 yards away, across the road).

Skara Brae

At the far-eastern reaches of Mainland (about a 20-minute drive from Maeshowe), this remarkable site illustrates how some Neolithic people lived like rabbits in warrens—hunkered down in subterranean homes, connected by tunnels and lit only by whale-oil lamps. Uncovered by an 1850 windstorm, Skara Brae (meaning roughly "village under hills") has been meticulously excavated and is very well presented.

Cost and Hours: £10.50—book online in advance to guarantee entry, daily 9:30-17:30, Oct-March 10:00-16:00, café and WCs, www.historicenvironment.scot.

Visiting Skara Brae: Begin your visit in the small exhibition hall, where you'll watch a short film and see displays on Neolithic life. Then head out and walk inside a reconstructed home from Skara Brae—with a hearth, beds, storage area, and live-bait tanks dug into the floor. Finally, walk across a field to reach the site itself. Museum attendants stand by to answer any questions.

The oldest, stand-alone homes at Skara Brae were built around 3100 BC; a few centuries later, the complex was expanded and connected with tunnels. You'll walk on a grassy ridge just above the complex, peering down into 10 partially ruined homes and the tunnels that connect them. For safety, all of this was covered with turf, with only two or three entrances and exits. Because sandstone is a natural insulator, these spaces—while cramped  and dank—would have been warm and cozy during the frequent battering storms. If you see a grate, squint down into the darkness: A primitive sewer system, flushed by a rerouted stream, ran beneath all of the homes, functioning not too differently from modern sewers. And all of this was accomplished without the use of metal tools. They even created an ingenious system of giant stone slabs on pivots, allowing them to be opened and closed like modern doors.

Before leaving, look out over the nearby bay, and consider that this is only about one-third of the entire size of the original Skara Brae. What's now a beach was once a freshwater loch. But with the rising Atlantic, the water became unusable. About 800 years after it was built, the village was abandoned; since then, most of it has been lost to the sea. This area is called Skaill Bay, from the Old Norse *skål*, for "cheers!"—during Viking times, this was a popular place for revelry...but the revelers had no clue they were partying on top of a Neolithic village.

And now for something completely different: Your ticket to Skara Brae also includes the **Skaill House,** the sprawling stone mansion on the nearby hilltop. Here you can tour some lived-in rooms (c. 1950) and see a fascinating hodgepodge of items once important to a leading Orkney family. Some items illustrate Orkney's prime location for passing maritime trade: The dining room proudly displays Captain James Cook's dinner service—bartered by his crew on their return voyage after the captain was killed in Hawaii (Orkney was the first place they made landfall in the UK). You'll also see traditional Orkney chairs (with woven backs); in the library, an Old Norse "calendar"—a wooden stick that you could hold up to the horizon at sunset to determine the exact date; a Redcoat's red coat from the Crimean War; a Spanish chest salvaged from a shipwreck; and some very "homely" (and supposedly haunted) bedrooms.

Nearby: About five miles south of Skara Brae, the sightseeing twofer of **Yesnaby** is worth a quick visit for drivers (watch for the turnoff on the B-9056). On a bluff overlooking the sea, you'll find an old antiaircraft artillery  battery from World War II, and some of Orkney's most dramatic sea-cliff scenery.

SCAPA FLOW: WORLD WAR II SITES

For a quick and fascinating glimpse of Orkney's World War II locations, worth ▲▲▲, drive 10 minutes south from Kirkwall on the A-961 (leave town toward St. Mary's and St. Margaret's Hope, past the Highland Park Distillery)—to the natural harbor called Scapa Flow (see the sidebar). From the village of St. Mary's, you can cross over all four of the Churchill Barriers, with  subtle reminders of war all around. The floor of Scapa Flow is littered with shipwrecks, and if you know where to look, you can still see many of them as you drive by.

Barrier #1 crosses from St. Mary's to the Isle of Burray. This narrow channel is where, in the early days of World War II, the German U-47 slipped between sunken ships to attack the *Royal*

Scapa Flow: Britain's Remote Wartime Naval Base

Orkney's arc of scattered islands forms one of the world's largest natural harbors, called Scapa Flow (SKAH-pah flow). The Norsemen named this area *skalpai floi*—"scabbard water," where a sword was sheathed—suggesting that they used this area to store their warships when not in use. And in the 20th century, Scapa Flow was the main base for Britain's Royal Navy.

During World War I, to thwart U-boat attacks, dozens of old ships and fishing vessels were requisitioned and intentionally sunk to block the gaps between the islets that define Scapa Flow. You can still see many of these "block ships" breaking the surface today.

At the end of World War I, a fleet of 74 German battleships surrendered at Scapa Flow. On the morning of June 21, 1919—days before the Treaty of Versailles was formally enacted—the British admiral took most of his navy out on a "victory lap" patrol. Once they were gone, the German commander ordered his men to scuttle the entire fleet rather than turn the ships over. By the time the British returned five hours later, 52 German ships littered the bottom of the bay. The British opened fire on the remaining German ships, killing nine Germans—the final casualties of World War I. While most of the ships were later salvaged for scrap, to this day, German crockery washes up on Orkney beaches after a storm. Seven ships remain underwater, making this one of Europe's most popular scuba diving destinations.

Oak—demonstrating the need to build these barriers. Notice that the Churchill Barriers have two levels: smaller quarried stone down below, and huge concrete blocks on top.

Just over the first barrier, perched on the little rise on the left, is Orkney's most fascinating wartime site: the **Italian Chapel** (£3.50, daily 9:00-17:30 in summer, shorter hours off-season). Italian POWs who were captured during the North African campaign (and imprisoned here on Orkney to work on the Churchill Barriers) were granted permission to create a Catholic chapel to remind them of their homeland. While the front view

Scapa Flow also played an important role in World War II. Even before Britain declared war on Germany, Luftwaffe reconnaissance flights had identified a gap in the sunken-ship barriers around the harbor. And on October 14, 1939—just weeks after war was declared—a Nazi U-47 slipped inside the harbor and torpedoed the HMS *Royal Oak*, killing 834 (including 110 seamen-in-training under the age of 15). To this day, the battleship—which had been fully loaded with fuel and ordnance—sits on the bottom of the bay, marked with a green warning buoy.

In April 1940, Luftwaffe planes flew from German-occupied Norway to bomb Orkney for three days straight in what's termed the "Battle of Orkney." But the islands were bulked up with heavy-duty gun batteries and other defenses, turning Orkney into a fortress. A sea of blimps called "barrage balloons"—designed to interfere with air attacks—clogged the air overhead. They even built a false fleet out of wood (also protected by barrage balloons) as a decoy for the Luftwaffe. The local population of 22,000 was joined by some 80,000 troops. Many surviving fragments from the Battle of Orkney can still be seen all over the island.

To ensure that no further surprises would sneak into the bay, First Lord of the Admiralty Winston Churchill visited here (just weeks before becoming prime minister) and hatched a plan to build sturdy barriers spanning the small distances between the islands south of Kirkwall. Throughout the wartime years, British workers and Italian prisoners of war labored to construct the "Churchill Barriers." The roads on top of the barriers opened just a few days after V-E Day, and today tourists use them to island-hop—and to learn about the dramatic history of Scapa Flow.

is a pretty Baroque facade, if you circle around you'll see that the core of the structure is two prefab Nissen huts (similar to Quonset huts). Inside, you can see the remarkable craftsmanship of the artists who decorated the church. In 1943, Domenico Chiocchetti led the effort to create this house of worship, and personally painted the frescoes that adorn the interior. The ethereal *Madonna e Bambino* over the main altar is based on a small votive he had brought with him to war. An experienced iron-worker named Palumbi used scrap metal (much of it scavenged from sunken WWI ships) to create the gate and chandeliers,

while others used whatever basic materials they could to finish the details. (Notice the elegant corkscrew base of the baptismal font near the entrance; it's actually a suspension spring coated in concrete.) These lovingly crafted details are a hope-filled symbol of the gentility and grace that can blossom even during brutal wartime. (And the British military is proud of this structure as an embodiment of Britain's wartime ethic of treating POWs with care and respect.) Spend some time examining the details—such as the stained-glass windows, which are painted rather than leaded. The chapel was completed in 1944, just two months before the men who built it were sent home. Chiocchetti returned for a visit in the 1960s, bringing with him the wood-carved Stations of the Cross that now hang in the nave.

Continuing south along the road, you'll cross over two more barriers in rapid succession. You'll see the masts and hulls of **shipwrecks** (on the left) scuttled here during World War I to block the harbor. As you cross over the bridges, notice that these are solid barriers, with no water circulation—in fact, the water level on each side of the barrier varies slightly, since the tide differs by an hour and a half.

At the far end of **Barrier #3,** on the left, watch for the huge wooden boxes on the beach. These were used in pre-barrier times (WWI) for boom floats, which supported nets designed to block German submarines.

After Barrier #3, as you climb the hill, watch for the pullout on the right with an orientation board. From this **viewpoint,** you can see three of the Churchill Barriers in one grand panorama.

Carrying on south, the next barrier isn't a Churchill Barrier at all—it's an ayre, a causeway that was built during the Viking period.

Finally you'll reach **Barrier #4**—hard to recognize because so much sand has accumulated on its east side (look for the giant breakwater blocks). Surveying the dunes along this barrier, notice the crooked concrete shed poking up—actually the top of a shipwreck. The far side of this sand dune is one of Orkney's best beaches—sheltered and scenic.

From here, the A-961 continues south past **St. Margaret's**

Hope (where the ferry to Gills Bay departs) and all the way to Burwick, at the southern tip of South Ronaldsay. From here you can see the tip of Scotland. Nearby is the **Tomb of the Eagles,** a burial cairn similar to Maeshowe, but less accessible (time-consuming visit, www.tomboftheeagles.co.uk).

More WWII Sites: For those really interested in the World War II scene, consider a ferry trip out to the **Isle of Hoy;** the main settlement, Lyness, has the Scapa Flow Visitors Centre and cemetery (https://hoyorkney.com). Near Lyness alone are some 37 Luftwaffe crash sites. A tall hill, called Wee Fea, was hollowed out to hold 100,000 tons of fuel oil. Also on Hoy, you can hike seven miles round-trip to the iconic **Old Man of Hoy**—a 450-foot-high sea stack in front of Britain's tallest vertical sea cliffs. (Or you can see the same thing for free from the deck of the Stromness-Scrabster ferry.)

FERRY PORT TOWNS

With more time, check out these two towns with connections to northern Scotland. **Stromness** is Orkney's "second city," with 3,000 people. It's a stony 17th-century fishing town and worth a look. Equal parts fishing town and tourist depot, its traffic-free main drag has a certain salty charm. If driving, there's easy parking at the harbor. If catching the ferry to Scrabster, get here early to enjoy a stroll.

St. Margaret's Hope—named for a 13th-century Norwegian princess who was briefly Queen of Scots until she died en route to Orkney—is even smaller, with a charming seafront-village atmosphere. Ferries leave here for Gills Bay.

PRACTICALITIES

This section covers just the basics on traveling in Scotland (for much more information, see *Rick Steves Scotland*). You'll find free advice on specific topics at RickSteves.com/tips.

MONEY

For currency, Scotland uses the pound sterling (£), also called a "quid": 1 pound (£1) = about $1.30. One pound is broken into 100 pence (p). To convert prices in pounds to dollars, add about 30 percent: £20 = about $26, £50 = about $65. (Check Oanda.com for the latest exchange rates.) While the pound is used throughout the UK, Scotland prints its own bills, which are decorated with Scottish landmarks and VIPs. These are interchangeable with British pound notes, which are widely circulated here.

You'll use your **credit card** for purchases both big (hotels, advance tickets) and small (little shops, food stands). Visa and Mastercard are universal while American Express and Discover are less common. Some European businesses have gone cashless, making a card your only payment option.

A **"tap-to-pay"** or "contactless" card is the most widely accepted and simplest to use: Before departing, check if you have—or can get—a tap-to-pay credit card (look on the card for the symbol—four curvy lines) and consider setting up your smartphone for contactless payment. Let your bank know that you'll be traveling in Europe, adjust your ATM withdrawal limit if needed, and make sure you know the four-digit PIN for each of your cards, both debit and credit (as you may need to use **chip-and-PIN** for certain purchases). Allow time to receive your PIN by mail.

While most transactions are by card these days, **cash** can help you out of a jam if your card randomly doesn't work, and can be useful to pay for tips and local guides. Wait until you arrive to get euros using your **debit card** (airports have plenty of cash machines). European ATMs accept US debit cards with a Visa or Mastercard logo and work just like they do at home—except they spit out local currency instead of dollars. When possible, withdraw cash from a bank-run ATM located just outside that bank (they usually charge lower fees and are more secure).

Whether withdrawing cash at an ATM or paying with a credit card, you'll often be asked whether you want the transaction processed in dollars or in the local currency. To avoid a poor exchange rate, always refuse the conversion and *choose the local currency*.

Although rare, some US cards may not work at self-service payment machines (such as transit-ticket kiosks, tollbooths, or fuel pumps). Usually a tap-to-pay card does the trick in these situations. Carry cash as a backup and look for a cashier who can process your payment if your card is rejected.

Before you leave home, let your bank know when and where you'll be using your credit and debit cards. To keep your cash, cards, and valuables safe when traveling, wear a **money belt**.

STAYING CONNECTED

The simplest solution is to bring your own device—mobile phone, tablet, or laptop—and use it just as you would at home (following the money-saving tips below). For more on phoning, see RickSteves.com/phoning. For a one-hour talk covering tech issues for travelers, see RickSteves.com/mobile-travel-skills. The following instructions apply in Scotland and across Great Britain.

To Call from a US Phone: Phone numbers in this book are presented exactly as you would dial them from a US mobile phone. For international access, press and hold the 0 key until you get a + sign, then dial the country code (44 for Scotland/Great Britain) and phone number (omit the initial zero that's used for domestic calls). To dial from a US landline, replace + with 011 (US/Canada international access code).

From a European Landline: Replace + with 00 (Europe international access code), then dial the country code (44 for Scotland/Great Britain) and phone number (omitting the initial zero).

Within Scotland/Great Britain: To place a domestic call (from a Scottish or British landline or mobile), drop the +44 and dial the phone number (including the initial zero).

Tips: If you bring your mobile phone, consider signing up for an international plan; most providers offer a simple bundle that includes calling, messaging, and data.

Use Wi-Fi whenever possible. Most hotels and many cafés offer free Wi-Fi, and you may also find it at tourist information offices (TIs), major museums, public-transit hubs, and aboard trains and buses. With Wi-Fi you can use your phone or tablet to make free or

Sleep Code

Hotels are classified based on the average price of a standard en suite double room with breakfast in high season.

$$$$	**Splurge:** Most rooms over £180
$$$	**Pricier:** £130-180
$$	**Moderate:** £100-130
$	**Budget:** £60-100
¢	**Backpacker:** Under £60
RS%	**Rick Steves discount**

Unless otherwise noted, credit cards are accepted and free Wi-Fi is available. Comparison-shop by checking prices at several hotels (on each hotel's own website, on a booking site, or by email). For the best deal, *always book directly with the hotel.* Ask for a discount if paying in cash; if the listing includes **RS%,** request a Rick Steves discount.

low-cost domestic and international calls via a calling app such as Skype, WhatsApp, FaceTime, and Google Meet. When you need to get online but can't find Wi-Fi, turn on your cellular network (or turn off airplane mode) just long enough for the task at hand.

Most **hotels** charge a fee for placing calls—ask for rates before you dial. You can use a prepaid international phone card (usually available at newsstands, tobacco shops, and train stations) to call out from your hotel.

SLEEPING

I've categorized my recommended accommodations based on price, indicated with a dollar-sign rating (see sidebar). Book your accommodations as soon as your itinerary is set, especially if you want to stay at one of my top listings or if you'll be traveling during busy times. This is particularly important—especially in smaller towns—because good-quality, good-value, characteristic B&Bs are in short supply—and they book up fast.

Compare prices at several hotels. You can do this by checking hotel websites and booking sites such as Hotels.com or Booking. com. After you've zeroed in on your choice, **book directly with the hotel itself.** This increases the chances that the hotelier will be able to accommodate special needs or requests (such as shifting your reservation). And when you book on the hotel's website, by email, or by phone, the owner avoids the commission paid to booking sites, giving them wiggle room to offer you a discount, a nicer room, or a free breakfast.

For family-run hotels, it's generally best to book your room directly via email or phone. Here's what they'll want to know: number and type of rooms; number of nights; arrival date; departure date; any special requests; and applicable discounts (such as a

Rick Steves discount, cash discount, or promotional rate). Use the European style for writing dates: day/month/year.

An "en suite" room has a bathroom (toilet and shower/tub) attached to the room; a room with a "private bathroom" can mean that the bathroom is all yours, but it's across the hall. If you want your own bathroom inside the room, request "en suite."

Some hotels extend a discount to those who pay cash or stay longer than three nights. And some accommodations offer a special discount for Rick Steves readers, indicated in this guidebook by the abbreviation "**RS%.**"

Compared to hotels, bed-and-breakfast places give you double the cultural intimacy for half the price. Personal touches, whether it's joining my hosts for afternoon tea or relaxing by a common fireplace at the end of the day, make staying at a B&B my preferred choice. Many B&Bs take credit cards but may add the card service fee to your bill (about 3 percent). If you'll need to pay cash for your room, plan ahead.

A short-term rental—whether an apartment, house, or room in a private residence—is a popular alternative, especially if you plan to settle in one location for several nights. Websites such as Airbnb, FlipKey, Booking.com, and VRBO let you browse a wide range of properties. Alternatively, rental agencies such as InterhomeUSA.com and RentaVilla.com can provide a more personalized service.

EATING

I've categorized my recommended eateries based on the average price of a typical main course, indicated with a dollar-sign rating (see sidebar).

The traditional fry-up or full Scottish breakfast comes with your choice of eggs, Canadian-style bacon and/or sausage, a grilled tomato, sautéed mushrooms, baked beans, toast and marmalade, and often haggis, black pudding, or a dense potato scone. As an alternative, most hotels serve a healthier continental breakfast as well—with a buffet of yogurt, cereal, fruit, and pastries; and many B&Bs offer vegetarian, organic, gluten-free, or other creative variations on the traditional breakfast.

To dine affordably at classier restaurants, look for "early-bird specials" (sometimes called "pre-theater menus"), which allow you to eat well but early, usually before 18:30 or 19:00 (sometimes on weekdays only).

Smart travelers use pubs (short for "public houses") to eat, drink, get out of the rain, and make new friends. Pub grub is Scotland's best eating value (although not every pub sells food). Pubs that are attached to restaurants are more likely to have fresh, made-to-order food. For about $20, you'll get a basic meal in con-

Restaurant Code

I've assigned each eatery a price category, based on the average cost of a typical main course. Drinks, desserts, and splurge items (steak and seafood) can raise the price considerably.

$$$$	**Splurge:** Most main courses over £20
$$$	**Pricier:** £15-20
$$	**Moderate:** £10-15
$	**Budget:** Under £10

In Scotland, carryout fish-and-chips and other takeout food is **$**, a basic pub or sit-down eatery is **$$**, a gastropub or casual but more upscale restaurant is **$$$**, and a swanky splurge is **$$$$**.

vivial surroundings. The menu is generally hearty and traditional: fish-and-chips, roast beef with Yorkshire pudding, and assorted meat pies, such as steak-and-kidney pie or shepherd's pie (stewed lamb topped with mashed potatoes), with cooked vegetables. But these days, you'll likely find more pasta, curried dishes, and quiche on the menu than traditional fare.

Meals are usually served from 12:00 to 14:00 and from 18:00 to 20:00, not throughout the day. Order drinks and meals at the bar, and pay at the bar (sometimes when you order, sometimes after you eat).

Most pubs have lagers (cold, refreshing, American-style beer), ales (amber-colored, cellar-temperature beer), bitters (hop-flavored ale, perhaps the most typical British beer), and stouts (dark and somewhat bitter, like Guinness).

While bar-hopping tourists generally think in terms of beer, many Scottish pubs are just as enthusiastic about serving whisky. If you are unfamiliar with whisky (what Americans call "Scotch" and the Irish call "whiskey"), it's a great conversation starter. Pubs often have dozens of whiskies available.

Tipping: At pubs and places where you order at the counter, you don't have to tip. At restaurants and fancy pubs with waitstaff, it's standard to tip about 10-12 percent; you can add a bit more for finer dining or extra-good service. Occasionally a service charge is added to your bill, in which case no additional tip is necessary (but check your bill to be sure).

TRANSPORTATION

By Train: Great Britain's train system is one of Europe's best...and most expensive. To see if a rail pass could save you money—as it often does in Britain—check RickSteves.com/rail. If you're buying point-to-point tickets, you'll get the best deals if you book in advance, leave after rush hour (after 9:30 weekdays), or ride the bus. Train reservations are recommended for long journeys or for travel on weekends or holidays (reserve online, at any train station, or by phone). For train schedules or to book, see NationalRail. co.uk. Germany's all-Europe website, Bahn.com, is also a good source for schedules.

By Car: A car is useful for scouring the remote rural sights, but it's an expensive headache in big cities. It's cheaper to arrange most car rentals from the US. For tips on your insurance options, see RickSteves.com/cdw. For navigation, the mapping app on your phone works fine. Bring your driver's license.

Speedy motorways (comparable to our freeways) let you cover long distances in a snap. Remember that the Scottish drive on the left side of the road (and the driver sits on the right side of the car). You'll quickly master Scotland's many roundabouts: Traffic moves clockwise, cars inside the roundabout have the right-of-way, and entering traffic yields (look to your right as you merge). Note that road-surveillance cameras strictly enforce speed limits by automatically snapping photos of speeders' license plates, then mailing them a ticket.

Be aware of Britain's rules of the road. Ask your car-rental company about them or check the US State Department website (www.travel.state.gov, search for your country in the "Learn About Your Destination" box, then select "Travel and Transportation").

By Bus: Long-distance buses (called "coaches" in Scotland) are about a third slower than trains, but they're also much cheaper—and go many places that trains don't. Most long-haul domestic routes in Scotland are operated by Scottish Citylink (www.citylink.co.uk). Some regional routes are operated by Citylink's Stagecoach service (www.stagecoachbus.com). In peak season, it's worth booking your seat on popular routes at least a few days in advance (at the bus station or TI, on the Citylink website, or by calling +44 0141 352 4444). At slower times, you can just hop on the bus and pay the driver.

HELPFUL HINTS

Travel Advisories: Before traveling, check updated health and safety conditions, including restrictions for your destination, on the travel pages of the US State Department (www.travel.state. gov) and Centers for Disease Control and Prevention (www.cdc. gov/travel). The US embassy website for Edinburgh is also a good source of information (see below).

Covid Vaccine/Test Requirements: It's possible you'll need to present proof of vaccination against the coronavirus and/or a negative Covid-19 test result to board a plane to Europe or back to the US. Carefully check requirements for each country you'll visit well before you depart, and again a few days before your trip. See the websites listed above for current requirements.

Emergency and Medical Help: For any emergency service—ambulance, police, or fire—call **112 or 999** from a mobile phone or landline. If you get sick, do as the Scots do and go to a pharmacist for advice. Or ask at your hotel for help—they'll know the nearest medical and emergency services.

For **passport problems,** call the **US Consulate in Edinburgh** (+44 131 556 8315, no walk-in passport services, https://uk.usembassy.gov/embassy-consulates/edinburgh) or the **Canadian Consulate in Edinburgh** (+44 1250 870 831 during business hours, www.unitedkingdom.gc.ca).

Theft or Loss: To replace a passport, you'll need to go in person to an embassy or consulate (see above). Cancel and replace your credit and debit cards by calling these 24-hour US numbers: Visa (dial +1 303 967 1096), Mastercard (dial +1 636 722 7111), and American Express (dial +1 336 393 1111). From a landline, you can call these US numbers collect by going through a local operator.

File a police report either on the spot or within a day or two; you'll need it to submit an insurance claim for lost or stolen items, and it can help with replacing your passport or credit and debit cards. For more information, see RickSteves.com/help.

Time: Scotland uses the 24-hour clock. It's the same through 12:00 noon, then keep going: 13:00, 14:00, and so on. Scotland, like the rest of Great Britain, is five/eight hours ahead of the East/West Coasts of the US (and one hour earlier than most of continental Europe).

Business Hours: Most stores are open Monday through Saturday (roughly 9:00 or 10:00 to 17:00 or 18:00). In cities, some stores stay open later on Wednesday or Thursday (until 19:00 or 20:00). On Sundays sightseeing attractions are generally open, many street markets are lively with shoppers, banks and many shops are closed, and public transportation options are fewer (for example, no bus service to or from smaller towns).

Sightseeing: Many popular sights come with long lines—not to get in, but to buy a ticket. Visitors who buy tickets online in advance (or who have a museum pass covering these key sights) can skip the line and waltz right in. Advance tickets are generally timed-entry, meaning you're guaranteed admission on a certain date and time.

For some sights, buying ahead is required (tickets aren't sold at the sight and it's the only way to get in). At other sights, buying ahead is recommended to skip the line and save time. And for many sights, advance tickets are available but unnecessary: At these uncrowded sights you can simply arrive, buy a ticket, and go in.

Use my advice in this book as a guide. Note any must-see sights that sell out long in advance and be prepared to buy tickets early. If you do your research, you'll know the smart strategy.

Given how precious your vacation time is, I'd book in advance both where it's required (as soon as your dates are firm) and where it will save time in a long line (in some cases, you can do this even on the day you plan to visit).

Holidays and Festivals: Great Britain celebrates many holidays, which can close sights and attract crowds (book hotel rooms ahead). For information on holidays and festivals, check Scotland's tourism website, VisitScotland.com. For a simple list showing major—though not all—events, see RickSteves.com/festivals.

Numbers and Stumblers: What Americans call the second floor of a building is the first floor in Europe. Europeans write dates as day/month/year, so Christmas 2024 is 25/12/24. For most measurements, Great Britain uses the metric system: A kilogram is 2.2 pounds, and a liter is about a quart. For driving distances, they use miles.

RESOURCES FROM RICK STEVES

This Snapshot guide is excerpted from my latest edition of *Rick Steves Scotland,* one of many titles in my series of guidebooks on European travel. I also produce a public television series, *Rick Steves' Europe,* and a public radio show, *Travel with Rick Steves.* My free online video library, Rick Steves Classroom Europe, offers a searchable database of short video clips on European history, culture, and geography (Classroom.RickSteves.com). My website, RickSteves. com, offers free travel information, a forum for travelers' comments, guidebook updates, my travel blog, an online travel store, and information on European rail passes and our tours of Europe. If you're bringing a mobile device, you can download my free Rick Steves Audio Europe app, featuring dozens of self-guided audio tours of the top sights in Europe, including the Edinburgh Royal Mile Walk audio tour, and travel interviews about Scotland. For more information, see RickSteves.com/audioeurope. You can also follow me on Facebook, Twitter, and Instagram.

ADDITIONAL RESOURCES

Tourist Information: www.visitscotland.com
Passports and Red Tape: www.travel.state.gov
Packing List: www.ricksteves.com/packing
Travel Insurance: www.ricksteves.com/insurance
Cheap Flights: www.kayak.com or www.google.com/flights
Airplane Carry-on Restrictions: www.tsa.gov
Updates for This Book: www.ricksteves.com/update

HOW WAS YOUR TRIP?

To share your tips, concerns, and discoveries after using this book, please fill out the survey at RickSteves.com/feedback. Thanks in advance—it helps a lot.

PRACTICALITIES

INDEX

INDEX

Our website enhances this book and turns

Explore Europe

At ricksteves.com you can browse through thousands of articles, videos, photos and radio interviews, plus find a wealth of money-saving travel tips for planning your dream trip. And with our mobile-friendly website, you can easily access all this great travel information anywhere you go.

TV Shows

Preview the places you'll visit by watching entire half-hour episodes of *Rick Steves' Europe* (choose from all 100 shows) on-demand, for free.

ricksteves.com

your travel dreams into affordable reality

Radio Interviews

Enjoy ready access to Rick's vast library of radio interviews covering travel tips and cultural insights that relate specifically to your Europe travel plans.

Travel Forums

Learn, ask, share! Our online community of savvy travelers is a great resource for first-time travelers to Europe, as well as seasoned pros.

Travel News

Subscribe to our free Travel News e-newsletter, and get monthly updates from Rick on what's happening in Europe.

Classroom Europe®

Check out our free resource for educators with 500 short video clips from the *Rick Steves' Europe* TV show.

Audio Europe™

Pack Light and Right

Gear up for your next adventure at ricksteves.com

Light Luggage

Pack light and right with Rick Steves' affordable, custom-designed rolling carry-on bags, backpacks, day packs and shoulder bags.

Accessories

From packing cubes to moneybelts and beyond, Rick has personally selected the travel goodies that will help your trip go smoother.

Experience maximum Europe

Save time and energy

This guidebook is your independent-travel toolkit. But for all it delivers, it's still up to you to devote the time and energy it takes to manage the preparation and logistics that are essential for a happy trip. If that's a hassle, there's a solution.

Rick Steves Tours

A Rick Steves tour takes you to Europe's most interesting places with great

great tours, too!

with minimum stress

guides and small groups. We follow Rick's favorite itineraries, ride in comfy buses, stay in family-run hotels, and bring you intimately close to the Europe you've traveled so far to see. Most importantly, we take away the logistical headaches so you can focus on the fun.

Join the fun

This year we'll take thousands of free-spirited travelers—nearly half of them repeat customers— along with us on 50 different itineraries, from Athens to Istanbul. Is a Rick Steves tour the right fit for your travel dreams?

Find out at ricksteves.com, where you can also check seat availability and sign up. Europe is best experienced with happy travel partners. We hope you can join us.

See our itineraries at ricksteves.com

A Guide for Every Trip

BEST OF GUIDES

Full-color guides in an easy-to-scan format. Focused on top sights and experiences in the most popular European destinations

Best of England
Best of Europe
Best of France
Best of Germany
Best of Ireland
Best of Italy
Best of Scotland
Best of Spain

COMPREHENSIVE GUIDES

City, country, and regional guides printed on Bible-thin paper. Packed with detailed coverage for a multiweek trip exploring iconic sights and venturing off the beaten path

Amsterdam & the Netherlands
Barcelona
Belgium: Bruges, Brussels,
  Antwerp & Ghent
Berlin
Budapest
Croatia & Slovenia
Eastern Europe
England
Florence & Tuscany
France
Germany
Great Britain
Greece: Athens & the Peloponnese
Iceland
Ireland
Istanbul
Italy
London
Paris
Portugal
Prague & the Czech Republic
Provence & the French Riviera
Rome
Scandinavia
Scotland
Sicily
Spain
Switzerland
Venice
Vienna, Salzburg & Tirol

Rick Steves books are available from your favorite bookseller.
Many guides are available as ebooks.

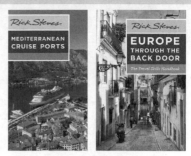

Photo Credits

Avalon Travel
Hachette Book Group
1700 Fourth Street
Berkeley, CA 94710

Text © 2022 by Rick Steves' Europe, Inc. All rights reserved.
Maps © 2022 by Rick Steves' Europe, Inc. All rights reserved.
Portions of this book originally appeared in *Rick Steves Scotland*, 4th Edition.

Printed in Canada by Friesens.
Third Edition. First printing February 2023.

ISBN 978-1-64171-535-5

For the latest on Rick's talks, guidebooks, tours, public television series, and public
radio show, contact Rick Steves' Europe, 130 Fourth Avenue North, Edmonds, WA
98020, +1 425 771 8303, RickSteves.com, rick@ricksteves.com.

Rick Steves' Europe

Managing Editor: Jennifer Madison Davis
Assistant Managing Editor: Cathy Lu
Editors: Glenn Eriksen, Suzanne Kotz, Rosie Leutzinger, Teresa Nemeth, Jessica
 Shaw, Carrie Shepherd
Editorial & Production Assistant: Megan Simms
Researcher: Cameron Hewitt
Contributor: Gene Openshaw
Graphic Content Director: Sandra Hundacker
Maps & Graphics: Orin Dubrow, David C. Hoerlein, Lauren Mills, Mary Rostad,
 Laura Terrenzio

Avalon Travel

Senior Editor and Series Manager: Maddy McPrasher
Editors: Jamie Andrade, Rachael Sablik
Proofreader: Patrick Collins
Indexer: Stephen Callahan
Production & Typesetting: Christine DeLorenzo, Lisi Baldwin, Rue Flaherty
Cover Design: Kimberly Glyder Design
Maps & Graphics: Kat Bennett, Lohnes & Wright

Let's Keep on Travelin'

Your trip doesn't need to end.

Follow Rick on social media!